AF564672

RIGHT TO PRIVACY UNDER INDIAN LAW

RIGHT TO PRIVACY UNDER INDIAN LAW

KIRAN DESHTA
LL.M., Ph.D.

DEEP & DEEP PUBLICATIONS PVT. LTD.
F-159, Rajouri Garden, New Delhi-110027

RIGHT TO PRIVACY UNDER INDIAN LAW

ISBN 978-81-8450-380-7

Typeset by S.S. COMPOSERS
3190, Mohindra Park, Shakur Basti, Delhi-110034.

Printed in India at MAYUR ENTERPRISES
WZ Plot No. 3, Gujjar Market, Tihar Village, New Delhi-110018.

Published by DEEP & DEEP PUBLICATIONS PVT. LTD.
F-159, Rajouri Garden, New Delhi-110027.
Phones: 25435369, 25440916
E-mail: ddpbooks@yahoo.co.in • ddpubs@gmail.com
Showroom:
2/13, Ansari Road, Daryaganj, New Delhi-110002 • Telefax: 23245122

Contents

Preface

Privacy is a part of vocabulary of every society. It is a human value enshrined in human behaviour. It goes with human desire. It gives sixth sense to every society and it preserves human autonomy under the umbrella of human dignity. It has traversed a long journey with a number of experiences. A review of Hindu scriptures proves the prevalence of ruler respecting the privacy of individuals in ancient India society. The kings were bound to uphold *Dharma* and to respect the privacy of the citizens. A person was not to be disturbed while meditating, sleeping or studying. Enjoyment of sex and food were recommended in a secluded place, where one may not be observed by others. Similarly, a male was enjoyed not to see, touch or meet other woman in a lonely place. Visits to others' house without owner's consent at odd hours and during nights were prohibited. The main door of the house was not to face the door of another house and the construction of the house was to be so devised that the householder should not be seen by unholy persons while performing religious rites, while dinning his house and passersby should not be able to see the valuables of the house. The Muslims always maintained the distinction between "public and private" and a high level of consciousness about privacy is reflected in their language, culture, architecture and other aspects of everyday life. The privacy of home is guaranteed under Islamic law as a core value and fundamental human rights, yet the privacy of home is not absolute, and can be regulated and restricted when it interferes with a compelling state interest. The privacy of home can be restricted when it interferes in serious manner with health, safety, rights and privileges of others or with the public affairs.

During the colonial period, the Indian legal system provided for inviolability of one's person, his family, home and correspondence. Various legislations of 19th century acknowledge the concept of privacy in India. The British Indian rulers used to shadow freedom fighters and the methodology of secret watch and domiciliary visits became part of police exercise. The relevant rules found their way into police manuals. The post-independence period in India witnessed emergence of many constitutional rights, the right to privacy is one of such right which has of late been accorded constitutional recognition in this period.

Right to privacy in India is a peculiar blend of constitutional, customary and common law right scattered over various legal fields. Privacy is not a static concept, but a dynamic one. Though, it varies time to time, culture to culture, it is always inevitable for the civilized society. Though, there is no express provision in the Constitution of India, right to privacy has got a secure position under it. Article 21 miraculously has been playing a major role in the safeguard of privacy as an essential ingredient of personal liberty. Though, there are several customary and constitutional provisions for right of privacy, without statutory protection this right cannot be protected in a meaningful way. Constitution provides only framework and constitutionally protected fundamental rights cannot be enforced against private person alone. Customary rules are very limited and inadequate. Statutory provisions, therefore, are more important to safeguard the privacy interest. In India, privacy has been recongnised in many cases as a fundamental right emanated under the Constitution of India, its content, extent and limit are not still clear. Statutory protection is piecemeal. The Courts of India have been taken the cherished concept of privacy to a new and unprecedented height with a zeal to translate the philosophy of right to life and personal liberty into reality. The right relating to privacy had to pass through a strenuous struggle during last many decades and it seems that it would still have to struggle hard. Truly admitting that the technological discoveries in modern times pose a serious threat to citizen's privacy. In this age of computer, it is very difficult to identify the infringement of the right for the purpose of taking action. The development of the concept of privacy has gone apace rapidly with the recent scientific and technological developments and have raised the spectre of new and frightening invasion of privacy. The recent communication explosion and revolutionary advance in communication technology which have put thrust into the hands of unscrupulous persons, gadgets by the use of which they have with impunity, pry into, intrude upon or invade the privacy of another's home without his consent or even knowledge-keeping in view these developments, a person's house is no longer inviolate or immune from wire-tapping, eavesdropping and bugging with the aid of sophisticated devices. Privacy, in such situations, dies an unnatural death. Further, in an age of revolutionized communications, privacy is clearly under seize but law-makers have shown scarce concern on the issue. In fact, the attitude of the legislators and the executive has been rather regressive. Hence, there is need for a constitutional amendment whereby right to privacy should either be added in Article 21 or a new clause should be added in Article 19, which would be subject to appropriate judicial control, so that balance is struck between individual's privacy and social exposure. Alternatively, if constitutional amendment is more difficult, a comprehensive and separate unified right of privacy Act is expected to be enacted which would not violate any provision of the Constitution. Even if privacy is made as a fundamental right, a separate legislation becomes necessary to regulate it. Right to privacy, therefore, should not rely on other laws. It should be developed as an independent right.

To write this book, inspiration and encouragement have been received from many quarters and would like to take this opportunity to thank them all. Firstly, I wish to place on record my heart-felt sense of gratitude to my learned *'Guru'*, Professor Kailash Thakur. Without his sincere and able guidance this work could not have been presented in the form it has now been done. I also wish to record my sense of gratitude to Professor O.P. Chauhan, Professor A.C. Pal, Professor H.R. Jhingta, Professor S.N. Sharma for their encouragement and critical comments rendered by them from time to time.

Over and above all, I owe, more than I could express my immense debt of gratitude to my parents, and parents-in-laws for giving their love and understanding. I am also thankful to Deepika (daughter) and Aarush (son) for their active co-operation while accomplishing this work. Thanks are also due to Mr. Surender Singh Deshta (Advocate) and Mr. Sanjay Deshta (Assistant Professor) for their help and encouragement. My husband, Dr. Sunil Deshta, Associate Professor, Department of Laws, H.P.U., Shimla gave me full liberty for my intellectual exercise and was ready to interfere with my work only when I tended to go on wrong track. I enjoyed the advantage of his critical judgment, vast knowledge and advice on many points. I really lack words to express my deep sense of gratitude to him.

The book has drawn ideas and materials from the works of many scholars on the subject, to name a few Warren and Brandeis; A.H. Robertson; Edward Shills; William Prosser; Alan F. Westin; S.K. Sharma; M.L. Upadhyay; Govind Mishra; Shrinivas Gupta; V.M. Apte; Ramanarayan Dutta Shastri; Hargovind Sastri; Medani Abdel Rehman Tegeldin; Thrity Patel; Faizan Mustafa and I.P. Messey.

I will be failing in my duty if I do not express my sincere thanks and gratitude to Shri G.S. Bhatia of M/s Deep & Deep Publications Pvt. Ltd., New Delhi-110027, who unhesitatingly agreed to publish this book.

Shimla DR. KIRAN DESHTA

List of Abbreviations

A.C. : Appeal Cases
A.I.R. : All India Reporter
A.P. : Andhra Pradesh
A.S.I.L : Annual Survey of Indian Law
Academy L.R. : Academy Law Review
Ala. : Alabama
All E.R. : All England Reports
All. : Allahabad
Alta App. Div.: Altanta Appeal Division
Ariz. L.R. : Arizona Law Review
Arz. : Arizona
B.J.A.L : British Journal of Administrative Law
Bom. : Bombay
Bom. L.J. : Bombay Law Journal
Bom. L.R. : Bombay Law Review
Brand. L.R. : Brandeis Law Journal
Brit. Med. J. : Britain Medical Journal
C.L.R. : Calcutta Law Reports
C.U.L.R. : Cochin University Law Review
C.W.N. : Calcutta Weekly Notes
Cal. : Calcutta
Cal. L.R. : California Law Review
Canadian B.R. : Canadian Bar Review
Ch. : Chancery
Ch.D. : Chancery Division
Col. L.R. : Columbia Law Review
Cornell L.R. : Cornell Law Review

Cr.P.C.	: Code of Criminal Procedure
Del.	: Delhi
Del. L.R.	: Delhi Law Review
ed.	: Edition
et. al.	: and others
Guj.	: Gujarat
H.C.R.	: High Court Reports
H.L.	: House of Lords
H.M.G.	: His Majesty's Government
Harv. L.R.	: Harvard Law Review
Him.	: Himachal Pradesh
I.L.R.	: Indian Law Reports
I.P.C.	: Indian Penal Code
Ibid.	: Ibidem (in the same place)
Id.	: Idem (the same)
Ind. L.R.	: Indiana Law Review
J.B.C.I.	: Journal of Bar Council of India
J.C.P.S.	: Journal of Constitutional and Parliamentary Studies
J.I.L.I.	: Journal of Indian Law Institute
J.K.	: Jammu and Kashmir
Jour.	: Journal
K.B.	: King's Bench
Ker.	: Kerala
L.Q.R.	: Law Quarterly Review
Lah.	: Lahore
M.P.	: Madhya Pradesh
M.P.L.J.	: Madhya Pradesh Law Journal
Mad.	: Madras
Mass	: Massachussetts
Mc. Gill L.J.	: Mc. Gill Law Journal
Media L.R.	: Media Law Review
Mod. L.R.	: Modern Law Review
Mys.	: Mysore
N.O.C.	: Notes of Cases
Ny. Univ. L.R.	: New York University Law Review

Op. cit.	: Opera citato (Already cited)
P&H.C.	: Punjab and Haryana High Court
Pat.	: Patna
Pub. Law	: Public Law
Punj.	: Punjab
Q.B.	: Queen's Bench
Raj.	: Rajasthan
S.C.	: Supreme Court
S.C.C.	: Supreme Court Cases
S.C.J.	: Supreme Court Journal
Supra	: Above
U.S.	: United States
W.L.R.	: Weekly Law Review
Yale L.J.	: Yale Law Journal

1

Introduction

Once a civilization has made a distinction between the "outer" and the "inner" man, between the life of the soul and the life of the body, between the spiritual and the material, between the sacred and the profane, between the realm of God and the realm of Caesar, between the Church and the State, between the rights inherent and inalienable and rights that are in the power of government to give and take away, between public and private, between society and solitude, it becomes impossible to avoid the idea of privacy by whatever name it may be called—the idea of "private space in which man may become and remain himself."[1]

Privacy is a natural need of a man to establish individual boundaries and to restrict the entry of others into that area. There are sufficient evidences in both oriental and occidental civilizations to support this view. The idea of privacy is as old as Biblical periods. The studies of animal behaviour and social organization suggest that man's need for privacy may well be rooted in the animal origins, and that men and animals share several basic mechanisms for claiming

---

1. Herbert Marcuse, One Dimensional Man, 10 (1964); Milton R. Konvitz, Privacy and The Law: A Philosophical Prelude, 31, *Law and Contemporary Problems*, 273 (1966).

privacy among their own fellows.[2] Bible describes the moment when Adam and Eve opened their eyes and they knew that they were naked; and they sewed fig leaves together and made themselves aprons.[3] The distance from the biblical garden to the statutory wilderness may have taken thousands of years to traverse because it is necessary for a secure relationship between individual and individual whether it is between man and wife, son and father or friend and or friend. In other words, it concretises relationship of love, friendship and trust. The concept of privacy in its broad sense covers a number of aspects, for example, non-disclosure of information, his sexual affairs, privacy of business secrets and non-observance of others, etc. It is a concept related to solitude, secrecy and autonomy. Privacy is an inseparable part of the vocabulary of every society.

"Privacy" has grown into a large and widely concept. Synonymous with autonomy, it has colonised traditional liberties, become entangled with confidentiality, secrecy, defamation, property, and the storage of information. Thus, the right to privacy can comprise public disclosure of private facts and intrusion upon individual's seclusion, solitude or private affairs.[4] The modern state collects all types of information about individuals and store them often in computerized form. In such a situation two types of difficulties may be envisaged. One relates to the apprehension of the individual that the authority may publish it. The other relates to the danger of supply of such material by the authority to strangers. In both cases the consent of the individual is not obtained before any eventual publication. The concerned individual may come to know about it only after the publication. Even if the right to privacy protects the person from any publication by the authority, does it-prevent the supply of such information to third parties.

---

2. Alan F. Westin, Privacy and Freedom, 8 (1970).
3. The Holy Bible American Standard Version (1929), Genesis 3: 7; Charles Freid, Privacy, 77 *Yale L.J.* 475 (1968) at p. 478; M.C. Pramodan, Right to Privacy, 14 *C.U.L.R.* 59 (1990); also see S.K. Sharma, Privacy Law: A Comparative Study, 25 (1994).
4. Raymond Wacks, Personal Information Privacy and the Law, 20-21 (1994).

In democratic societies there is a fundamental belief in the uniqueness of the individual, his basic dignity, his worth as a human being. Psychologist and sociologists have linked the development and maintenance of the sense of individuality to the human need for autonomy. One of the accepted ways of representing the individual's need for an ultimate core of autonomy has been to describe the individual's relation with others in terms of a series of zones or regions of privacy leading to a 'core self'. This core self is pictured as surrounded by a series of layer consecutive circles. The inner circle shelters the individual's ultimate secrets, those hopes, fears and aspirations that are beyond sharing with anyone unless the individual comes under such stress, that he must pour out these ultimate secrets to secure emotional belief. The most serious threat to individual autonomy is that someone will penetrate this inner zone and learn this ultimate secrets either by physical or other means. This deliberate penetration of an individual's protection shell, his psychological armour will leave him naked to ridicule and will put him under the control of those who know his secrets.

The seminal idea of privacy as a 'right' originated in United States of America in 1888 when Thomas Cooley, the American scholar named this then extremely nebulous concept as privacy, defining it simply as 'a right to be let alone'.[5] A couple of years later, in 1890 Samuel D. Warren and Louis D. Brandeis cultivated the notion with the initial analysis of the concept of privacy.[6] There still remain confusion as respects the nature of interest which privacy is designed to protect. There is a school of thought of which Dean William L. Prosser is the most outstanding spokesman that privacy is not an independent value at all but a composite of interest in reputation, emotional tranquillity and intangible property. The view of Dean Prosser has been adopted by Salmond in his book 'Law of Torts',[7] although

5. Thomas M. Cooley, Torts 91 (1888).
6. Samuel D. Warren and Louis D. Brandeis, The Right to Privacy, 4 *Harvard Law Rev.* 193 (1890).
7. Salmond, The Law of Torts, 15th Edition at pp. 44 and 46; also see William L. Prosser, Privacy 48 *Cali. L.R.* 383-423 (1960).

English common law does not recognise invasion of privacy as a tort in cases in which the American courts do. According to Dean Prosser, the four distinct torts, which are discovered in these cases are:

(i) Intrusion upon a person's solitude or seclusion or into his affairs.
(ii) Public disclosure of embarrassing facts of a person's private life.
(iii) Appropriation to a person's advantage of another's name or likeness.

The interests protected in these cases are interests in freedom from mental distress, in public disclosure and false light cases, the interest in reputation and in appropriation cases, the interest in reputation and in appropriation cases, proprietary interest in the name and likeness: From this angle the prized right of privacy shrinks in its stature so that it becomes a mere application to novel circumstances of the traditional legal rights to protect well identified and established social values. In this view, privacy is not an independent legal right protecting a fundamental human value. Assaults on privacy are transmuted into a species of defamation, infliction of mental distress and misappropriation. Accordingly, there is no new tort of invasion of privacy but only new ways of committing old torts. In other words, the social value or the interest in privacy is not an independent one but only a composite of the value society places on protecting mental, tranquillity, reputation or intangible forms of property.

The development of the concept of privacy has gone a pace rapidly with the recent scientific and technological developments and have raised the spectre of new and frightening invasion of privacy of another home without his consent or even knowledge. Owing to these developments, a person's house is no longer inviolate or immune from wire-tapping, eavesdropping and bugging with the aid of sophisticated devices.[8]

8. Justice R.S. Sarkaria, Freedom of the Press: Defamation and Privacy, 15 *Press Council of India Review* 11 (1994).

With respect to the area of an individual existence, the right to privacy protects one's identity, integrity and intimacy. Identity includes one's name, gender, appearance, feelings, honour and reputation, and so on. Privacy, however, is not an absolute right. Only arbitrary or unlawful interferences are prohibited; in order to know whether a given interference actually violates the right to privacy, we have to balance it with certain vital interests, such as national security, health, morals, the prevention of crime or the rights and freedoms of others. The same holds true if states prohibit trans-sexuals from changing sex. Forced medical treatment which interferes with the individual's integrity might, however, be justified in the interests of the rights of others, as in the case with mandatory withdrawal of blood for the purpose of determining paternity. Intimacy is at the very heart of privacy and means that certain private characteristics, actions or data should be kept secret. In view of the threats caused to privacy by electronic data processing, states are under an obligation to adopt data protection laws with effective supervision measures. Interference with sexual life and autonomy cannot be justified merely on the ground of morals or health. Both the European Courts of Human Rights and the Human Rights Committee, therefore, found a general prohibition of homosexuality a violation of right to privacy.

Respect for a person's private and family life, his home and correspondence is guaranteed in almost identical terms by the Universal Declaration of Human Rights, the Covenant on Civil and Political Rights, the European Convention on Human Rights and the divers regional Conventions on human rights in preparation in various regions of the globe outside Europe. This notion may seem to be self-evident, for it is one of those which we find at the very origin of the idea of human rights, and it constitutes one of the foundations of political democracy as it has developed from *Magna Carta* and successive declarations of human rights. The life of the individual in a society has to strike a balance between freedom and discipline. There has been a spurt in technique of surveillance, and when a large organisation can employ them for political or industrial espionage the result can be spectacular. If the techniques are focused by police or private detectives or press on the individual they can certainly embarrass and discomfit. Moreover, although they can to some extent be countered, and although some of them are at times necessary, their widespread use would make life meaner. All individuals would have constantly to live in a state of strain, even those with nothing to hide. The dislike of surveillance is instinctive; even well intended parental surveillance ultimately becomes irksome. Perhaps it all goes back to some primitive ancestor who knew that the only eyes which followed him continuously were those of a stalking predator.

At the same time, the dangers of surveillance should not be seen out of perspective. It is true that any given individual could be subjected to embarrassingly penetrating surveillance, but the cost is so high that only a small proportion of individuals could be kept under surveillance all the time, even in a totalitarian state. Moreover, although the new surveillance devices would be an aid to a dictator or to a ruling clique. But it is important for a free society to know that these aids to tyranny exist so that it can be on its guard, and what is essential to that society is that it should possess enough men of foresight and courage to resist tyranny, whether technically aided or not. The same applies to all other forms of threat to privacy: interrogation under stress, personality tests, data banks and tempering with the subconscious.

The increase in the flow of information induced by the computer threatens the individual's ability to control the flow of information about himself—in other words, his privacy is endangered. Undoubtedly new laws will be required. During 1969 a private member's Bill, the Data Surveillance Bill, was introduced in the House of Commons with the aim of providing legislation 'to prevent the invasion of privacy through the misuse of computer information.' The Bill did not become law but nevertheless included interesting new proposals, such as registration of computer-operated data banks and the compulsory supply of print-outs which may be embodied in future legislation.[9] Several federal statutes

9. G.B.F. Niblett, Computers and Privacy in A.H. Robertson (ed.) *Privacy and Human Rights*, 73 (1972).

"restrict the accumulation, storage, and distribution of information."[10] For example, the Privacy Act of 1974 regulates the collection and use of personal information possessed by the federal government.[11] The Act permits the government to collect only "relevant" or "necessary" information[12] and limits disclosure of individual's records.[13] However, the Act explicitly restricts its provisions from prohibiting the release of any material for which disclosure is required under the Freedom of Information Act.[14] The Freedom of Information Act allows private citizens to access government records, subject to several exceptions.[15] In addition, the Privacy Act only regulates information gathered by the government and does not apply to personal information collected and distributed by private entities.[16]

In United States of America, the Congress dealt with the problem of States selling driver's license records by enacting the Driver's Privacy Protection Act of 1994,[17] which regulates the disclosure and sale of personal information contained in the records of state motor vehicle department. This Act applies to States and private individuals,[18] and imposes penalties for failing to comply with its requirements. Also the Computer Fraud and Abuse Act of 1986 imposes criminal penalties on individuals who knowingly access a computer without authorisation, intentionally obtain

---

10. Kurt M. Saunders and Bruce Zucker, Counteracting Identity Fraud in the Information Age: The Identity Theft and Assumption Deterrence Act, 8 *Cornell J.L. & Pub. Pol'y* 661, 669 (1999); see also Stephanie Byers, The Internet: Privacy Lost, Identities Stolen 40 *Brandeis Law Journal* 149 (2001).
11. See Saunders and Zucker, *op. cit.*, at p. 669; See also Nicole M. Buba, Note, Waging War Against Identity Theft: Should the United States Borrow From the European Union's Battalion? 23 *Suffolk Transnatt' LL. Rev.* 633, 644 (2000)
12. Nicole M. Buba, *op. cit.* at p. 644.
13. Fred H. Cate, The Changing Face of Privacy Protection in the European Union and the United States, 33 *Ind. L. Rev.* 173, 210 (1999).
14. *Id.*
15. *Id.*
16. Nicole M. Buba, *op. cit.* at p. 644.
17. Stephanie Byers, *op. cit.* at p. 149.
18. *Id.* at p. 150.

information from a financial institution or the government, with the intent to commit a fraud, and as a result, cause damage.[19] However, the Act is limited in scope and application rendering it an ineffective means of battling widespread misuse of information and the occurrence of privacy crimes, such as identity theft.[20]

Further, the Electronic Communications Privacy Act of 1986 prohibits the unauthorized interception of, disclosure of, or access to "electronic communications services and for knowingly divulging the content of such communications while in storage."[21] The prohibition relates to any electronic communication, such as telephone conversation or e-mail, or even of any conversation in which the participants exhibit 'an expectation that such communication is no subject to interception under circumstances justifying such an expectation.'[22] In addition, the Fair Credit Reporting Act regulates the collection and use of personal information possessed by credit reporting agencies.[23] Recent legislation passed by Congress specifically addressing identity theft is the Identity Theft and Assumption Deterrence Act of 1998. This Act expressly criminalizes identify theft, and classifies private citizens as direct victims of such conduct. Criminal liability for identity theft is imposed on an individual who knowingly transfers or uses, without lawful authority, a means of identification of another person with the intent to commit, or to aid or abet, any unlawful activity that constitutes a violation of federal law or that constitutes a felony under any applicable state or local law.[24] In addition to these the legislation the Identity Theft Prevention Act of 2000 was introduced in the United States Senate on March 30, 2000. The Act's stated purpose is "to prevent identity fraud in consumer credit transactions and credit reports, and for

19. *Ibid.*
20. Nicole M. Buba, *op. cit.* at p. 645.
21. Saunders and Zucker, *op. cit.*, at p. 669.
22. Fred H. Cate, *op. cit.* at p. 214.
23. Saunders and Zucker, *op. cit.*, at p. 670.
24. Kristen S. Provenza, Identity Theft: Prevention and Liability, 3 *N.C. Banking Inst.* 325 (1999).

other purposes."[25] The Bill would amend the Social Security Act to subject a person to a civil monetary penalty for falsely using or selling a social security number not belonging to that person. Again, such legislation does not sufficiently deal with the problem of the easy availability of personal information on the internet.

Hence, the majority of the federal states do not solve the privacy problems presented by the Internet because they only govern the disclosure of personal identifiable information, and not the collection or use of such information.[26] Federal law, although recognising and addressing the problem of identity theft, is insufficient to deal with the procedures used by perpetrators to gather confidential information.[27] Therefore, it is abundantly clear that neither current nor proposed laws sufficiently deal with or regulate these procedures in the United States and there is a need of effective and achievable privacy protection laws.

On the other hand, the European Union has taken a major step in the direction of protecting citizen's personal information. The European Union adopted the Data Privacy Directive,[28] which is a comprehensive directive governing the collection and use of personal identifiable information.[29] Article 1 of the Directive sets out the objective that "Member States shall protect the fundamental rights and freedoms of natural persons, and in particular their rights to privacy with respect to the processing of personal data." Thus, the directive immediately and explicitly recognizes a right to privacy.

In England Justice Committee examined the whole subject of privacy. The Committee suggested comprehensive

---

25. S. 2328, 106th Cong. (2000).
26. Jonathan P. Cody, Note, Protecting Privacy Over the Internet: Has the Time Come to Abandon Self-Regulation? 48 *Cath. U.L. Rev.* 1183, 1200 (1999).
27. Kristen S. Provenza, *op. cit.* at p. 326.
28. Jonathan P. Cody, *op. cit.* at p. 1212.
29. Council Directive 95/46/EC of 24 October 1995 on the Protection of individuals with regard to the Processing of Personal Data on the Free Movement of such Data, 1995 (Article 1).

legislation on the civil side, and recommended that to make use of electronic, optical or other artificial devices as means of surreptitious surveillance should be made a criminal offence except in certain clearly defined circumstances. The Committee also recommended further investigation as regards criminal sanctions for industrial espionage.[30] Again the subject was examined by Younger Committee[31] and in some cases they recommended there should be legislation to create either a new offence in order to deal with new threats to privacy, for instance new technical surveillance devices; or a right of access by an individual to information held about him by a credit rating agency. In other cases they thought that more effective administrative controls would provide better protection of privacy.[32]

India till date does not have a proper data protection law. In May 2000, the Government passed the Information Technology Act, a set of laws intended to provide a comprehensive regulatory environment for electronic commerce. The Act also addresses computer crime, hacking, damage of computer source code, breach of confidentiality and viewing of pornography. Chapter X of the Act creates a Cyber Appellate Tribunal to over see adjudication of Cyber-crimes such as damage to computer system (Section 43) and breech of confidentiality and privacy (section 72). At the time of legislating on Cyber laws for India, Parliament appears to have largely neglected the issue of privacy of personally identifiable information. Section 72 of the Information Technology Act of 2000, which is the sole provision dealing with the issue, is very narrow in scope. Save as otherwise provided in this Act or any other law for the time being in force, any person, who in pursuance of any of the powers conferred under this Act, rules or regulations made thereunder, has secured access to any electronic record, book, register, correspondence, information, document or other material without the consent of the person concerned discloses such electronic record, book, register,

30. See Justice Report (Privacy and the Law), 1970.
31. Report of the Committee on Privacy (1972).
32. *Ibid.*

correspondence, information, document or other material to any other person shall be punished with imprisonment for a term which may extend to two years, or with fine which may extend to one lakh rupees or with both. Thus it prescribes a penalty for breach of privacy of any electronic record, but applies only to offences by authorities, etc. Thus, there exists huge gap between the privacy needs of individuals and existing legislative protection in India. On the contrary, privacy has been legislatively restricted by provisions in the Information Technology Act of 2000,[33] the Telegraph Act of 1885[34] and the proposed Communications Convergence Bill.[35]

Thus far, the whole data protection discourse and the effort to increase privacy standards in India has taken place only in the context of retaining India's huge potential for business process outsourcing. There has not yet been any wider discussion surrounding the privacy implications of the government's collection, retention and use of personal data. For historic and cultural reasons, the motives of the government in handling personal data are not suspected. Hence, a comprehensive privacy law is urgently needed, not only to safeguard India's economic interests, but equally, if

---

33. Section 69 of the Information Technology Act gives tremendous powers to the Controller of Certifying Authorities to direct the interception of any information transmitted through any computer resource, if he is satisfied that it is necessary or expedient to so to do in the interests of the sovereignty or integrity of India, the security of the state, friendly relations with foreign states, public order, or to prevent incitement of the commission of any cognizable offence.
34. Despite numerous phone-tap scandals resulting in the Supreme Court's laying down guidelines for wiretapping in People's Union for Civil Liberties (PUCL) *v.* Union of India, (1997) 1 SCC 301, Para 18. The court laid guidelines for tapping under the Act to create adequate privacy safeguards against official abuse. Illegal taps by government agencies still continues. The mail of many prominent NGOs in Delhi and strife-torn areas continues to be subjected to interception and censorship.
35. The Bill aims to create a "super regulator", the Communications Commission for India, to oversee voice and data communications. Chapter XIV of the Bill has been criticized for allowing law enforcement to intercept any communication under a very low standard.

not more importantly, to protect the privacy of its citizens against the increasingly orwellian powers of the government. Till date Parliament has not enacted any Act relating to privacy. It remains to be seen what would be the conditions to restrict it. There are other legislations which afford protection of privacy which would be highlighted in coming chapters.

The right to privacy has been brought into conspicuous prominence in the legal literature in view of the perpetuating debate amongst the legal thinkers and Judges. However, very scarce systematic documented information in the form of books on legal aspects of privacy is available. The difficulty is further compounded because of the absence of any specific legislation and organizational rules ensuring privacy and confidentiality. Hence, to make an extensive and comprehensive study of the subject, this study is proposed to be undertaken with the following objectives in mind.

To find out the systematic evolution of privacy in its historical perspective.

To explore the legal provisions of the Indian legal system to identify and highlight the status of the right and extent of the protection enshrined in those legal provisions. Apart from the statutory analyses the thrust of the study would be to assess the constitutional position of this right under our Constitution more particularly Part III dealing with the Fundamental Rights.

As the privacy is no longer regarded as an abstract concept. Identifiable with a national culture, a political system and a specific period of time, the concern for its protection in modern democratic societies characterized by enormous sophisticated bureaucratic structure and greatly advanced technological communications and information system, has become more intense, the computer age as the present era is known greatly threatened to make privacy impossible and present new challenges for any legal system which tend to protect this right. The focus of the present study would be to highlight the emerging challenges of new technological age, a social transformation and point out as to how and to what extent the legal system has cope up with the further extension and protection of the right to privacy.

The right to privacy is not specially spelled out in our Constitution. Judges none-the-less have considered the existence of such a right in numerous cases and regarded it as implicit in the fundamental freedom to life and personal liberty in numerous judicial determinations. The focus of this study would be to present the views of the Judges in particular instances as a reflection of judicial attitude towards privacy as a right and how and why and to what extent it is to be protected against invasions or intrusions. This would include a critical evaluation of judicial response in the furtherance and extension of this right.

The study shall proceed on the following hypotheses:

Whether right to privacy should be included in Part III of the Constitution of India so as to give explicit constitutional recognition to this right as one of the fundamental rights?

How far the judiciary has contributed in the growth of this right?

Whether there is a necessity to protect right to privacy from the potential threat of interference emanating from contemporary technological innovations?

Since the present study is not based on empirical experience, the author has selected India as a whole for the present study. The main focus of study is on the theoretical aspect which has been analyzed on the basis of material collected from different sources which mainly include Constituent Assembly Debates, Reports of Law Commission, recommendations of the Second Press Commission, the Nordic Conference of Jurists on Right to Respect for Privacy, 1967 and the Report of Younger Committee, 1972. This study is conducted in various libraries. It consists of studying various literatures available in this field. While dealing with particular aspect of privacy a brief reference of American and British Legal provisions are also given. Basically on the topic of conceptual basis of privacy Western luminaries contribution has been taken as a fundamental basis. However, the oriental concept of right to privacy is also included in several appropriate places. Constitutional stand of this right is discussed with reference to customary and statutory provisions. Further, the study is a critical evaluation of decided case law. As primary sources Constitution of India, USA and United Kingdom, Act of Parliament and judicial pronouncements have been taken and as a secondary sources different literatures, that is, books, articles, case comments, encyclopaedias, Corpus Secundum Juris, dictionaries and newspapers, have been consulted. Further, to simplify and unify the citation system, the same system has been adopted as it is directed generally for cases in different countries law reports.

In order to achieve the objectives of the study, the book is divided into seven chapters. Chapter 1 introduces the subject-matter. To make an extensive and comprehensive study of the subject, a brief description reflecting on objective of the study, hypotheses raised and methodology applied, is the focal point of Chapter 1.

Chapter 2 proceeds to examine the meaning, definitions, classification, functions and conceptual preliminaries and theoretical exposition of the right of privacy.

Chapter 3 contains a systematic description of the genetical evolution of the right of privacy in India. Efforts have been made to trace the genesis of privacy from the ancient period onwards. The chapter has been divided into three important heads, i.e., Privacy in Hindu Period, Privacy in Islamic Law and Privacy in British and Post-British Period.

Chapter 4 is an attempt to discuss in detail the legal framework of right to privacy in India. It talks about customary rules of privacy and provides constitutional support to clarify its stand. Besides customary rules and constitutional protection, several other statutory provisions recognise right to privacy directly or indirectly.

Chapter 5 is devoted to limitation on the right to privacy. Right to privacy, like other rights, is not an unqualified right. It brings into the limelight the general limitations which are reognised by the courts, jurists and legal luminaries in the field.

Chapter 6 deals with the judicial response. The American courts have been more evolutionary as far as "right to privacy" is concerned. There has been vivid, varied and distinct recognition and enforcement of this right in USA. In

English courts, "right to privacy" has yet to gain recognition as independent existing right. The English jurisprudence has tried to give effect to this right but under one or other existing rights. The Supreme Court of India has risen to the occasion and considered the "right to privacy" in catena of cases. It has been clearly enunciated in judicial pronouncements that right to privacy is a part of the fundamental right guaranteed under the Constitution in its Article 21.

Chapter 7 contains the appraisal of the study with critical approach of the right of privacy. Further, a few suggestions have also been made to reform the law with respect to the privacy of individual group and association.

2

Privacy: Meaning, Classifications and Philosophical Basis

I. MEANING OF PRIVACY

Privacy is a culturally limited concept. It varies with the times, the historical context, the state of culture and the prevailing judicial philosophy.[1] The customs related to privacy differ greatly from culture to culture, from situations to situations and from social system to social system.[2] The question 'what is privacy' has therefore, remained a problem for those who have made an attempt to define it and a few scholars have even abandoned their efforts to define it.[3] The concept of privacy in its broad sweep covers number of aspects, for example, non-disclosure of information about oneself, his sexual affairs, privacy of business secrets and non-observance by others, etc.

---

1. Hyman Gross, Privacy—Its Legal Protection, 1976; Alan F. Westin, Privacy and Freedom 7(1970); William L. Prosser, Privacy, 48 *California Law Review*, 383-423 (1960); also see Chandra Pal, Right to Privacy—Emerging As a Constitutional Right, 18 *Civil and Military Law Journal*, 42 (1982).
2. Arnold Simmel, Privacy, 12 *International Encyclopaedia of the Social Sciences*, 481 (1968).

The right of privacy is defined as the right to be let alone, the right of a person to be free from unwarranted publicity and the right to live without unwarranted interference by the public in matters with which the public is not necessarily concerned. The term right of privacy is a generic term encompassing various rights recognised to be inherent in the concept of ordered liberty and such a right prevents governmental interference in intimate personal relationships or activities, freedom of the individual to make fundamental choices involving himself, his family, and his relationships with others. Privacy laws prohibit an invasion of a person's right to be let alone (for example, not to be photographed in public) and also restrict access to personal information (for example, income tax returns, credit reports, etc.) and overhearing of private communications (for example, electronic surveillance). The right of privacy, simply put, is merely the right to live as one chooses.[4]

The concept of right to privacy does not lead itself to easy logical definition. This is so partly because as Tom Gaiety said in his article, "Redefining Privacy,"[5] the concept was thrown up in great haste from a miscellany of legal rock and stone and partly because of inherent difficulties in defining such an elusive concept. The difficulty arises out of the fact that it is not unitary concept but is multidimensional susceptible more for enumeration than definition. But it can be confidently asserted that any plausible definition of right to privacy is bound to take human body as its first and most basic reference for control over personal identity. Such a definition is bound to include body's inviolability, integrity and intimacy of personal identity including marital privacy.

There is no consensus in the legal and philosophical literature on a definition of privacy. For some, privacy is a psychological state, a condition of being apart from others

3. For example, A.H. Robertson in his book Privacy and Human Rights did not attempt to define it.
4. Pravin Anand and Gitanjali Duggal, Privacy in Michael Henry (ed.), International Privacy, Publicity and Personality Laws, 233(2001).
5. 12 *Harv. Cil. Rights Civil Lib. Rev.*, p. 233; see also S.K. Sharma, Privacy Law—A Comparative Study, 97(1994).

closely related to alienation.[6] For others, privacy is a form of power, the control we have over information about ourselves,[7] or the condition under which there is control over acquaintance with one's personal affairs by one enjoying it[8] or the individual's ability to control the circulation of information relating to him.[9] The cultural and societal variance of privacy can be observed from the fact that to a foreigner visiting an Indian village for the first time will have a feeling that there is absolutely no privacy in India, because village life in India is always alive with people all the time and in all the places. Everyone is related to every other person as uncle and aunt and anybody will enter anybody's houses. To him it may be invasion of privacy but to the villagers it is their culture to see their guests are taken care of even when not requested. On the other hand, an Indian visiting for the first time a western country would stand shocked by their culture and freedom in all matters. There is respect for privacy in all cultures as how the people living there expect it. For Europeans, their correspondence and their papers may be more sacred and secret than their own families. An Englishman may allow one or two women to share his compartment but not his confidential papers. But in India marriage, family and home are more sacred than individual rights. It is not the individual privacy that is protected but it is the privacy of the group as family privacy or community privacy that is protected. Inviolability of home is acknowledged even to the extent of denying rights to some of the members of the family. Many of the fundamental rights such as right to equality and certain other freedoms are denied to women because family and marriage are more sacred than individual rights and freedoms.[10]

---

6. Michael A. Weinstein, The Uses of Privacy in the Good Life, XIII, *Privacy, Nomos,* 94 (1971).
7. Charles Fried, An Anatomy of Values, 140(1970).
8. Hyman Gross, Privacy and Autonomy, XIII, *Privacy, Nomos,* 169.
9. Arthur R: Miller, The Assault on Privacy, 40 (1972).
10. Vany Adithan, Right to Privacy Under Art. 21-B, II *Madras Law Journal* 29 (2003).

While dealing with the subject of privacy William Cohen and John Kaplan have touched the genesis of the concept of privacy as follows:[11]

Once a civilization has made a distinction between the 'outer' and 'inner' man, between the life of the soul and the life of the body, between the spiritual and the material, between the sacred and profane, between the realm of God and the realm of Caesar, between the Church and the State, between rights inherit and inalienable and the rights that are in the power of government to give and take away, between public and private, between society and solitude, it becomes impossible to avoid the idea of privacy by whatever name it may be called—the idea of a private space in which man may become and remain himself.

Cohen and Kaplan have nearly covered all the aspects of privacy but still it is difficult to define the concept of privacy in exact words. The dictionary meaning[12] of privacy is seclusion; a place of seclusion; retreat; retirement; avoidance of notice or display; secrecy; a private matter. There may be cases where a complaint is made about the public disclosure of embarrassing private facts about an individual or where a person is placed in a false light in the public eye by publishing untrue statements about him. The remedy for such actions would be under the law of defamation or copyright. There may be cases in which a person may make use of other person's name or identity. In all the cases, a person's right to privacy is affected which is an aspect of liberty and for which remedy is available in the law of torts.

Hence, whether the word privacy implies positive or negative meaning depends upon the social, cultural background in which the concept of privacy has developed. It could be said that privacy is a dynamic concept and it takes its contents from the culture it thrives in. It starts with life and protects human dignity. It is akin to the concept of

---

11. William Cohen and John Kaplan, Constitutional Law—Civil Liberty and Individual Rights, 516 (1982).
12. Chambers 20th Century Dictionary (New Edition).

natural justice which is in accordance with natural human law. Although the concept is not well defined, it can be intellectually perceived with majority consensus.

II. DEFINITIONS OF RIGHT TO PRIVACY

The concept of privacy is not amenable to precise definition. In public law, traditionally 'privacy' means freedom from official intrusion. However, today with the development of science and technology and other pressures, the term 'privacy' has received extended meaning. Privacy in general means 'the right to be let alone.' The expression was used by Justice Thomas Cooley in 1888. According to him the right to respect for private life is the right to be let alone.[13] A couple of years later, in 1890 Samuel D. Warren and Louis D. Brandeis cultivated the notion with the initial analysis of the concept of privacy.[14] Political, social and economic changes, they argued, entail the recognition of new rights, the common law, in its eternal youth, grows to meet the demands of society. In very early times, the law gave a remedy only for physical interference with life and property. Later, there came a recognition of man's spiritual nature, of his feelings and his intellect. Gradually the scope of these legal rights broadened; and now the right to life has come to mean the right to enjoy life, the right to be let alone.[15] Describing the desirability and necessity for such protection, they argued:

Recent inventions and business methods call attention to the next step which must be taken for the protection of the person, and for securing to the individual what Judge Cooley calls the right "to be let alone." Instantaneous photographs and newspaper enterprise have invaded the sacred precincts of private and domestic life; and numerous mechanical devices threatened to make good the prediction that "what is whispered in the closet shall be proclaimed from the house-tops." . . . The press is overstepping in every direction the

---

13. Thomas M. Cooley, Torts, 91 (1888).
14. Samuel D. Warren and Louis D. Bradeis, The Right to Privacy, 4 *Harvard Law Review*, 193 (1890).
15. *Ibid.*

obvious bounds of propriety and decency. Gossip is no longer the resource of the idle and of the vicious, but has become a trade, which is pursued with industry as well as effrontery. To satisfy the prurient taste the details of sexual relations are spread broadcast in the columns of daily papers. To occupy the indolent, column upon column is filled with idle gossip, which can only be procured by intrusion upon the domestic circle. The intensity and complexity of life, attendant upon advancing civilization, have rendered necessary some retreat from the world, and man, under the refining influence of culture, has become more sensitive to publicity, so that solitude and privacy have become more essential to the individual; but modern enterprise and invention have, through invasions upon his privacy, subjected him to mental pain and distress, far greater than could be inflicted by mere bodily injury.[16]

Warren and Brandeis borrowed the view of Thomas M. Cooley and defined privacy as a right to be let alone. This definition emphasizes a person's right to be let alone or his withdrawal from the rest of the society. It has a negative meaning. In this point of view, the alleged right of privacy is clearly a privilege rather than a claim, at least in so far as they are stated in this unrestricted fashion. The object of privacy from Warren and Brandeis point of view is to protect 'inviolate personality'. It may be observed that the main thrust of Warren and Brandeis article revolves on two points. In the first place, they have advocated the necessity or desirability of affording the legal protection of privacy and secondly, the courts should grant such protection by extending the application of already existing principles of the common law. In the traditional division of law (into: law of persons, law of things and law of obligations) privacy, belongs to the first, i.e., the law of persons. The interest in privacy, they have argued is an interest of personality, not an interest of property. In the light of the discussion, it does not appear much convincing that "the common law of right to intellectual and artistic property are but instances and

16. *Id.* at 196.

applications of general right to privacy." The same right is later described by them as an "instance of the more general right to be let alone." It has rightly been commented that analytically, there is not interest in arguing as the 'real' meaning that Warren and Brandeis ascribed to 'privacy'. The existence of the Prosser-Bloustein controversy is sufficient to suggest, however, that Warren and Brandies were not clear about the meaning, or that what they wrote could legitimately be interpreted in more than one way.[17] It further observed that the Warren and Brandeis interpretation of privacy as a "right to be let alone" that protects man's "inviolate personality" is unsatisfying. Their definition is too imprecise for judicial construction and principled application, let alone incorporation into public policy.[18] Being first and seminal contribution, Warren and Brandeis article has generated a lot of controversies in the subsequent juristic thought. Harry Kalven has commented that the impact of the article resides not so much in the power of its argument as in the social status it gave to the tort.[19] There are other definitions which support this view in a way or other. For example, the right of privacy has also been defined as the right to be free from unwarranted publicity,[20] to live a life of seclusion[21] and to live without unwarranted interference by the public in matter with which the public is not necessarily concerned.[22] Adam Carlyle Breckenridge has defined privacy as a person's personal possession.[23] Edward Shills has defined privacy as "Zero relationship" between two or more persons in the sense that there is no interaction or communication between them if they so choose.[24]

---

17. Ruth E. Gavison, Privacy and Its Legal Protection (Unpublished thesis submitted to the University of Oxford for Ph.D. in 1975).
18. David O'Brien, Privacy and Law and Public Policy, 4(1979).
19. Harry Kalven, J.R., "Privacy and Tort Law—Were Warren and Brandeis Wrong?" 31 *Law and Contemporary Problems*, 333-339 (1966).
20. Roach *v.* Harper, 143 W. Va 860, 105 SC 2d 564.
21. Frith *v.* Associated Press (DC SC) 176 F Supp. 671.
22. Glancy, The Invention of the Right to Privacy, 21 *Ariz. L.R.*1(1979).
23. Adam Carlyle Breckeridge, The Right to Privacy, 1 (1970).
24. Edward Shills, Privacy—Its Constitution and Vicissitudes, 31 *Law and Contemporary Problems*, (No. 2 Spring) 281 (1966).

William L. Prosser, reviewed a number of cases, and said, "right to privacy is a compound of four different torts." These are as follows:[25]

(i) Intrusion upon the plaintiff's seclusion or solitude or into his private affairs,
(ii) Public disclosure of embarrassing private facts about the plaintiff,
(iii) Publicity which places the plaintiff in a false light in the public eyes, and
(iv) Appropriation for defendant's advantage, of the plaintiff's name or likeness.

William L. Prosser's analysis clearly highlighted four interests represented by four torts which questioned the view of Warren and Brandeis. Prosser's classification of privacy interests raised much controversy over the theoretical and legal foundations of privacy. If Prosser's analysis was correct, the Warren and Brandeis were wrong. Instead of a single interest, there were four interests represented by four torts, none of which bore a distinctive interest in privacy. By re-analyzing Prosser's classification, Bloustein attempted to show that the principle of "inviolate personality" was still the fundamental interest in privacy cases. He argued that the injury is to our individuality to our dignity as individuals, and the legal remedy represents a social vindication of the human spirit, thus, threatened rather than a recompense for the loss suffered.[26]

Like Warren and Brandeis, Bloustein assumed that privacy interests have an intrinsic value, and for this reason they involve more than mere protection of instrumental value, such as protection of property, reputation and mental suffering. It is highly been commented that although Bloustein's critique usefully emphasizes that Prosser's re-examination cannot be accepted unconditionally, his definition, like that of Warren and Brandeis, remain

25. William L. Prosser, Privacy, 48 *California Law Review* 389 (1960).
26. Edward J. Bloustein, Privacy as an Aspect of Human Dignity: An Answer to Dean Prosser, 39 *N.Y.U.L. Rev.* 962 (1964)

imprecise. The problem with Bloustein's analysis, however, is not that his "explanation is so wide as to be meaningless" but that he does not define and analyse privacy itself. Rather, his approach consists of a broad characterization of the reason privacy is of value at all namely, that privacy is associated with human freedom and dignity. Bloustein describes the right to privacy by reference to the ends that enjoyment of privacy is supposed to promote such as individuality, human dignity and liberty. He concludes that the focal point of Warren and Brandeis article was indeed freedom from publicity, but argues that the same rationale holds for all affronts to human dignity.

Commenting upon the Articles of William L. Prosser and Edward J. Bloustein, Hyman Gross observes:[27]

> It is clear from a reading of the cases which Dean Prosser and Professor Bloustein examine that what is at stake in all of them is an interest in the state of affairs we have described as privacy. All involves improperly getting to know something personal or making it known to others. Dean Prosser concludes, however, that an assortment of different interests have been improper packaged together in one tort box labelled "invasion of privacy." Professor Bloustein's answer is that only one interest is involved in all-human dignity. Both notions lead though by different paths, to a conceptual indeterminacy regarding privacy.

However, Hyman Gross himself maintains that the conceptual vacuum surrounding the notion of privacy is because of the different uses of the word 'privacy' in law and ordinary language. The law does not determine that privacy is but what situations of privacy will be afforded legal protection, or will be made private by virtue of legal protection. Privacy, no less than good reputation or physical safety, is a creature of life in a human community and not the contrivance of a legal system concerned with its protection. Privacy does not exist because of legal recognition

27. Hyman Gross, The Concept of Privacy, 42 *N.Y.U.L. Rev.* 46 (1967).

but depends upon habits of life.[28] He distinguishes privacy in week or derivative sense and privacy in strong sense. Privacy, in week sense is used only as a synonym for another terms viz. mental repose (unwanted telephone calls or to hear what is going on in the next apartment), physical solitude (remaining out of public gaze or glimpse), physical exclusiveness and autonomy (planing a family, deciding about one's children's education or about Church affiliation, etc.).

For privacy in strong sense there is no exact synonym. But defining privacy Hyman Gross appears to oscillate between viewing it as a "condition of life" and as a "form of control". In his first article he defines it in the following words:

Privacy is the condition of human life in which acquaintance with a person or with affairs of his life which are personal to him is limited.[29]

In another article, he describes privacy as:

> The condition under which there is control over acquaintance with one's personal affairs by one enjoying it. . .[30]

Hyman Gross further explains the meaning of 'control' in the context of privacy. According to his analysis if A voluntarily exposes himself to B, by either giving B some information or enabling B to overhear A's conversation, and if B is bound by one convention obligating him not to disclose the information thus acquired. A losses no 'control' over the information, although he opens himself to a risk of loss of 'control'. Voluntary exposure without the presence of restrictive convention, or acquisition of information about A against his wish despite his efforts to prevent it are instances of loss of control.[31]

28. *Id.* at 36.
29. *Ibid.*
30. Hyman Gross, Privacy and Autonomy, XIII *Privacy Nomos* 169 (1971).
31. *Id.* at 170-171.

Hyman Gross's analysis of 'control' is open to criticism for he uses two different senses of 'control' viz., (a) the control an individual has over the flow of information about himself from himself, and (b) the control over the communication of information about oneself by others. Even though others are obliged not to disclose the information, it can hardly amount to 'control' the information. This duality of senses exists for all those who define privacy in terms of control over informations (e.g. Charles Fried, Aurther Miller and Richard B. Parker) except Edward Shils who defines it as the existence of a boundary through which information does not flow from the persons who possess it to others. The actions of the former are not reported to, or observed or recorded or otherwise perceived by the latter.[32]

Similarly privacy, writes Weinstein, like alienation, loneliness, ostracism and isolation, is a condition of being-apart-from-others.[33] It is a voluntary limitation of communication to or from others for the purpose of undertaking activity in pursuit of a perceived good.[34] Commenting upon this definition, Richard B. Parker observes:[35]

> If privacy is defined as a psychological state, it becomes impossible to describe a person who has had his privacy temporarily invaded without his knowledge, since his psychological state is not affected at all by the loss of privacy. It is interesting and important to study what it is like to experience various gains and losses of privacy. One of the reasons the law protects privacy in certain situations is to protect us as individuals from suffering mental distress. But privacy should not be defined as, for example, freedom from various sorts of mental distress, or as the experience of being apart from others. Such definitions of privacy will be unable to cover those situations where we lose or gain privacy with no corresponding change in our mental state.

---

32. *Supra* n. 24 at 282.
33. Michael A. Weinstein, *op. cit.*, p. 88.
34. *Id.* at 104.
35. Richard B. Parker, A Definition of Privacy 27 *Rutgers L. Rev.* 278-279 (1974).

Commenting upon the above definition of Richard B. Parker, Ruth E. Gavison in his thesis 'Privacy and its Legal Protection' writes that it is true that Weinstein speaks of privacy as it 'appears in consciousness' but he does not define it as a state of consciousness, but as a condition of life. It seems that Weinstein has not committed the mistake concerning the nature of privacy while Parker accuses him of.[36]

Charles Fried offers the following definition:[37]

> Privacy is not simply an absence of information about us in the minds of others; rather it is the control we have over information about ourselves . . . The person who enjoys privacy is able to grant or deny access to others . . . Privacy, thus, is control over knowledge about oneself.

Gary L. Bostwick[38] suggests that privacy is divisible into three components, i.e. (a) repose, (b) sanctuary, and (c) initimate decisions. Of these three components he holds that the last one is an eminently more dynamic privacy concept as compare to repose and sanctuary. Professor Tribe[39] stressed another fundamental facet of right to privacy problem. He wrote *inter alia*: "of all decisions as person makes about his or her body the most profound and intimate relates to two sets of questions first, whether, when and how one's body is to become the vehicle for another human being creation."

Similarly other important definition is given by Alan F. Westin. He defines privacy as "the claim of individuals, groups or institutions to determine for themselves, when, how and to what extent information about them is communicated to others."[40] Commenting on Westin's

---

36. *Supra* n. 17 at 33.
37. *Supra* n. 7 at 140; also see Charles Fried, Privacy, 77 *Yale Law Journal*, 475-483 (1965).
38. 64 *California Law Review*, pp. 1447 and 1466.
39. Professor Tribe, American Constitutional Law, p. 921.
40. Alan F. Westin, Privacy and Freedom, 7 (1970).

definition of privacy, Professor Louis Lusky points out that literally, it declares my privacy to be invaded, or at least affected somehow, if my one neighbour tells my second neighbour (without my consent) that I am vegetarian or that I am suffering from fever, or that I like oyster. The more troublesome aspect of the Westinian definition, according to him, is that it confuses through over simplification. So Louis Lusky redefines Westin's definition as "privacy is the condition enjoyed by one who control the communication of information about himself."[41]

Arthur Miller defines privacy as a control over information. For him, privacy is the individual's ability to control the circulation of information relating to him—a power that often is essential to maintaining social relationship and personal freedom.

The definitions of privacy in terms of 'control over information about ourselves' have been criticized as being overbroad and narrow. Richard B. Parker is perhaps the only one who has addressed himself with the question as to what criteria a definition of privacy should meet. He maintains that ideally a definition of privacy should be as true (fit the data) as beautiful (simple) and as useful (applicable) as possible.[42] By "data" he means "our shared institutions of when privacy is or is not gained or lost." It may be that our shared concept of privacy may not have common characteristics. Thus the simplest definition may have to include a list. A third criterion which a definition of privacy should meet is applicability by lawyers and courts.[43] In the light of the above premises Richard B. Parker gives his own definition in the following words:

> Privacy is control over when and by whom the various parts of us can be sensed by others.[44]

41. Louis Lusky, Invasion of Privacy: A Clarification of Concepts, LXII *Colum. L. Rev.* 693 (1972).
42. *Supra* n. 35 at 277.
43. *Ibid.*
44. *Id.* at 281.

These definitions emphasize on communication of circulation of private information. For them if there is no communication or disclosure of information that cannot amount to invasion of privacy. For this reason, these definitions are inadequate because there may be invasion of privacy without having communication to others also.

For example, in certain situations, when a private 'eye' a photographer tracks an individual, that person's privacy may be invaded but in such instance there is no communication or disclosure of personal information. Many private interests that have been constitutionally recognised involve neither dissemination nor acquisition of personal information. If somebody plays music in public buses or a beggar goes from door to door, there is no communication of private information which may constitute violation of privacy. It is not covered by these definitions. There are other definitions which would be worthwhile to mention here.

Privacy is an outcome of a person's wish to withhold from others certain knowledge as to his past and present experience and actions and his intentions for the future. The wish for privacy expresses a desire to be an enigma to others or more generally a desire to control others perception and beliefs *vis-à-vis* self-concealing person.[45] This definition highlights the psychological aspect of privacy.

In the United Kingdom both the Justice Report, 1970 and the Younger Committee Report, 1972 pointed out that the difficulty of finding a precise and logical formula which could either circumscribe the meaning of the word 'privacy' or define it exhaustively. Each, however, suggested a working definition. Justice Report defines privacy as "that area of a man's life which in any given circumstances, a reasonable man with an understanding of the legitimate needs of the community would think it wrong to invade."[46]

The Younger Committee conceived of the rights of the privacy as having two main aspects:

---

45. Sidney M. Tourad, Some Psychological Aspects of Privacy, 31 *Law and Contemporary Problems* (No. 2 Spring) 307 (1966).
46. Justice Report (Privacy and the Law) 5 (1970).

> "The first of these is freedom from intrusion upon oneself, one's home, family and relationships. The second is privacy of information, that is the right to determine for oneself how and to what extent information about oneself is communicated to others."[47]

The Indian scholars,[48] who have written articles on privacy, have preferred to rely upon the definition given by the western scholars rather than contributing their own. Shriniwas Gupta, of course, initiated the question regarding the concept of privacy in India but concluded with the following observations:

> Our ancient law in *Dharmshashtras* also recognised the concept of privacy. Really, the law of privacy has been well-expounded in the commentaries of the old law. Kautilya in his *Arthashastra* has prescribed a detailed procedure to ensure right to privacy while ministers were consulted. But neither in ancient law nor in the present law the term 'privacy' has anywhere been defined nor any judicial pronouncement has so far come to make the position clear.[49]

Pannalal Dhar says that the right to privacy is a right whose contours still remained undefined.[50] Professor P.K. Tripathi relates the right to privacy with the idea of

---

47. The Younger Committee Report (Report of the Committee on Privacy) 10 (1972).
48. B. Shanta Kumari, 'Infringement of Privacy As An Actionable Tort, VIII *The Year Book of Legal Studies* 92 (1972); F.S. Nariman, The Right To Be Let Alone, XVII *The Indian Advocate* 76 (1977); Anirudh Prasad, New Dimensions of Right to Privacy under the Indian Constitution, XIV, *J.C.P.S.* 252 (1980); Shriniwas Gupta, Right to Privacy: A Kind of Personal Autonomy, *Lex et. Juris*, August 30, 1988; Dilkbir Kaur Bajwa, Right to Privacy: Its Origin and Ramifications, 26 *CMLJ* 48 (1990).
49. Shriniwas Gupta, Right to Privacy: A Kind of Personal Autonomy, *Ibid.*, Shriniwas Gupta, Right to Privacy Is An Aspect of Human Dignity, 17 *Lawyer* 67.
50. Pannalal Dhar, Right to Privacy, *AIR Journal Section* (Raj.) 145 (1987).

exclusion.[51] To exclude others has remained by and large, the main theme of privacy.

Govind Mishra defines privacy as a fundamental right of the citizens to exclude governmental acts, omissions and things which tend to annoy or embarrass them and which affect the promotion and maintenance of their dignity.[52] However, it is not an exhaustive one. He accept that privacy is a culturally limited concept.[53]

But surprisingly enough, Professor Upendra Baxi has raised a very basic question as to whether 'privacy' is a value of human relations in India. He observes:

> But the question arises at a more general level whether privacy is a value of human relations in India. Everyday experience in Indian setting suggests otherwise, Marriage parties and midnight music, wedding processions and morning '*bhajans*', unabated curiosity at other people's illness or personal vicissitudes, manifestation of good neighbourliness through constant surveillance by the next door neighbour (large number of Indian houses do not use curtains) are some of the common experiences. A question may arise whether privacy is not after all a value somewhat alien to Indian culture.[54]

There are many other scholars who have also subscribed to the opinion expressed by Professor Baxi.[55]

An attempt has been made to cover most of the definitions of the privacy in the Nordic Conference of Jurists on the Right to Respect for Privacy which was held in May

---

51. Speech for symposium organised at the Campus Law Centre, Faculty of Law, University of Delhi on February 17, 1982 quoted in Govind Mishra, Privacy: A Fundamental Right under the Indian Constitution, 8 & 9, *Del. L. Rev.*, p. 139.
52. Govind Mishra, *op. cit.*, p. 139.
53. *Id.* at 138.
54. K.K. Mathew on Democracy, Equality and Freedom, Introduction, lxxiv, note 262.
55. Sir Zelman Cowan, Justice V.R. Krishna Iyer, Sri V.N. Gadgil, M.P. and Mr. Ranjit Lal, a journalist.

1967. Privacy is not made of one particular interest only. This consists of many interests and hence the right to privacy should be meant as the right of the individual to protect his life against:

(i) the interference with his private, family and home life;
(ii) the interference with his physical or mental integrity or his moral or intellectual freedom;
(iii) the attacks on his honour or reputation;
(iv) being placed in a false light;
(v) the disclosure of irrelevant, embarrassing facts relating to his private life;
(vi) the use of his name, identity or likeness;
(vii) the interference with his correspondence;
(viii) the spying, prying, watching and besetting;
(ix) misuse of his communication, written or oral; and
(x) the disclosure of information given or received by him in circumstances of professional confidence.

In United States of America, a judicially approved definition of the right of privacy is that it is the right to be free from the unwarranted appropriation or exploitation of one's personality, the publicizing of one's private affairs with which the public has no legitimate concern, or the wrongful intrusion into one's private activities in such manner as to outrage or cause mental suffering, shame, or humiliation to a person of ordinary sensibilities.[56]

The Western scholars have also subscribed to the view that privacy is very closely knitted with the life-style of the people. People have different life-styles in different civilizations. And, so long there are different civilizations existing on the globe, there cannot be uniform human behaviour. This is the reason which defies a universally accepted definition of privacy. After having observed all definitions one can draw an inference about the right of privacy.

---

56. Rubenfeld, The Right of Privacy, 102 *Harv. L. Rev.* 737 (Fall 1989).

It is a condition of individuals, groups or institutions to determine themselves when and to what extent information about them is communicated to others. It includes protection from interference with his physical or mental integrity or his moral or intellectual freedom. It encircles a person's inner zone. It gives authority to a person to decide for himself how much he will share with others his thoughts, his feelings and the facts of his personal life. The concept of privacy will increasingly insinuate itself into our law as a means of describing the 'interest',[57] claim,[58] power,[59] or right[60] which is infringed.

The long search for 'definition' or 'privacy' has triggered a continuing debate that is often sterile and ultimately, futile. The debate is sterile for four main reasons. Firstly, the premises upon which the proposed definition are based are materially different. Thus, for example, those who assume 'privacy' to be 'right' have not really joined issue with those who conceive it to be a 'condition', 'state', 'area of life' and so on. The former are asserting a normative statement about the desirability of whatever it is that the particular writer regards as privacy, while the latter merely proffering a descriptive statement about privacy. Secondly, the objectives of the arguments tend to differ. For example, Dean Prosser's famous essay, which marshalled several hundred privacy cases, was a successful attempt to demonstrate that the American law recognised four distinct torts under the umbrella of 'privacy'. In his well-known rejoinder Edward Bloustein seized upon Dean Prosser's atomisation of 'privacy' and insisted that there is a single interest at the heart of the law's protection, namely 'human dignity'. But in exposing the disparate interests protected Prosser is merely describing the law; in his reply Bloustein whatever the merits of his argument, is engaged in seeking, at a higher level of abstraction, a wider explanation for the law's concern to protect privacy.

---

57. Louis Lusky, Invasion of Privacy, *op. cit.*, p. 693.
58. Alan F. Westin, Privacy and Freedom, 7 (1970).
59. Richard B. Parker, *op. cit.*, pp. 275 and 280.

Thirdly, the arguments as to the desirability of 'privacy' frequently proceed from different standpoints. Some see privacy as an end itself, while others regards it as instrumental in the securing of other desirable social ends such as 'creativity', 'love' or 'emotional release'. The former position, though it is central to any argument in favour of privacy, does not adequately explain why it should prevail over competing interests such as free speech.[60] The later position is based on unproven empirical speculation. If they are to have any force, the two arguments must be seen together rather than in opposition. Fourthly, the definitions usually beg more questions than they are designed to answer. For instance, privacy is widely defined in terms of 'control' over who has information about or access to the individual. But in order to evaluate such definitions we need to know, for instance, what purpose, if any, is served by the exercise of this control. Normally the answers point to arguments in favour of the individual's right or claim to or interest in limiting the exposure to which he is subject, or in the circulation of facts about him. Another defect of the 'control' definition is that it fails to account for the act that if I want you to know a fact about me and I am unable to communicate it to you then, according to the definition of 'privacy' in terms of control, I should have lost privacy for I have lost control over the circulation of information about myself. Equally, if I succeed in total disclosure of any private life to you I should not have lost privacy. Neither of these can be correct.[61]

The debate is ultimate futile for, in those legal systems which recognize a common law right to privacy (for its equivalent), privacy is entrenched in a vocabulary of the courts, where it is accorded statutory protection then privacy is simply what the legislature says it is.

---

60. D.N. McCormick, Privacy: A Problem of Definition, 1 *Brit J. of Law and Society*, 75 (1974).

61. E.L. Beardsley, Privacy, Autonomy and Selective Disclosure, XIII *Privacy Nomos* 56 (1971); Raymond Wacks, The Poverty of Privacy, 96 *Law Quarterly Review* 75-76 (Jan-Oct. 1980); S. I. Ben, Privacy, Freedom and Respect for Persons, XIII *Nomos* 1; also see Edward J. Bloustein, *op. cit.*

III. CLASSIFICATION OF PRIVACY

Absolute privacy, except for the individual living alone on an island, had never existed. In the small towns and villages where most people lived before the industrial revolution, there was little or no privacy.[62] The details of one's wealth or health could not be hidden for long .from other community members. Indeed someone seeking privacy from the others might have been looked with suspicion. Hence, the quest for privacy is inherent in man. It is a natural need to establish individual boundaries and to restrict the entry of others into that area. There are moments in every man's life when he does not want intrusion on privacy threatens that liberty. Therefore, the concept of privacy can be classified under the following heads:

(i) Intimate Privacy
(ii) Family Privacy
(iii) Social Privacy
(iv) Individual Privacy

(i) Intimate Privacy

According to the western view "intimacy is the sharing of information about one's action, beliefs, or emotions, which one does not share with all, and which one as the right not to share with anyone."[63] Emerson goes on to elaborate on the zones of personal information which privacy law should include such as the things which deals with intimacy. He says, "so far as the privacy tort (of 'public disclosure') is concerned, protection would be extended only to matters relating to the intimate details of person's life: those activities, ideas, or emotions which one does not share with others or shares only with those who are closest. This would include sexual relations, the performance of bodily functions, family relations, and the like."[64]

---

62. Jeremy Refkin, Biosphere Politics, 154 (1992).
63. *Supra* n. 11 at p. 524.
64. T. Emerson, The Right of Privacy and Freedom of Press, 14 *Harv. Cr-CLL Rev.* 343(1979).

On account of a different culture, the Indian society in which we live the concept of intimate privacy somewhat differs from the Western one. It is observed that most intimate form of privacy exists amongst married couples, but since marriage constitute a family, the intimate privacy can also be classified under the head 'family privacy'. Hence the intimate privacy relates to the inner and outer mechanisms in the minds of the individuals, their beliefs and actions which they desire to treat as private. It does not however, mean that these intimate aspects are never disclosed at all. Many a time the thoughts, emotions, beliefs or actions are confined to the trusted ones like intimate discreet friends, parents, spouses, etc.

The individuals sharing this intimate informations, actions, beliefs, etc. would not favour any leakage, disclosure or exposure to their privacy. To safeguards this particular type of privacy the help of constitutional provisions is not necessary, nor does a situation arise when the safeguard of the law is deemed essential. The intimate privacy generally covers the grounds of sexual intimacies, personal beliefs, and such other things the society would not approve.

(ii) Family Privacy

A concept of family privacy can cover a wide area beginning from the privacy between a married couple, extending to a joint family living together and ending with all the blood relations of the family though they may not be living together. It is often seen that a family secret is assiduously guarded by the members of a family although they might be living in different towns. In India during the olden times people lived in joint families and it was only when our society became progressively urbanized that the institution of a joint family underwent changes because of changing forms of social institutions and not through the need for privacy. The social customs and the cultural background were such that the families were auto-adjusted to certain kinds of privacy and the individuals never even felt the need of intervention of law or that of any court. The safeguards were in built in the very customs themselves. There was segregation of males and females and unwritten social rules automatically created and granted privacy. A friend or a relative visiting the house would do so without encroaching upon the permissible limits of privacy.

It was only after the fragmentation of the joint family under the on slought of urbanization and its economic impact, that people became self-centered. In order to share selfishly the privileges of wealth and pleasurable living—not necessarily a happy and contended living that different factions in the family made the need for privacy a dominant tool for their segregation. As a result of this, plausibly the need for family privacy has assumed significance and law has been compelled to favour the clamorous demand for it and the judicial activism has become a collaborator.

(iii) Social Privacy

The third type of privacy is social privacy. This privacy can further be sub-divided into three categories:

(A) Political/Legal Privacy
(B) Professional Privacy
(C) Community Privacy

(A) Political/Legal Privacy

Under this privacy, certain intimate liberties are protected from the intrusions of the government. The intrusions by the government are regulated by means of law and the law in turn either gives or takes away rights to certain liberties which will have considerable bearing on privacy. The examples of regulations are: Procedure of search and seizure; Publications of news; Eavesdropping/wire tapping; Taking photographs; Birth control; National security, Public nudity (exposure); Sexual relationship beyond marriage; Privacy of court proceedings (trial in camera); and Tax recovery and income. Since these subjects need a separate and quite an elaborate discussion the author has only mentioned the areas in which human society can lay claim to privacy as can be seen from the American legal literature. So long as the Indian society is not enveloped by the American evaluations and devaluations, it is not likely to make any hard demands on the Indian Constitution and Article 21 will not have to reach its elastic limits to finally break down, while bearing the burden of privacy.

(B) Professional Privacy

One of the areas in which privacy of an individual can get affected is that of the professional and through the professions. When a professional acquires knowledge of private activities of an individual, it cannot be safeguarded unless professional privacy is made possible. A professional may also have his own privacy of vocation to safeguard. Hence, in the case of professionals safeguard to privacy may become essential on two scores: Firstly is own professional privacy, and secondly, the professional privacies of his clients.

Generally in India, lawyers, doctors, chartered accountants, consultants, document copiers, magicians, astrologers, etc. are the professionals who have the opportunity to possess knowledge about the privacy of their patrons. The above as well as other categories of professionals including businessmen may have their trade secrets, inventions, special methods of operations and so on and so forth. They assiduously strive to guard their secrets and privacy for continual success as well as for avoiding competition. The safeguard of professional privacy therefore becomes vitally important to them because with protection to their privacy, they can hope for protection to their life and personal liberty.

A doctor revealing about the disease of his patient to his employer may result in the termination of the service of the patient rendering him without the means of his livelihood or a discreet doctor having carried out an abortion for a maiden, can come into trouble by one leak in his professional privacy. Similarly, a lawyer or a chartered accountant can violate the privacy of his client by several means. In *R.M. Malkani's case*,[65] the Coroner's attempts to extract bribe from Dr. Adatia has been a typical case of an attempt to violate professional privacy.

Hence professional privacy needs to be safeguarded vehemently not only because it can affect the professional,

---

65. R.M. Malkani *v.* State of Maharashtra, AIR 1973 SC 157.

but because it can also affect lives of individuals who seek help of the professionals. In the context of modern living, professionalism has come to stay in a long and important way and hence it would adequately need and deserve all legal safeguards. By protecting professional privacy, we will be in a position to protect right to life and personal liberty.

(C) Community Privacy

The concept of community privacy has a very limited field because a society is composed of conglomeration of communities and social laws generally govern major aspects. But there are certain community privacy which may need intervention of law for their safeguard. A Hindu Brahmin community would not approve of a slaughter house for beef in the midst and cluster of their business and residential colony. Nor would Christians and Muslims approve of a ban on cow slaughter. For them beef eating is their privacy of food and dietary habit and they would not wish to surrender this community privacy. Similarly, every community can have some peculiar customs and rituals private to their own community, which they would not like to expose to public gaze or interference.

Many communities hold certain beliefs and religious dogmas from which they adopt their special ways of living. Any interference from outsider to this way of life, they are unwilling to tolerate and, therefore, they would need the right to privacy for their community collectively. Especially in Britain in the recent times there are secret organized groups of people involved with the supernatural. They are composed of interested believers, worshippers and practitioners, and they are known as Covens or witches of members of black mass cults. There are other such groups constituting membership of Voodoo priests, magicians, cabalistic, etc. They staunchly follow the beliefs, rights and rituals which are generally carried out in strict secrecy.[66] Whether these beliefs are well founded or they are misconceived cannot be the subject matter of any rationalist court but situations may arise

66. Based on 'Supernatural' by Douglas Hill and Pat William (New American Library).

when the court would be called upon to determine the right of privacy of these secret societies or groups. In India fortified by Articles 25 and 26 coupled with Article 21, these groups can certainly claim privacy for their practices without any blanket bar on superstitions.

For instance in *Saifudin Saheb* v. *State of Bombay*,[67] our Supreme Court has held that the head of the Dawoodi Bohra Community has the right to ex-communicate any member of the community. The power of ex-communication is vested in him for the purpose of enforcing discipline and for keeping the denomination as an entity. The court further held that the community as a whole has a right through its religious head to manage its own affairs in matters of religion under Article 26(b) of the Constitution. The person who is ex-communicated may be affected but the power of ex-communication is mainly for the purpose of ensuring the preservation of the community and it is prime significance in religious life of every member of the group. This is community privacy.

But ex-communication of a member of a community affects many of his civil rights and to that extent his personal liberty is also affected. An individual cannot be treated as a pariah and he has the right to follow the dictates of his own conscience. Article 21 as it is being interpreted today was not available at the time when this case arose. Otherwise the court could have granted the right of privacy to an individual in religious matters.

Even in modern sophisticated society, the members of Masonic Lodge take oath of secrecy and they jealously guard its privacy. To this extent community privacy may also become an important subject for the consideration of our juridical minds.

(iv) Individual Privacy

The most susceptible area is the privacy of individuals. An individual by nature at some time or the other in his daily existence craves for brief periods of privacy for mental peace, quiet, meditation, enjoyment of hobbies, cultivation of personality, both by cosmetically means as well as by

67. AIR 1962 SC 853.

rehearsals and practices such as speech modulation, physical exercise, etc. Thus quest for privacy is inherent in every human being. Man's pursuit of seclusion is in reality his pursuit for privacy and since privacy is an integral part of one's life the right to life cannot be complete with any abnegation of right to privacy.

In our complex society as per individual idiosyncrasy the manifestation of demand for right to privacy may appear even in paradoxical forms. Whereas on the one hand the Indian women may go for choice of apparels which expose their bodies to the public gaze to the minimum in the American society, the women may want to bare their bodies to the maximum and making the right to privacy paradoxical. Any attempt on the part of the authority to forbid the exposure of their anatomy on grounds of obscenity may well be construed by these women as an infringement of their right to privacy of their bodies which they wish to exhibit publicly. Women when they do not mind exposing their anatomy in public, they are assiduous defenders of their age, which they wish to hide by all means.

Any effort on the part of the government or the society to restrict the right to privacy of an individual who wishes to choose his own way of life, associations, profession, faith, religion and so on and so forth would definitely mean to him that his privacy is at stake. Generally governments, journalists, social scientists, employers and relatives constitute a class of intruders of individual privacy.

IV. FUNCTIONS OF PRIVACY

One of the principal arguments advanced in support of the doctrine of privacy by its original exponents is that the increased complexity and intensity of modern civilization and the development of spiritual sensibilities have rendered people more sensitive to publicity and have increased their need of privacy, while the great technological improvements in the means of communication have more and more subjected the intimacies of people's private lives to exploitation by those who ponder to commercialism and to prurient and idle curiosity. A legally enforceable right of privacy is deemed to be a property protection against this type of encroachment upon the personality of the individual.[68] The role and functions of privacy are described by Alan F. Westin which would be apposite to discuss here. Westin has described four functions of privacy in democratic societies. These can be grouped conveniently under four headings—personal autonomy, emotional release, self-evaluation, and limited and protected communication. Since every human being is a whole organism, these four functions constantly flow into one another, but their separation for analytical purposes helps to clarify the important choices about individual privacy that American law may have to make in the coming years.

These functions are comparable with 'values' of Emerson which are essential to the maintenance of a system of free expression, the concept with which personal liberty is most often in conflict. Emerson's those values are democratic values, namely, individual self-fulfilment, the pursuit of truth, participation in social and political decision-making and the maintenance of both change and stability in society.[69] Alan F. Westin's functions and Thomas Emerson's values are similar means towards the same end of liberal democracy but the functions of privacy and values of free expression are so frequently in conflict that any resolution usually rests in the balancing of priorities. In the succeeding pages the author will elaborate the functions of privacy as put forward by Westin.

(i) Personal Autonomy

In democratic societies there is a fundamental belief in the uniqueness of the individual, in his basic dignity and worth as a creature of God and a human being and in need to maintain social processes that safeguard is sacred individuality. Psychologists and sociologists have linked the development and maintenance of this sense in individuality to the human need for autonomy—the desire to avoid being

68. Towe, A., Growing Awareness of Privacy in America, 37 *Mont. L. Rev.* 39 (Winter 1976)
69. Thomas I. Emerson, Towards a General Theory of the First Amendment (1966).

manipulated or dominated wholly by others.[70] Social theorists, viz., R.E. Park, Kurt Lewin and Erving Goffman at the centre of traditional liberalism seek to defend individual claims against general societal interests. They say the individual is inviolable and they believe the 'core self' is protected by zones of privacy. And autonomy is threatened by those who penetrate the inner zone. The most serious threat to the individual's autonomy is the possibility that someone may penetrate the inner zone and learn his ultimate secrets either by physical or psychological means. This deliberate penetration of the individual's protective shell, his psychological armor, would leave him naked to ridicule and shame and would put him under the control of those who knew his secrets.[71] Autonomy is also threatened by those who penetrate the core self because they do not recognize the importance of ultimate privacy or think that the casual and uninvited help they may be rendering compensates for the violation.[72]

The autonomy that privacy protects is also vital to the development of individuality and consciousness of individual choice of life. Leontine Young noted that "without privacy there is no individuality. There are types only who can know what he thinks and feels if he never has the opportunity to be alone with his thoughts and feelings?"[73] This development of individuality is particularly important in democratic societies since qualities of independent thought, diversity of views and non-conformity are considered desirable traits of individuals. Such independence requires time for sheltered experimentation and testing of ideas for preparation and practice in thought and conduct without fear of ridicule or penalty and for the opportunity to alter opinions before making them public. The individual's sense that it is he who decides when to "go public" is a crucial aspect of his feeling

---

70. Alan F. Westin, Privacy and Freedom, 33 (1970).
71. *Ibid.*
72. *Ibid.*
73. Leontine Young, Life Among the Giants, (1966) quoted by Alan F. Westin, *Id.* at p. 34.

of autonomy. Summing up the importance of privacy for political liberty, Clinton Rossiter has also stressed the feature of autonomy:

> Privacy is a special kind of independence, which can be understood as an attempt to secure autonomy in at least a few personal and spiritual concerns, if necessary in defiance of all the pressures of modern society . . . It seeks to erect an unbreachable wall of dignity and reserve against the entire world. The free man is the private man, the man who still keeps some of his thoughts and judgments entirely to himself, who feels no-over-riding compulsion to share everything of value with others, not even those he loves and trusts.[74]

(ii) Emotional Release

Emotional release, the second function, stems from the need the individual has to seek relief from physical and emotional stress. Life in society generates such tensions for the individual that both physical and psychological health demand periods of privacy for various types of emotional release. At one level, such relaxation is required from the pressure of playing social roles. Social scientists agree that each person constantly plays a series of varied and multiple roles, depending on his audience and behavioural situation.[75] They remind us that the life demands a variety of roles, and no person can successfully play these different parts without some relief. In this also privacy shields the individual from having always to comply with social norms. As Alan F. Westin sees it: "if there is no privacy to permit society to ignore these deviations—if all transgressions were known—most persons in society would be under organizational discipline or in jail, or could be manipulated by threats of such action.[76]

Another aspect of release is the "safety-valve" function afforded by privacy. Most persons need to give vent to their

---

74. Clinton Rossiter, The Pattern of Liberty, quoted by Alan F. Westin, *Ibid.*, also quoted by S.K. Sharma, Privacy Law—A Comparative Study, 86 (1994).
75. Goffman, Presentation of Self 56-57, quoted by Alan F. Westin, *Ibid.*
76. *Supra* n. 70 at 35.

anger at "the system", "city hall", "the boss", and various others who exercise authority over them, and to do this in the intimacy of family or friendship circles, or in private papers, without fear of being held responsible for such comments. This is very different from freedom of speech or press, which involves publicly voiced criticism without fear of interference by government and subject only to private suit. Rather, the aspect of release concerned here involves commentary that may be wholly unfair, frivolous, nasty and libelous, but never socially measured because it is uttered in privacy. Without the aid of such release in accommodating the daily abrasions, most people would experience serious emotional pressure.

Surveillance of bodily and sexual functions by outsiders is practiced with social approval only in what sociologists call "total institution"—such as jails, mental institutions, and monasteries—or on volunteers in medical or behavioural science experiments. Even then, prisoners and patients usually complain about being watched and seek ways to escape the constant surveillance of guards.[77]

Finally, emotional release through privacy plays an important part in individual life at times of loss, shock, or sorrow. In such moments society provides comfort both through communal support by gathering of friends and through respect for the privacy of the individual and his intimates. Privacy also performs a protective function at moments of less intense stress, during the periods of anxiety and uncertainty which are part of daily life.[78] Privacy, in short, allows us to be ourselves at low risk.

(iii) Self-Evaluation

Self-evaluation is another function which privacy enhances. Every individual needs some evaluation of his action. What he has done? What he has to do? What is the purpose of his life? It can be achieved only by self-evaluation. For this privacy is required. In a state of solitude, a person is able to evaluate information that bombards him or his daily

---

77. *Id.* at 36.
78. *Ibid.*

routine in order to act as appropriately and as consistently as possible. Every individual needs to integrate his experiences into a meaningful pattern and to exert his individuality on events. To carry on such self-evaluation, privacy is essential. At the intellectual level, individuals need to process the information that cannot be processed while there are still "on the go". Alan Bates has written that privacy in such circumstances enables a person to "assess the flood of information received, to consider alternatives and possible consequences so that he may then act as consistently and appropriately as possible."[79] Westin argues that privacy provides the time to anticipate problems, recast doubts, and originate solutions. Creative human beings always affirmed man's need for contemplation. Persons must learn to live with themselves before they can live with others.

(iv) Limited and Protected Communication

Limited and protected communication is the final function of privacy which provides the individual with the opportunities he needs for sharing confidences and intimacies with those he trusts. Everybody wants to keep secret the matter of spouse, family, personal friends and business secrets. It is based on utilitarian principle. This is founded upon the principle of necessity, in the interest and administration of justice.[80] Limited communication is accepted between husband and wife, attorney and client, doctor and patient, etc. Common law recognizes the need to protect certain confidential relationships that can flourish in the state of intimacy. Psychological distance as respected in a successful marriage, is as important as spatial distance. Similarly, distance is observed in relation between teacher and student, parent and child, minister and communicant and many others.

Having discussed the above functions of privacy Alan F. Westin observes that privacy functions basically as an

79. Alan P. Bates, Privacy, *Nomos*, XIII, 97.
80. William S. Strong, The Grave's a Fine and Private Place, XXIX, *Society*, No. 2, Jan.-Feb. 6 (1992).

instrument for achieving goals of self-realization.[81] As such, it is only part of the individual's complex and shifting system of social needs, part of the way he adjusts his emotional mechanism to the barrage of personal and social stimuli that he encounters in daily life. Individual have needs for disclosure and companionship every bit as important as their needs for privacy. To be left in privacy when one wants companionship is as uncomfortable as the inability to have privacy when one craves it. The balance of privacy and disclosure will be powerfully influenced, of course, by both the society's cultural norms and the particular individual's status and life situation. The basic point is that each individual must, within the larger context of his culture, his status, and his personal situation, make a continuous adjustment between his needs for solitude and companionship; for intimacy and general social intercourse; for anonymity and responsible participation in society; for reserve and disclosure. A free society leaves this choice to the individual, for this is the core of the "right of individual privacy"—the right of the individual to decide for himself, with only extra-ordinary exceptions in the interests of society, when and on what terms his acts should be revealed to the general public.[82]

Westin does not only emphasized privacy. He seems that companionship and disclosure are also very important. Man always does not want to live in isolation; most of time he lives in society. So social life, he argues, is equally important from the point of view of privacy. For this reason the balance between privacy and disclosure is required.

It is rather difficult to add anything more to such a detailed description of the functions of privacy as Westin mentioned. However, his entire description is predicted upon a civilized social life. He has not deliberated over the role of privacy in the transformation of a natural society to a civilized one. For civilization itself is the progress towards a society of privacy. The savage's whole existence is public.

81. *Supra* n. 70 at 39.

82. *Id.* at 39-42.

Civilization is the process of setting man free from men.[83] The more one knows about a person, the greater one's power to damage him.[84] To sum up, the functional justification of privacy as a human right lies in protecting human beings against emotional disturbances of anxiety, humiliation, embarrassment, disgrace, inconvenience, annoyance, shame and feeling of indignities. It protects morals and ideas of decency.

V. PHILOSOPHICAL BASIS OF RIGHT TO PRIVACY

Philosophical literature has given scant attention to the problem of privacy as such; the framework of reference within which privacy has so recently and widely become a matter of controversy is a distinctly contemporary one.[85] The notion of privacy is not a new one. It is inherent in human behaviour. It is a notion of an original sovereignty over oneself. It is an activity that touches the very nature of man; the man's nature is, to a considerable degree, made and not given. Man constantly transcends himself, and in the process of transcendence he discovers in himself new dimensions, new heights, and new depths. He reaches eminencies never before dreamed of, and debasements to which no one before had fallen.[86] The Chorus of Atigone and the Psalmist thousands of years ago noted the wonder that is man—man in tension, man in the process of becoming, emergent man.[87] Every human being has his shell and we must take the shell into account. Here 'shell' means the whole envelope of circumstances.[88] Thus, the notion of 'shell' is the fundamental base of privacy.

---

83. Ayn Rand, The Fountainhead 660 (1986),
84. Stanley I. Ben, Privacy, Freedom and Respect for Persons, XIII *Privacy, Nomos,* p. 6.
85. Glen Negley, Philosophical Views on the Value of Privacy, 31 *Law And Contemporary Problems,* 319 (1966).
86. Milton R. Konvitz, Privacy and the Law: A Philosophical Prelude, 31 *Law And Contemporary Problems,* 274-275 (1966).
87. *Id.* at 275.
88. Henry James, The Portrait of a Lady, 287-88 (1881).

The right to privacy has its foundations in the instincts of nature. It is recognised intuitively, consciousness being witness that can be called to establish its existence. Any person whose intellect is in a normal condition recognizes at once that as to each individual member of society there are matters private and here are matters public so far as the individual is concerned. Each individual as instinctively resents any encroachment by the public upon his rights which are of a private nature as he does the withdrawal of those rights which are of a public nature. A concept of privacy in matters purely private is therefore derived from natural law.[89]

Some jurists, as well as courts have suggested the natural law as the basis of right of privacy. In the Anglo-American system, the absence of any "positive law" as far back as in 1905, led the court to grant relief on the basis of "nature justice and reasons." Hence, the court held that the right of privacy was founded on the "instincts of nature" and is entitled to be recognised as a legal right under the conception of natural justice. The courts, on the basis of this held that each individual as instinctively resents any encroachment by public upon the rights which are of private nature as he does the withdrawal of those of his rights which are of a public nature. A right of privacy in matters purely private is, therefore, derived from natural law. Indian courts, however, do not recognise any natural right of privacy and believe that such a right can be acquired only as a customary easement. There is yet another school which recognises the right of privacy in the guise of well established rights as those relating to property, contracts or libel.

When Justice Douglas wrote for the Supreme Court, in *Griswold* v. *Connecticut*,[90] that various constitutional guarantees create "zones of privacy", he was quite right in pointing out that the court was delaying "with a right of privacy older than the Bill of Rights." Indeed, "Zones of privacy" can be found marked off, hinted at, or groped for in some of our oldest legal codes and in the most influential philosophical writings and traditions.

---

89. Pavesich *v.* New England Life Ins. Co., 122 Ga 190, 194 (1905).
90. 381 U.S. 479, 486 (1965).

Almost the first page of the Bible introduced us to the feeling of shame as a violation of privacy. After Adam and Eve had eaten the fruit of the tree of knowledge, "the eyes of both were opened, and they knew that they were naked; and they sewed fig leaves together and made themselves aprons."[91] Thus, mythically, we have been taught that our very knowledge of good and evil—our moral nature, our nature as men—is somehow, by divine ordinance, linked with a sense and a realm of privacy.[92] When, after the Flood, Noah became drunk, he "lay uncovered in his tent," and Ham violated his father's privacy by looking upon his father's nakedness and by telling his brothers about it. His brothers took a garment, "laid it upon their shoulders and walked backward and covered the nakedness of their father. Their faces were turned away, and they did not see their father's nakedness.[93]

This distance from the biblical garden to the statutory wilderness may have taken thousands of years to traverse; but surely that distance and the distance between the "zone of privacy" which two of Noah's three sons respected and "the sacred precincts of marital bedrooms", which the Supreme Court of United States sought to protect in Griswold, cannot conceptually be great.

Once a civilization has made a distinction between the 'outer' and the 'inner' man, between life of the soul and life of the body, between the spiritual and the material, between the realm of God and the realm of Caesar, between rights inherent and inalienable and rights that are in the power of government to give and take away between public and private, between society and solitude. It becomes impossible to avoid the idea of privacy by whatever name it may be called—the idea of a private space in which man may become and remain himself.[94]

Privacy is a natural need of man to establish individual boundaries and to restrict the entry of others into that area.

---

91. Genesis 3: 7 (Revised Standard Version).
92. Helen M. Lynd, On Shame and the Search for Identity. Ch. 2 (1958).
93. Genesis 9: 20-27 (Revised Standard Version).
94. Herbert Marcuse, *op. cit.*, p. 10.

There are sufficient evidences in both oriental and occidental civilizations to support this view. Biblical reference is given to support the privacy concept in occidental philosophy and *Vedas, Puranas* and different ancient sources are cited to support its ancient origin in oriental philosophy.[95]

Any claim to a right to privacy has ancient origins, but general recognition of that right is relatively modern. Further more, governmental guarantees to protect a right to privacy are even more recent.[96] Though the concept of privacy was fully recognised in ancient Indian society, there was no concept as a right in the manner we define it now. The ancient Indian society, in general, was duty-oriented and, therefore, the right of an individual can be inferred from the duties thus imposed.[97] Though, India is culturally different from that of United States and United Kingdom, they share the same jurisprudential outlook in certain legal tenets. The extent and scope of privacy may vary among them, but value of privacy is the same to them. Although, both civilization, oriental and occidental, recognise the value of privacy, most of the discussions on this topic have taken place in Western society particularly in United States of America. In ancient Indian literature privacy was recognised in a duty-based way. The ancient Indian society was duty-bound and there was no hard and fast 'right' concept which is relatively younger. It is difficult to trace the antecedents of each facet of the right with any precision. Right is rather modern phenomenon; it was unknown to the Greeks and Romans. Alan R. White ascribes its late arrival as partly due to delayed but now pronounce, prominence given to the individual.[98] One can identify at least the major sources of the right to privacy and, at the same time, can see more clearly the countervailing claims or interests that must be taken into account.[99] It is also

95. A detailed survey of authority is given by Govind Mishra in Privacy and the Indian Legal System 12 *Del. L. Rev.* 46 (1990).
96. Alan F. Westin, *op. cit.*, p. 8.
97. *Supra* n. 95 at 62.
98. Alan R. White, Rights 2 (1984).
99. William M. Beaney, The Right to Privacy and American Law, 31 *Law and Contemporary Problems*, 256 (1966).

true that the concept of duty which dates back to classical times as well, emphasizes the individual. Hence, in ancient Indian society the individual was bound to perform the duty which maintained the social relation.

How and to what extent, has the concept of privacy reached the level of legal right? What are the fundamentals of this right? Various scholar's views have to be taken into account in this respect. The usual starting point in any discussion of the legal concept of privacy, though not necessarily the correct one, is the famous article, "The Right to Privacy" by two Boston lawyers Samuel D. Warren and Louis D. Brandeis in 1890.[100] But if Warren and Brandeis were less than prescient in dealing with the countervailing power of the press, they were more convincing in their efforts to show that some existing English and American torts previously classified by the courts under property, contract, or implied trust rubrics were most meaningfully described as rights of privacy. What was truly creative was their insistence that privacy—the right to be let alone—was an interest that man should be able to assert directly and not derivatively from his efforts to protect other interests.[101] To protect man's "inviolate personality" against the intrusive behaviour so increasingly evident in their time, Warren and Brandeis thought that the law should provide both a criminal and a private remedy.[102] They did not reject the property aspects of privacy, but rather pleaded for a distinct right. Further, they wanted to extend the scope of jurisprudence to protect not the reputation already covered by libel law—but the feelings of individuals who had been subjected to some form on intrusion. They elaborated the proposition as follows:

Thus in early times, the law gave remedy only for physical interference with life and property, for trespass *vi et armis*. Then the right to life served only to protect from battery in its various forms; liberty meant freedom from actual restraint and the right to property secured to the

---

100. 4 *Harv. Law Rev.* 193 (1890).
101. *Supra* n. 99 at 257.
102. *Ibid*; See also Harry Kalven JR, *op. cit.*, pp. 326-41.

individual, his land and cattle, later there came a recognition of spiritual nature of his feelings and his intellect. Gradually, the scope of these legal rights has come to mean the right to enjoy the life—the right to be let alone.[103]

The individual shall have full protection in person and in his property is a principle as old as the common law; but it has been found necessary from time to time to define a new and exact nature and extent of such protection. Warren and Brandeis described the common law as having evolved steadily to protect man from physical interference with life and property. This 'right to life' they noted, served only to protect the individual against trespass and battery. But as Justice Thomas M. Cooley had asserted "battery involves many elements of injury not always present in beaches of duty. There is very likely a shock to the nerves, and the peace and quiet of the individual is disturbed for a period of greater or less duration.[104] Samuel D. Warren and Louis D. Brandeis traced these early actions to such concepts as nuisance, slander and libel, and intangible property, the products and processes of the mind. However, new inventions are business methods required that a next step be taken to protect the right to be let alone. The authors then detailed their criticism of the press.[105]

Instantaneous photographs and newspaper enterprise have evaded the sacred precincts of private and domestic life; and numerous mechanical devices threaten to make good the prediction that what is whispered in the closet shall be proclaimed from house tops . . . The press is overstepping in every direction the obvious bounds of propriety and of decency.

Warren and Brandeis explained their underlying rationale of privacy thus:

> "The intensity and complexity of life, attendant upon advancing civilization have rendered necessary some

---

103. Warren and Brandeis, *op. cit.*
104. Richard F. Hixan, Privacy in a Public Society 30 (1987).
105. *Supra* n. 103 at 194-95.

> retreat from the world, the man, under the refining influence of culture, has become more sensitive to publicity, so that solitude and privacy have become more essential to the individual; but modern enterprise and invention have, through invasions upon his privacy, subjected him to mental pain and distress for greater than could be inflicted by mere bodily injury." The spreading of gossip both belittled and perverted the relative importance of things, "dwarfing the thoughts and aspirations of people." Easy of comprehension, appealing to the weak side of human nature which is never wholly cast down by the misfortunes and frailties of our neighbours . . . Triviality destroys at once robustness of the thought and delicacy of feeling. No enthusiasm can flourish, no generous impulse can service under its blighting influence.[106]

In advancing the thesis, Warren and Brandeis made no effort to hide the fact that they were more interested in the moral, or spiritual, not material side of law. Our law recognizes no principle upon which compensation can be granted for mere injury to the feelings.[107] They found such a principle in the doctrine of common law copyright, which gives the author or artist exclusive ownership. But they said, the statutory right is of no value unless there is publication and the common law right is lost as soon as there is publication. Thus, they summarized: the principle which protects personal productions . . . against publication in any form, is in reality not the principle of private property, but that of an inviolate personality. They deduced, therefore, that "a general right to privacy for thoughts, emotions and sensations . . . should receive the same protection, whether expressed in writing or in conduct, in conversation, in attitudes or in facial expression."

---

106. *Id.* at 195-96.
107. *Id.* at 196-97.

Warren and Brandeis did not make their right unqualified. They placed several limitations on their new right. These are follows:

Firstly, the right to privacy did not prohibit the publication of any matter of public or general interest. But what is public or general interest they left it for future generations to decide. They did not decide it.

Secondly, they insisted that their right did not prohibit the communication of any matter, "though in its nature private" under circumstances that would render it a privileged communication as defined by the law of Slander and Libel. This would include statements made at public meetings or in courts. The publication of which clearly serve a public purpose.

Thirdly, their law of privacy did not grant redress for any wrong suffered by oral publication of private matter.

Fourthly, the right ceased when the individual published the facts himself, or consented to their publication. Truth, long a defence in libel actions, did not afford a defence in a privacy suit, the authors said, "It is not for injury to the individual's character that redress or prevention is sought, but for injury to the right of prìvacy." Nor finally, was the absence of malice an acceptable defence.

The increased recognition of a right to privacy has brought corresponding praise for Warren and Brandeis as originator of a new legal right.[108] At the same time, their contribution has been criticised as having lacked sufficient legal[109] and factual[110] basis for the right they are credited with launching. A more fundamental critique of privacy law in general attempts to reduce this "new" right to its component interests and then to assess whether these interests deserve legal protection.[111] Finding some aspects of privacy to be, for

---

108. P. Dionisopoulos and C. Ducat, The Right to Privacy 20 (1976).
109. Pratt, The Warren and Brandeis Argument for a Right to Privacy 161, 179 *Pub. L. Rev.* (1975).
110. Barron, Warren and Brandeis, The Right to Privacy, 4 *Harv. L. Rev.* 193 (1890).
111. Davis, What Do We Mean by "Right to Privacy?" 4 *S.D.L. Rev.* 1 (1959); Harry Kalven, *op. cit.*, p. 326; Posner, The Right to Privacy, 12 *G. A.L. Rev.* 393 (1978).

example, merely extensions of property and reputation, the educationist approach suggests that what Warren and Brandeis invented did not constitute and independently protectible right.[112]

Both praise and criticism proceed on the assumption shared by modern courts,[113] commentators,[114] and legal historians,[115] that "courts had not prior to 1890 granted relief expressly for invasion of a right of privacy."[116] Warren and Brandeis, however, deserve either full credit nor blame for the law's recognition of privacy as a protectible interest. They did not purport to add a novel right to the legal universe, but instead drew upon some of the established legal doctrines protecting personal privacy to propose and extension of remedies against the press. They were moved in their effort by a personal grievance on the part of one of them against yellow press. Their work was thus something of a lawyer's catharsis rather than objective scholarship or judicial craftsmanship.[117]

Later the concept of privacy has been studied by so many scholars and jurists. Eminent among them who have contributed to the conceptual basis of privacy are William L. Prosser, Edward J. Bloustein and Alan F. Westin. These scholars have highlighted a conceptual basis of privacy. Similarly, Garry L. Bostwick and Judee K. Burgoon added some conceptual literature in the field. The author will make an endeavour to discuss their views in relation to right to privacy in the following pages.

---

112. Davis, *op. cit.* at pp. 7-12.
113. See, e.g. Flores *v.* Mosler Safe Co., 7 N. Y. 2 d 276, 280, 164 N.E. 2d 853-855, 196 N.Y.S. 2d 975, 978 (1959); Nader *v.* General Motors Corp. 31 A.D. 2d 392, 397, 398 N.Y.S. 2d 137, 143 (1969).
114. A. Miller, The Assault on Privacy 169 (1971); W. Prosser, Handbook of the Law of Torts 117 (1971), Davis *op. cit.* at p. 3.
115. L. Friedman, A History of American Law 548 (1973); O' Counor, The Right to Privacy in Historical Perspective, 53 *Mass. L.Q.* 101, 109-10 (1968).
116. Bullings *v.* Atkinson, 489 S.W. 2d 858, 859 (Tex. 1973).
117. Clark C. Havighurst, Foreword in 31 *Law and Contemporary Problems* 251 (1966).

William L. Prosser, elaborated on Warren and Brandeis's private-facts tort and, based upon more than two hundred court cases, found three other distinct categories: intrusion, false light and appropriation. According to Prosser, it is not one tort, but a complex of four. The law of privacy comprises four distinct kinds of invasion of four different interests of the plaintiff, which are tied together by the common name, but otherwise have almost nothing in common except that each represents an interference with the right of the plaintiff, in the phrase coined by Justice Cooley, "to be let alone."[118] His effort was to reduce privacy law to manageable proportions.

Edward J. Bloustein extended privacy to an "interest in preserving human dignity and individuality."[119] His concept although laudable, imposes an incredible burden on juridical system that normally relies upon precision. Somewhere between Prosser's specific torts and Bloustein's broad conception Alan F. Westin comes. He defines privacy as ". . . the claims of individuals, groups of institutions to determine themselves when, how and to what extent information about them is communicated to others." He also includes "the voluntary and temporary withdrawal of a person from the general society through physical or psychological means . . . in a condition of anonymity or reserve."

Dean Prosser incorporated four torts in his book entitled, Handbook of Law of Torts and Restatement.[120] According to him, privacy is not an independent value at all but a composite of interest in reputation, emotional tranquillity and intangible property.

William L. Prosser defined the Samuel D. Warren and Louis D. Brandeis's private facts-tort of which they were primarily concerned this way:

> One who gives publicity to a matter concerning the private life of another is subject to liability to the other

118. William L. Prosser, *op. cit.*, p. 962.
119. Edward J. Bloustein, *op. cit.*, p. 962.
120. William L. Prosser, Handbook of the Law of Torts (1968).

for invasion of his privacy, if the matter is publicized is of a kind that (a) would be highly offensive to a reasonable person, and (b) is not of legitimate concern to the public.

Actually this tort was rather slow to appear in the decisions. Although there were earlier instances,[121] in which other elements were involved, its first real separate application was in a Kentucky case[122] in 1927 in which the defendant put up a notice in the window of his garage announcing to the world that the defendant owed him money and would not pay it. But the decision which has become the leading case, largely because of its spectacular facts, in *Melvin* v. *Reid*,[123] in California in 1931. The plaintiff has been a prostitute, whose original name was Gabrielle Darley, and the defendant in a sensational murder trial. After her acquittal she had abandoned her life of shame, become rehabilitated, married a man named Melvin, had led a life of rectitude in respectable society, among friends and associates who were unaware of her earlier career. Seven years afterward the defendant made and exhibited a motion picture, which created the true story and ruined her new life by revealing her past to the world and her friends. The court held that this was an actionable invasion of her right of privacy.

For William Prosser, the second tort, is intrusion. It occurs when an expectation of seclusion is breached, normally the invasion of someone's physical solitude. This category related to common law trespass, is what most people think of when they discuss privacy invasion, although the protection of private information is now also a widespread concern. Strong statutory law protects against such devices as wire-tapping, bugging and photography. Intrusion upon seclusion pertains generally to unauthorized prying into someone's

---

121. Douglas *v.* Stokes, 149 Ky. 506, 149 S.W. 849 (1912); Thompson *v.* Adelberg and Berman, 181 Ky. 487, 205 S.W. 558 (1918); and Peed *v.* Washington Times, 55 Wash L. Rep. 182 (D.C. 1927).
122. Brents *v.* Morgan, 221 Ky. 765, 299 S.W. 967 (1927).
123. 112 Cal. App. 285, 297 Pac. 91 (1931).

private affairs. The basic recovery rule has three components: the intrusion must (i) be highly offensive to a reasonable person; (ii) be intentional; and (iii) occur in a place where the plaintiff has a reasonable expectation of privacy. For three reasons, this tort fails to protect people from the potentially privacy invasive practices of credit bureaus. The common law intrusion upon seclusion tort appears inhospitable to consumer violation of privacy claims against credit bureaus. A consumer who complains that a credit bureau has violated his privacy must look elsewhere for relief.

The third form of invasion of privacy, which Warren and Brandeis again do not appear to have had in mind at all, consists of publicity that places the plaintiff in a false light in the public eye. It seems to have made first appearance in 1816, when Lord Byron succeeded in enjoining the circulation of a spurious inferior poem attributed to his pen.[124] The principle frequently, over a good many years, has made a rather nebulous appearance in a line of decisions[125] in which falsity or fiction has been held to defeat the privilege of reporting news and other matters of public interest, or of giving further publicity to already figures. It is only of late years that it has begun to receive any independent recognition of its own. One form in which it occasionally appears is that of publicity falsely attributing to the plaintiff some opinion or utterance. Another form in which this form of the tort-frequently has made appearance is the use of the plaintiff's picture to illustrate a book or an article with which he has no reasonable connection. Still another form in which the tort occurs is the inclusion of the plaintiff's name, photograph and finger prints in a public "rogues' gallery" of convicted criminals, when he has not in fact been convicted of any crime.

---

124. Lord Byron *v.* Johnston, 2 Mer. 29, 35 Eng. Rep. 851 (1816).
125. Peay *v.* Curtis Pub. Co., 78 F. Supp. 305 (D.D.C. 1948); Martin *v.* Johnson Pub. Co., 157 N.Y.S. 2d 409 (Sup. ct. 1956); Samuel *v.* Curtis Pub. Co., 122 F. Supp. 327 (N.D. Cal. 1954); Metzer *v.* Dell Pub. Co., 207 Misc. 182. 136 N.Y.S. 2d 888 (Supp. ct. 1955) and Hazlitt *v.* Fawcett Publications, 116 F Supp. 539 (D. Conn. 1953).

Hence, false light involves the publication of erroneous information that creates a wrong impression about an individual's life or behaviour. The information may not be unflattering, but it, however, injures personal dignity. The offence is often unintentional or unplanned. An aspect of this category, fictionalization, is something a dramist, for example, might do make the story more appealing. Whether intentional or not, the publication or broadcast of false information is considered an invasion of personal privacy.

Appropriation is the fourth tort. There is little indication the Warren and Brandeis intended to direct their article at the fourth branch of the tort, that exploitation of attributes of the plaintiff's identity. It means the unauthorised use of one's name or likeness for commercial purposes. But Bloustein says, right of privacy protects human dignity not the commercial interests. Appropriation is quite a different matter from intrusion, disclosure of private facts or a false light in the public eye. The interest protected is not so much a mental as a proprietary one, in the exclusive use of the plaintiff's name and likeness as an aspect of his identity. It seems quite pointless to dispute over whether such a right is to be classified as "property". If it is not, it is at least, once it is protected by law, a right of value upon which the plaintiff can capitalize by selling licenses. Its proprietary nature is clearly indicated by a decision that an exclusive license has been called a "right of publicity".

William Prosser says that the plaintiff has to show that the information was in fact private and that the defendant spread the information widely. The action may be defeated by showing that the public has legitimate interest in the information. Therefore, the private facts torts usually involves the mass media because of this mass publication requirement. Bloustein rejects Prosser's reputational and emotional distress arguments and says that the tort, in preserving some "right to be let alone" really protects individual dignity and integrity and prevents the loss of individual freedom and independence. However, he supports the mass publicity requirement. He believes that individual dignity is damaged not when friends, who are assumed to know better, learn things that may change their opinion of us. Private gossip, he says, does not damage individual dignity in general. But Diane Zimmerman does not agree with this view. He observes, such conclusions are questionable because exposure of private information to people who have no special interest or first hand knowledge is likely to be more damaging than information circulated widely among strangers by the media. How we are viewed by the people we know is likely to be of greater concern than is the opinion of strangers.[126]

Alan F. Westin begins his defense with the premise that, despite obvious differences among cultural norms, it is still possible to describe the general functions that privacy performs for individuals and groups in democratic nations. The functions are part of what Westin identifies as four basic states of individual privacy: solitude, intimacy, anonymity and reserve.

In the state of solitude, Westin says, the individual is separated from the group and freed from the observation of other person. Solitude is the place where the individual communes with himself or with some supernatural force. It is the ultimate state of personal privacy.[127]

Westin's second state, 'intimate state' where an individual acts as part of a small unit that claims and is permitted to exercise "corporate seclusion" in order to achieve "a close, relaxed and frank relationship between two or more individuals." Typically, such units include husband and wife, the family a circle of friends, or certain work-place relationships.[128] Whereas solitude is a natural and solitary experience, the state of intimacy is at risk without the understood trust of others who also have a stake in the relationship. Common law already protects the confidentiality of many such arrangements for example, those between physician and patient, attorney and client, and husband and wife. Legislated law recognizes similar intimacies, such as that between a journalist and an undisclosed source of news.

---

126. Diae L. Zimmerman, Requirement for a Heavy-weight: A Farewell to Warren and Brandeis Privacy Tort, 68 *Cornell L. R.* 333 (1983), see also, Harry ·D. Krause and Paul Marcus, Privacy 26 *The American Journal of Comparative Law* 377-92 (Supp. 1978).
127. Alan F. Wenstin, Privacy and Freedom 31 (1970).
128. *Ibid.*

But the promise of the intimate state is not so much a matter of the right of privacy as it is a matter of understood trust and confidence.

In a state of anonymity the individual may appear in public places or perform public acts but still seek, and find freedom from identification and surveillance. As Westin describes the anonymous person:[129]

He may be riding a subway, attending a ball game, or walking the streets; he is among people and knows that he is being observed: but unless he is well known celebrity, he does not expect to be personally identified and held to the full rules of behaviour and role that would operate if he were known to those observing him.

The individual merges into the "situational landscape" and the sense of relaxation and freedom that one may seek in open spaces and public places is destroyed by the knowledge or fear that one is under systematic observation or surveillance.

Reserve, which Westin defines as the most subtle state of privacy, is the creation of a psychological barrier against unwanted intrusion, as when we feel the need to limit information about ourselves with the help and discretion of the people around us. "Even in the most intimate relations, Westin writes, "communication of self to others is always incomplete and is based on the need to hold back some parts of one's self as either too personal and sacred or too shameful and profane to express.[130]

Similarly, Bostwick has made a significant contribution in relation to right of privacy. According to him privacy rights are: repose, sanctuary and intimate decision.[131] His approach is similar to that of Dean Prosser which is a reductionist one. We can compare the idea of Bostwick with that of P. Alan Dionisopoulous and Craig R. Ducat. They have propounded three types of privacies namely: place-oriented, person-oriented and privacy as it inheres in certain

129. *Ibid.*

130. *Id.* at 32.

131. Gary L. Bostwick, "A Taxonomy of Privacy: Repose: Sanctuary and Intimate Decision", 64 *Cal. L.R.* 1447 (1976).

human relationships.[132] Bostwick's privacies of repose and sanctuary are place-oriented concepts and his privacy of initiate decision is person-oriented and relational.

The privacy of repose, according to him, is the freedom from anything that disturbs or excites, the opposite of calm, peace, or tranquillity, sometimes the right of repose is in conflict with other protected rights—"freedom from being talked to can be guaranteed only if others are prevented from talking".

Similarly, Bostwick's privacy right associated with sanctuary is meant to prohibit other persons from seeing, hearing and knowing. Where the zone of repose serves to blockout unwanted stimuli, the sanctuary zone attempts to keep things within its boundaries.

His third right related to intimate decisions, is more dynamic than either of the others and implies less "freedom from" and more "freedom to". The landmark decision in this context is *Griswold* v. *Connecticut,*[133] where the court invalidated the state's birth control law as a violation of marital privacy. Bostwik, meanwhile summarizes his privacy rights as follows: "Repose maintains the actor's peace; sanctuary allows an individual to keep somethings private; and intimate decision grants the freedom to act in an autonomous fashion.[134]

Like several luminaries, several non-judicial academicians have also developed a research interest in privacy. Prominent among them is Judee K. Burgoon who belong to communication studies.

Burgoon,[135] who reviewed current literatures and research findings, identifies four broad dimensions: physical privacy, social privacy, psychological privacy and informational privacy. Her physical privacy is the degree to which one is physically inaccessible to others. It is, she

---

132. See details in R. Allan Dionisopoulos *et. al.*, The Right to Privacy, Essays and Cases (1976).
133. 381 US 479 (1965).
134. Bostwick *supra* n. 61 at 1482.
135. See detail in Judee K. Burgoon, "Privacy and Communication" Michael Burgoon (ed.) Communication Year Book 6 (1982).

argues, necessary for the optimal functioning of the individual within society and for society itself. Her social privacy is similar to that of Westin's notion of limited or protected communication which is often the consequence of the physical dimension. This kind of privacy allows for "situational exigencies" and individual differences.

Burgoon affirms that psychological privacy is dependent upon each person's interpretation of any given situation. These dimensions are an extra legal aspect of the private life. By nature, psychological privacy, pertains only to the individual and not groups.

Burgoon's informational privacy is related to interpersonal communication. This aspect is the most talked about and the most problematic aspect of privacy today. It is what most people have in mind when they speak of privacy intrusion. It is the topic of highly academic discussion which has been taking place in so many seminars. Closely allied with the psychological dimensions, informational privacy also has a political dimension that transcends ideology.

Communication scholars are primarily interested in the actual ways people cope with complex modern society. Legal scholars too frequently rely upon the ways people ought to act or might act regarding, in this instance, their individual or collective perception of privacy. Communication scholars attempt to learn what people do in their everyday habitats and every day lives.[136]

Out of four dimensions mentioned above, only informational privacy is clearly beyond the exclusive control of the individual. Thus, in order to reduce the threat of invasion it has been necessary to enact appropriate legislation. As for the other dimensions, however, studies have shown a high degree of individual self-control over physical, social and psychological privacy. So legal protection of this aspect is not that much necessary, if not irrelevant.[137]

Prosser and Bostwick describe the application of law to personal autonomy, property and other liberties that have

136. *Id.* at 232.

137. *Ibid.*

come to be associated with privacy. Prosser's tort become Bostwick's generic rights in translation. Bloustein, however, is not satisfied with it. He insists that there is a single interest behind the law's protection, what he calls "human dignity". Westin wants a narrow but absolute "claim" to control individual, group and institutional information. His approach seems both the normative and descriptive.

Westin's claims were criticised by Louis Luskey who suggests that privacy is more a condition than a right. He says we must begin to break down our unitary concept and seek more useful and precise terminology. We must identify those aspects of privacy that are absolute, and separate them from the contingent ones. Luskey believes we can then more readily deal with the legal aspects, for 'right' implies legal right and clearly not all privacy can legalised.[138]

In short, the conceptual basis of privacy is an original sovereignty over oneself. Privacy is the recognition of individual autonomy and inviolate personality. It seeks protection of human dignity in a clear tune. Reputation and integrity of a person can be preserved out of the conceptual basis of privacy. It obeys the sacred relation with spouse family and recognizes a person's home as his castle. Privacy harmonizes social and individual relation. It gives place for genuine human emotions. It does not allow commercial exploitation of an individual's personality. Finally, it encircles a person's inner zone with a view to restore his status at par of his fellow member of society.

The interests protected in Prosser's four torts are interests in freedom from mental distress, in public disclosure and in false light cases, the interest in reputation and in appropriation cases, proprietary interest in name and likeness, from this angle and prized right of privacy shrinks in its stature so that it becomes a mere application to novel circumstances of the traditional legal rights to protect well identified and established social values. In this view, privacy is not an independent legal right protecting a fundamental human value. Assault on privacy are transmuted into a

138. Louis Lusky, Invasion of Privacy: A Clarification of Concepts, 72 *Columbia L.R.* 693 (1972)

species of defamation, infliction of invasions of mental distress and misappropriation. Accordingly, there is no new tort of invasion of privacy but only new ways of committing old torts. In other words, the social value or the interest of privacy is not an independent one but only a composite of the value society places on protecting mental tranquillity, reputation or intangible forms of property.

When scientific and technological developments have raised the spectre of new and frightening invasion of privacy, it is all the more necessary to have conceptual basis of the elements of the wrong and the nature of the remedy. Confusion here will have disastrous effect on the development of this new but important branch of the law. Moreover, any conceptual disarray will offend the primary canon of all science; that a single general theory is to be preferred to a congeries of disparate rules. Privacy has psychological, social and political dimensions. This means that it has overtones beyond the legal orbit.

VI. SCOPE AND EXTENT OF RIGHT OF PRIVACY

The right of privacy is a right whose contours still remained undefined. From the right to live one's life it is claimed that one has the right to do what one likes to do with one's own life without governmental interference. The insistence has always been for a private space in which man may become and remain himself. While common law principle in democratic countries makes every man's house his castle, Kantian philosophy stresses the spiritual aspect of life apart from mere physical existence with right to personal dignity necessary for man's full spiritual development. It is bare material aspect, the right to privacy stresses on the personal intimacies of home, family, marriage, motherhood, procreation and even child bearing, consistent with the concept of personal dignity. In the grossest terms, the right to privacy stresses the right to use of contraceptives, use or abuse of sex, and the right to personal habits howsoever obnoxious.

Bruno Battelheim has observed that a wish to have privacy was closely associated with "increased value placed on private property", and those without property were liable to be so without privacy.[139] One ultimately looks to the Bill of Rights of the United States Constitution and the interpretation given by the courts to determine the extent of one's rights to freedom of various sorts. The right to privacy, however, is not spelled out in the Constitution. The word "privacy" is not used at all. Judges nonetheless have considered the existence of the right of privacy. The primary object and purpose is to show how far government in the United States has gone in invading the right to personal privacy, and how far government has gone also to protect that right. It is to examine how government is prevented, in the words of Justice Brandeis from "obtaining disclosure in court of what is whispered in the closet"; how government is restricted from intrusions into the privacy of the home of the person; how the right of privacy is frequently in conflict with other claimed liberties and governmental power, and finally, to show how some intrusions of privacy have become accepted as necessary in the interest of public health, safety, morals and the general welfare.

Prior to 1965, references were frequently made to "privacy" or the "right to privacy", but these phrases were used as little more than flourishes of rhetoric. They added nothing to already existing rights. Legal researchers could look in vain for a case and outcome of which rested strictly upon privacy concepts. Two important essays published in 1890 in the United States are said to be responsible for the development of this right in the United States of America. An article in *Scriber's* magazine written by the editor of the *New York Evening Post* described a growing tension between the urge for privacy and the increased tendency of the press to cater to the public curiosity about other peoples affairs.[140] In December of the same year, the *Harvard Law Review* published an article by Samuel D. Warren and Louis D. Brandeis that launched a new legal concept which eventually

---

139. Bruno Bettelheim, The Right to Privacy is a Myth, *Saturday Evening Post*, July 27, 1968, pp. 8-9.

140. E.L. Godhin, The Rights of Citizen-IV, To His Reputation, *Scriber* 58, (1890).

broadened into the principle of information privacy.[141] However, the privacy right, in its present form of development is commonly understood as the right to be let alone and is broadly described as the "right to an inviolate personality."

The American courts have been more evolutionary as far as "right of privacy" is concerned. There has been vivid, varied and distinct recognition and enforcement of this right in that country. The English jurisprudence has tried to give effect to this right but under one or the other existing rights. In English court, "right to privacy" has yet to gain recognition as independent existing right. However, there is a ray of hope because the jurists like Winfield has mentioned infringement or violation of privacy as a tort though a "doubtful tort". This recognition by Winfield goes in with this definition of tort as different from the "pigeon-hole" definition of Salmond. Even apart from the nomenclature the concept has crept in the decisions of English Courts. In India, this right of privacy has its roots in *purdah* system prevalent since good old days and has not so far developed in its modern form.

Not surprisingly, most reference to privacy in United States of America have occurred in Fourth Amendment Litigation. In declaring the right of all "to be secure in their persons, houses, papers and effects, against unreasonable searches and seizures," the Constitution provides the primary support for a privacy right. *Boyd* v. *United States*[142] particularly shows that the Supreme Court, as early as 1885 recognized privacy as the underlying principle of the Fourth amendment prohibition against unlawful searches and seizures. Writing for the court, Justice Bradley recognised a concern for privacy as being part of heritage of British common law. Use of Fourth Amendment as a vehicle for the right of privacy was inhibited in the 1920s because of the heavy reliance placed on it by bootleggers during prohibition. Law is never created in a vacuum, and the interpretation of

---

141. 4 *Harvard Law Review* 193 (1890).
142. 116 U.S. 616 (1885).

law, like the making of it, is shaped by the pressures and prejudices of the times. During 1920s much "bad" law was written by judges anxious to support the "noble experiment". In particular, Chief Justice Taft narrowed the Fourth Amendment to assist federal agents in keeping America dry.[143] The high point of his fight for prohibition came in the court opinion in *Olmstead* v. *United States*.[144] There Taft condoned obtaining incriminating evidence through the tapping of telephones even though no provision of law or court order authorized it. It took over forty years for the Supreme Court to overrule completely this unfortunate precedent. The fourth amendment was seen as protecting individuals from only one type of intrusion on their privacy—the trespass or physical intrusion into a house with seizure of material objects.

In the area of traditional searches and seizures, the Supreme Court has had little trouble in recognizing a right of privacy as the underlying interest protected by the fourth amendment. With *Wolf* v. *Colorado*,[145] the court extended the federal right against unreasonable search and seizure to the states through the fourteenth amendment.

The Supreme Court prior to 1965, offered little protection to the privacy of the individual. But social needs outpaced the law as modern science and technology increased the power of government to manipulate or interfere in the lives of the individuals to an extent not thought possible at the inception of the republic.

Griswold v. *Connecticut*[146] gave its first and greatest recognition as a constitutional limitation on the power of both state and federal government to interfere in the lives of individuals. For the first time, the court found that the right of privacy to be sufficient importance to overturn a state law, that is, a Connecticut law prohibiting sale or distribution of contraceptives to any person. The court found that right of

143. William Beaney, The Constitutional Right to Privacy, 1962, *Supreme Court Review*, 212, 218, No. 24.
144. 277 U.S. 438 (1927).
145. 338 U.S. 25 (1949).
146. 381 U.S. 508 (1965).

privacy to be a substantial constitutional right formulated not by only one amendment but by the specific guarantees of at least five amendments (the first, third, fourth, fifth and ninth) that "have penumbras, formed by emanations from those guarantees that help give them life and substance . . . various guarantees create zones of privacy.[147]

In one of the most controversial cases, the Supreme Court found unconstitutional a Texas abortion statute which, like laws in force in most states, forbade procuring or attempting an abortion except "by medical advice for the purpose of saving the life of the mother." In *Roe* v. *Wade*,[148] Justice Blackmun said that the state regulation violated the due process clause of the fourteenth amendment which was found to protect the right of privacy against state action. The right of privacy was said to be the basis of a woman's qualified right to procure an abortion free from state interference during most of her pregnancy. As in the Griswold case, the court appeared to go out of its way to reach the constitutional issue despite traditional theories of judicial restraint that usually preclude reaching of constitutional questions particularly when state law is involved. While finding privacy to be a "fundamental law", Justice Blackmun's decision for the Court did not clarify the definitional basis of that right. In some ways, the decision seemed to narrow the scope of the right by cataloguing "certain area of zones of privacy." This list of area in which the right of privacy was found to have some application include marriage,[149] procreation,[150] contraception,[151] family relationship,[152] and child rearing and education.[153] Justice

147. *Ibid.*

148. Roe *v.* Wade, 410 U.S. 112 (1973).

149. Loving *v.* Virginia, 388 U.S. 1, 12 (1967).

150. Skinner *v.* Oklahoma, 317 U.S. 535, 541-42 (1942).

151. Eisenstadt *v.* Baird, 405 U.S. 438, 453-54 (White concurring), 460, 463-65 (1972).

152. Prince *v.* Massachusetts. 321 U.S. 158, 166 (1944), Cf. United States *v.* Kahn, 415 U.S. 143 (1974).

153. Pierce *v.* Society of Sisters, 268 U.S. 510, 535 (1925); Meyer *v.* Bebraska 262 U.S. 390, 399 (1923).

Blackmun concluded that "right of privacy, whether it be founded in the Fourteenth Amendment's concept of personal liberty and restriction upon state action, as we feel it is, or, as the District Court determined in the Ninth Amendment's reservation of rights to the people, is broad enough to encompass a woman's decision whether or not to terminate her pregnancy."[154] Like written guarantees, privacy rights were found to be subject to limitation when they conflicted with a "compelling state interest." For the first trimester of pregnancy, the Court held the state can only regulate abortion procedures in a manner reasonably related to maternal health but must leave decisions relating to effectuating of an abortion to the woman and her physician. After that point, the state interest increases as the potentiality of human life increases until, in the last trimester, it can limit abortions to those cases in which it is medically necessary in order to preserve the life or health of the mother.

The cases in which the right to privacy has been controlling center predominantly in the area of contraception and abortion. If this trend continues, we may witness the limitation of constitutional privacy rights to mere marital privacy (thus providing little protection against governmental intrusion upon privacy interests not related to sex and family and not completely covered by other constitutional guarantees). The explanation for this development is to be found partly in judicial politics. *Roe* v. *Wade* and its companion case, *Doe* v. *Bolton*, demonstrate that the Supreme Court is divided over the question as to whether there is a constitutional right of privacy and, if it exists, what it means and from where it arises. Justice Stewart, in his concurring opinion in Roe, suggested that the right of privacy developed in Griswold was merely a device to avoid admitting reliance on the due process clause of the fourteenth amendment and the "substance due process doctrine" which Justice Douglas had said in 1963 "could not be used to substitute the court's social and economic beliefs for that of elected legislative bodies.[155] If Justice Stewart is correct that there is no right of

154. Roe *v.* Wade 410 U.S. at 153 (1973).

155. *Id.* at 167, n. 2, quoting Kartz *v.* United States, 389 U.S. 347, 350, 351.

privacy apart from traditional constitutional guarantees, then protection from many forms of invasion of privacy will have to come from legislative action rather than from the courts relying on existing constitutional prohibitions. Four examples at the federal level reflect this prospect.

First, the Privacy Act of 1974,[156] marked enactment of the first comprehensive law to regulate use of records of personal information collected and maintained by the federal government. This landmark legislation, which gives citizens the right to see and copy most records about them stored by federal agencies and the right to challenge and correct any inaccurate information, also prohibits non-routine dissemination and disclosure of personally identifiable information, unless requested by or consented to by the file subject. Each federal agency is required to publish annual notices in the Federal Register as to the existence and nature of personal records maintained by it including a description of categories of individuals on whom records are maintained, the routine uses and users of the system, and procedures concerning access to and for correction of such records.

The Privacy Act also established a Privacy Protection Study Commission, prohibited sale of mailing lists by federal agencies, and prohibited denial of privileges or benefits by any governmental agency because of an individual's privileges or benefits by any governmental agency because of an individual's refusal or disclose his social security number, unless disclosure is specifically required by law or the system in question had been established prior to January 1, 1975. Violations of the Act are punishable by criminal penalties or by civil suits brought against the agency involved by persons adversely affected by Act violations.

Second, title 3 of the Omnibus Crime Control and Safe Streets Act of 1968[157] broke new ground by specifying criminal and civil sanctions against persons who engage in unauthorized wiretapping of electronic surveillance. More

156. Privacy Act of 1974; Public Law No. 91-579, Dec. 31, 1974, 88 Stat. 1896.

157. Omnibus Crime Control and Safe Streets Act; Public Law No. 90-351, June 19, 1968; 82 Stat. 1128.

important, the Act significantly advances privacy interests by prohibiting virtually all electronic surveillance activities conducted without court authorization and under some degree of judicial control.

Third, the Fair Credit Reporting Act of 1970[158] marked the first attempt by the federal government to control the accuracy of investigative reports made on millions of Americans each year by credit reporting agencies. While the Act does not permit the report-subjects to see the contents of the actual dossier compiled on them, it does require notice to be given to the subjects of such reports. This step is mandated when the report forms part of the basis for denial of insurance, credit, or employment. Criminal and civil damages are available to report-subjects when the credit agency fails to make a reasonable effort to purge inaccurate information from the file. Bills, such as S. 2360, 93rd Congress have been introduced to require written authorization from the subject before an investigative report is begun, and upon completion, to supply him with a copy of the report at the expense of the agency.

Fourth, concern for the detrimental effects that unwarranted dissemination of criminal records can have on an individual's reputation and rights led to enactment of a floor amendment to the Crime Control Act of 1973. Affected are all state law enforcement agencies collecting, storing, or disseminating criminal history information through support received from the Law Enforcement Assistance Administration (LEAA). They must "assure that the security and privacy of all information is adequately provided for and that information shall only be used for law enforcement and criminal justice and other lawful purposes.[159] All LEAA research or statistical information identifiable to a specific private person is barred from use for any purpose other than that for which it was collected. Further, it is immune from legal process, and cannot be used in any judicial or

158. Fair Credit Reporting Act, Public Law No. 93-508, Title VI, Sec. 601, October 26, 1970, 84 Stat. 1128.

159. Crime Control Act of 1973; Public Law No. 93-83, Sec. 524, August 6, 1973, 87 Stat. 197, 215.

administrative proceeding without the consent of the person furnishing the information. In view of the increasing reliance of all state law enforcement agencies on LEAA funds, this new requirement is likely to mark the first significant protection for computerized criminal records.

The rapid advances made by the Ninety-third Congress in the privacy area towards the end of its session indicate that Watergate, revelation of political surveillance by the F.B.I. and of possible misuse of tax returns by the Internal Revenue Service may have caused a consensus to form. With the resignation of President Nixon, the last barriers to bipartisan cooperation in this area appeared to have been removed and the demand for new laws to protect privacy reached a crescendo comparable to that achieved by environmental concerns a few year earlier.

In 1974 alone, more actions were taken to provide formal protection to privacy than had been achieved in all of the prior history of the United States. President Ford, who as vice-president had chaired a presidentially created Domestic Council Committee on the Right of Privacy, began his new administration with a pledge that, "there will be no illegal tapping, eavesdropping, bugging or break-ins by my administration. There will be hot pursuit of tough laws to prevent illegal invasions of privacy in both government and private activities.[160] Shortly thereafter, he issued an executive order limiting White House access to income tax returns[161] and indicated interest in bills introduced in the Senate and House to provide more extensive restrictions on access to tax returns.[162] In addition to passage of the Privacy Act, Congress enacted the "Family Educational Rights and Privacy Act of 1974"[163] which would deny federal funds to any educational institution that prevented parental access to a child's school

160. U.S. Congress, Presidential Message, President Gerald R. Ford, August 12, 1974, 120 Cong. Rec. H8161 (1974)

161. Ex. Ord. No. 11805, Sept. 24, 1974, 39 Fed. Reg. 34261 (1974)

162. U.S. Congress, House of Representatives, H.R. 16602, 93rd Cong. (1974)

163. Elementary and Secondary Education Act, Public Law No. 93-389, 512, 88 Stat. 464, 571 Aug. 21, 1974 as amended by Public Law No. 93-568, sec. 2, 88 Stat. 1855, 1858 Dec. 31, 1974.

records or permitted to release of a student's record without parental consent to anyone but another school official or in compliance with a court order. Among over 300 other privacy Bills introduced in the Ninety-third Congress relating to privacy, serious consideration was given to a Bill to establish rules on the use of dissemination of criminal records[164] and the Bill to prohibit military surveillance of civilian activities.[165]

It is a peculiarity of the American policy-making process that the Supreme Court is able to open new avenues of reform by posting directional markers reading "legal rights and liberties." But the more substantial work of smoothing the way for citizens to make use of their rights if often left for legislative follow-up. Of course, executive action and administrative policy also play a role which citizens expect to be constructive. Unfortunately, that has not always been the case; witness the assorted crimes assembled under the title of "Watergate." These politically mitigated invasions of privacy and related scandals have damaged public trust and confidence in government. The "Bill of Complaints" against Watergate-style abuses has generated significant demands for a more secure right to privacy. Popularly esteemed rights and liberties often grow out of deeply felt complaints against very specific executive abuses in the wake of terrorist attacks of 11th September 2001, the privacy concerns have suffered a jolt in the United States, Canada and other countries. In the name of national-security, anti-terrorism and detection and prevention of serious crimes, the right to privacy is being compromised. The proposed U.S. Policy on Informational Exchange and Financial Privacy aims at obtaining information about the global financial activities of terrorists. It also proposes sharing of this information with reliable democracies. There is indeed a proposal to sign an International Convention on Privacy and Information Exchange.

On the other hand, Great Britain has no general right to privacy. The equitable action for breach of confidence,

---

164. U.S. Congress, Senate, S. 2963, 93rd Cong. (1974).
165. U.S. Congress, Senate, S. 2318, 93rd Cong. (1974).

remains the principal means which provides protection against the gratituitous publication of personal information. The Younger Committee in 1972 decided against proposing a general right in privacy and made several specific recommendations instead, few of which become law. Neither the court nor Parliament have been particularly active in finding or making law to protect privacy. The Committee did accept that the most effective protection of privacy in the whole of existing law, is the equitable remedy for the breach of confidence. On positive development on the issue of privacy in England was the passing of Data Protection Act in 1984. The Act was concerned with personal information automatically processed, with no distinction between the public and private sectors, but no information about legal persons such as companies, nor information in manual files. National security was in category of exemption. The new Data Protection was passed in 1998 which replaced the 1984 Act and is an improvement on the Act of 1984.

India is far behind both Britain and the United States in active judicial enforcement, or even public discussion, of privacy laws. The lack of demands for judicial enforcement of the laws safeguarding privacy, and the further lack of public debate on the threat to the right of privacy, may mislead a casual observer to believe that there are no laws safeguarding this human rights in India. Nevertheless, research in Indian law on the subject reveals propositions which are somewhat startling. The following instances are more demanding than American and the British law:

Firstly, Section 509 of the Indian Penal Code of 1860 specifically makes it a crime to intrude upon the privacy of a woman intending to insult her modesty.

Second, in the case of re-Ratanmala,[166] the court ruled legally inexcusable the behaviour of a police officer (accompanies by witnesses to observe a raid on a brothel). They proceeded to a bedroom of a girl pushed upon the door, as the court observed, ". . . without even the civility of a knock or warning to her to prepare for the intrusion." Thus,

166. AIR 1962 Mad 31.

even a prostitute is entitled to elementary decencies.[167]

Third, the fact that a man can command the view of the interior of his neighbour's house does not entitle him to gaze at his neighbour's home at all times. Elaborate easement legislation covers this situation.

Fourth, case law shows that a police officer searching a dwelling without a warrant must take precautions. Prior to the search, he should record reasons why the search cannot be made after obtaining a warrant and state what he expects to find as a result of the search. Strict compliance with this law is necessary to insure against humiliation and reckless searches in disregard of citizen's rights.[168]

The above mentioned propositions supports the conclusion that in the body of Indian law there exists a number of safeguards which enforce the right of privacy of the individual.[169] From the Indian point of view, the problems for further present day development of the law of privacy grow out of factors associated with the nature of the courts and the nature of debates over public policy. One reason why Indian law especially the law of torts, is slow to develop can be traced to the exorbitant expenses associated with litigation. This discourages speculative actions, and offended parties often simply refrain from making demands on the judicial system to meet the need of changing times. A plaintiff tends to go to court only if there is established law to grant him redress. Since the scope of development of law through adjudication is narrow, the judicial function becomes mechanical on the view that cases that do arise are covered by precedent. Developments in India law tend to arise out of petitions for constitutionally provided writs, criminal cases,

---

167. State of Maharashtra *v.* Madhulkar Narain Mardikar, AIR 9191 SC 207; State *v.* Gurmit Singh, AIR 1996 SC 1393; State *v.* Gangula, AIR 1997 SC 1588.
168. State of Rajasthan *v.* Rehman, AIR 1960 SC 210.
169. See, Mohd. Hussain Saheb *v.* Chartered Bank, AIR 1964 (1) Mad. 1012, for discussion on secrecy of Bankings; Indian Evidence Act, 1872, Sections 121-129 and 132 on privileged communications; Sections 24, 25, 26 and 29 on confessions, Section 33 of the Special Marriage Act, 1959; Section 53 of the Indian Divorce Act, 1869 (in camera proceedings), Sections 16, 95, 127-A, 128 Representation of Peoples Act (Secrecy of Ballot).

and through legislation. A second inhibition on contemporary development of privacy protection lies in the fact that if it has not been isolated by influential spokesmen and policy makers as an urgent subject for debate and policy reform.

In the recent years there has appeared in nearly all countries a common concern to protect the individual's private life from the ever more numerous attacks on it. Such attacks are the work both of the individuals and of the authorities. Whereas the right to respect for private life, the home and communications loudly proclaimed, we find that the rules of law on which the right is based are unfortunately, as Professor Nelson remarks not without some bitterness, destined paradoxically not to be applied, or at least not regularly or to their full extent. The Report of the European Convention on Human Rights and the Right to Respect for Private Life, the Home and Communications is concerned with the extent of the protection afforded under its right by the European Convention on the Human Rights to persons under the jurisdiction of the fifteen states parties to the treaty.

VII. EFFECTS OF RIGHT TO PRIVACY

Privacy as a basic human rights touches upon fundamental needs and values associated with man's gregarious nature. Today, all democratic societies have come to realize that privacy is at the heart of all human rights. Certainly the level of technological and economic development creates pressures to protect these privacy values through legal enforcement techniques. But even in the absence of such development, the value of and the basic human right to privacy may prevail irrespective of legal recognition. On the other hand, active claims for legal enforcement of the right seem to have very direct relationship to the degree of threat posed to its survival. Certainly, this relationship holds at the level of legal development, and it supports the thesis that human rights such as privacy, although recognized by laws, are enforced only when the danger to underlying values is perceived. The values, themselves, may also be shared and implied in cultural norms, but often they are not articulated as legal norms until threatened.

Right to privacy is basic to every individual. Eclipse of privacy means eclipse of human dignity also. Justice Mathew rightly stated that "there can perhaps be no objection in regarding intrusion upon our privacy as a dignity tort. The harm caused by this intrusion is incapable of being repaired and the loss suffered in dignity is not susceptible of being made good of damages. The injuries to spiritual element in our otherwise mundane composition."[170] India has essentially been a gregarious society wherein cooperation and not competition, society and not solitude have been the dominant themes of its culture and civilization. Therefore, sometimes it is doubted whether privacy is a value of human relations in India. Certainly it is wrong to suppose that the concept of privacy is alien to Indian culture. A man's house is his castle is a supreme and valid truth which is valued in all cultures and civilizations and India is no exception to it. No matter due to various social and economic factors, the right to privacy in India had not received that recognition in public law as it has received in other technologically advanced countries.

VIII. SUM-UP

It may thus be summed up that the long search for a definition of 'privacy' has produced a continuing debate that is often sterile and ultimately futile for, in those legal systems recognise a common law right to privacy (or its equivalent), privacy is entrenched in the vocabulary of courts, where it is accorded statutory protection then privacy is simply what the legislature says it is. The foregoing study also discusses the functions of privacy as described by Alan F. Westin. It is revealed that the entire description is predicated upon a civilized social life. Professor Westin has not deliberated over the role of privacy in the transformation of a natural society to a civilized one. It is abundantly clear from the foregoing

---

170. Vide his Article, The Right to be Let Alone, 4 SCC Journal Section 3(1979).

study that the conceptual basis of privacy is an original sovereignty over oneself. Privacy is the recognition of individual autonomy and inviolate personality. It seeks protection of human dignity in a clear tune. Reputation and integrity of a person can be preserved out of the conceptual basis of privacy. It obeys the sacred relation with spouse, family and recognises a person's home as his castle. Privacy harmonizes social and individual relation. It gives place for genuine human emotions. It does not allow commercial exploitation of an individual's personality. Finally, it encircles a person's inner zone with a view to restore his status at art of his fellow member of society. Further, the contours of right to privacy remained undefined and an attempt has been made to analyse the scope, extent and effects of this right.

3

Genesis of Right to Privacy: The Indian Scenario

I. INTRODUCTION

Once a civilization has made a distinction between the "outer" and the "inner" man, between the life of the soul and the life of the body, between the spiritual and the material, between the sacred and the profane, between the realm of God and the realm of Caesar, between the church and State, between rights inherent and inalienable and rights that are in the power of government to give and take away, between public and private, between society and solitude, it becomes impossible to avoid the idea of privacy by whatever name it may be called—the idea of "private" space in which man may become and remain "himself".[1] The idea of privacy is as old as Biblical periods. Numerous meanings crowd in on the mind that tries to analyse privacy: The privacy of private property; privacy as a proprietary interest in name and image; privacy as the keeping of one's affairs to oneself; the privacy of internal affairs of a voluntary association or of a

1. Herbert Marcuse, One Dimensional Man 10 (1964); Milton R. Konvitz, Privacy And The Law: A Philosophical Prelude, 31 *Law and Contemporary Problems*, 273 (1966).

business corporation; the privacy of sexual and familial affairs, etc.[2] The studies of animal behaviour and social organization suggest that man's need for privacy may well be rooted in the animal origins, and that men and animals share several basic mechanisms for claiming privacy among their own fellows.[3] Almost the first page of Bible introduces us to the feeling of shame as a violation of privacy. After Adam and Eve had eaten the fruit of the tree of knowledge, "the eyes of both were opened, and they knew that they were naked, and they sewed fig leaves together and made themselves aporons."[4]

The distance from the biblical garden to the statutory wilderness may have taken thousands of years to traverse because it is necessary for a secure relationship between man and wife, it concretises interpersonal relationship of love, friendship and trust.[5] Privacy is one of the concepts which is closely connected with human dignity. Since privacy is the essence of human beings its history begins with the history of human beings. Historical evidences show that it was prevailing as a social value in every civilization. Our ancient law of Dharmaśastras also recognised the concept of privacy. Really the law of privacy has been well expounded in the commentaries of old law. Hence, an attempt is being made in the following pages to trace the history of privacy in India from Hindu period to modern period.

II. CONCEPT OF PRIVACY IN HINDU PERIOD

India has essentially been gregarious society wherein cooperation and not competition, society and not solitude have been dominant themes of its culture and civilization.

---

2. Charles Fried, "Privacy", 77 *Yale L.J.* 475 (1968) at p. 478; Edward Shils, "Privacy: Its Constitution and Vicissitudes," 31 *Law and Contemporary Problems* 281, (1966), see also, M.C. Pramodan, "Right to Privacy", 14 *CULR* 59 (1990).
3. Alan F. Westin, Privacy and Freedom, 8 (1970).
4. Charles Freid, *op. cit.*, p. 478; see also M.C. Pramodan, *op. cit.*, p. 59; S.K. Sharma, Privacy Law: A Contemporary Study, 25 (1994).
5. Charles Freid, *op. cit.* p. 477

Hence, sometimes it is doubted whether privacy is a value of human relation in India. Certainly it is wrong to suppose that the concept of privacy is alien to Indian culture.[6] Although no study seems to have been made examining the rules regarding the respect for privacy in the ancient Indian society, yet a careful scrutiny of general life-style and the duties imposed on the individuals in their inter-personal relationships, reveal remarkable rules respecting one's privacy which not only cover those aspect of privacy what Professor Alan F. Westin observes,[7] but, in several respects, surpass them also. In ancient times, people had a close community life. The ancient law giver of the Hindus declares, "*Sarvas Swe Swe Grihe Raja*" which means every man is a king of his own house. The Dharmasastras of ancient India and their commentaries expounded the laws of privacy in Indian sub-continent. The kings were bound to uphold *Dharma* and to respect the privacy of the citizens.[8]

Ancient Indian theory of knowledge based on *Upanishads* which suggested mediation or *upasana*. Its aim is gradually to withdraw the aspirant's mind from external

---

6. I.P. Massey, Constiutionalization of Right to Privacy in India in B.P. Sehgal (ed.), pp. 310-311.
7. Professor Alan F. Westin observes that man relies on physical senses-touch, taste, smell, sight and hearing—to define his daily boundaries of privacy. The veil is a symbolic realization of the need for privacy in every society. The eyes and the mouth are instruments that "expose," the individual and diminish his psychological privacy. The privacy protecting "masks" in many societies as also the use of the fan by women to cover the mouth and eyes when establishing their relations with men or the use of dark glasses today among high personages in the near and middle East, Latin America or Hollywood. "Modesty about natural functions" and the sexual relations are added to the above list where privacy is needed and found in all societies. Most societies have rules limiting free entry into the house by non-residents, as well as rules governing the outsider's conduct once he enters. Virtually, all societies have rules for concealment of the female genitals and restrictions on the time and manner of female genital exposure. For more details see Alan F. Westin, Privacy and Freedom (1970), pp. 9-15.
8. E. Jeremy Hutton *et. al.* The Right of Privacy in the United States, Great Britain and India in Richard P. Claude (ed.) Comparative Human Rights, 151 (1976).

things and direct it inward—to make him more and more introspective so that he may get rid of his dependence on the objective world.[9] Meditation is not possible without concentration and concentration is possible if the person concentrating is not disturbed. Thus, from the very dawn of the Vedic culture, disturbing a meditating sage came to be regarded as a sin or a wrong of the highest order in the Indian society. There are several legends which establish it beyond doubt that disturbing mediation was considered a wrong or a sin. Lord Shiva, while in meditation, is said to have been disturbed by *Kamdeva*, the god of love and sex in the Indian mythology, who was burnt as punishment thereof when Lord Shiva opened his third eye.[10]

Further, in matters of religious and spiritual pursuits interference or disturbance of any kind was prohibited. Similar was the case with the study of Vedas. The following text of the Rigveda clearly established the concern and awareness of privacy in the ancient Indian society.

य आस्ते यश्च चरति यश्च पश्यति नो जनः।
तेषां सं हन्मो अक्षाणि यथेदं हर्म्यं तथा।।[11]

(One ought to build such house which may sustain and protect the inmates in all seasons and be comfortable. The passers-by may not see the inmates not the inmates see them).

The Griha Sutras, Arthashastra and the epics of the Ramayana and the Mahabharata contain elaborate rules for the construction of a house so that privacy is prominently preserved. Hence, an earnest attempt is being made to see how privacy developed under different periods in India:

---

9. S. Radhakrishnan (ed.), The Cultural Heritage of India, (1970), Vol. 1, pp. 349-50; Govind Mishra, "Privacy and the Indian Legal System," *Del. L. Rev.* 1990, Vol. 12, p. 60; see also Govind Mishra, Right to Privacy in India, 17 (1994).
10. Kalidas, Kumarsambhavam, 3/17.
11. Rigveda, Mandal 7, Sukta 55, Hymn 6; see Maharshi Dayanand Sarswati Rigveda Bhasa Bhasya Sampurna (1st edn.)

(i) Privacy in the Griha Sutras

The Griha Sutras contain elaborate rules for the construction of a house. The house generally consisted of a number of rooms, such as a bed-room (*sayaninya*), a store room, a kitchen (*bhakta-sarana*), a hall or drawing room (*sabha*) and compound.[12] V.M. Apte in his book[13] supports the above view and maintains that a bed-room, a drawing room, provision room and a nursery used to be the part of a house. The main door of the house was not to face the door of another house and construction of the house was to be so devised that the house-holder should not be seen by unholy persons while performing religious rites, while dinning in his house and passers-by should not be able to see the valuables in the house.[14] Even in the selection of a site for a dwelling house, the main consideration, it appears, was to avoid the right of persons or things that formed impediments to the studies of the Vedas.[15] In these regulations and prohibitions lies the awareness and concern of the society to exclude possible right of a stranger, to preserve the sanctity of the house, to respect one's privacy in performance of religious rites, for the study of the Vedas and for dinning purposes.[16] Further, the need or the purpose of having a separate bed-room or a nursery reflects a modicum of privacy in its rudimentary form, a fore-runner of the modern psychiatrists thesis.[17]

---

12. Ram Gopal, India of Vedic Kalpasutras, p. 151.
13. V.M. Apte, Social and Religious Life in the Griha Sutras, p. 142.
14. *Id.* at 141.
15. *Id.* at 180.
16. The members of the denomination known as "Ramanuj Sampradaya" do not eat and drink in presence of any one else. This practice is still prevalent in Southern India.
17. Privacy in the bed-room is a necessity for both children and parents and faulty sleeping arrangements represent a subtle form of sexual abuse, observes psychiatrist Gabrial V. Laury of the State University of New York. "Such arrangements are generally made by well meaning parents who are unaware that their child has become an individual with his own personality, his own sexuality and with a right to modesty and privacy." "Privacy begins with birth," advises Dr. Sugar: keep an infant in a bed-room separate from yours. Many parents keep infants in their bed-room as a convenience for night

To reiterate, it is also evident that the house-holders were anxious to preserve their privacy in performance of their religious acts, for the Vedic studies and for dinning purposes. It is abundantly clear from the ancient texts that these considerations were found to influence their choice in selecting the site for dwelling house. A *Snataka* was prohibited to have a look at a naked woman (even if she is his wife) except during sexual intercourse. He was prohibited to take his meal together with his wife.[18] Dr. V.M. Apte while describing social and religious life in Sutra period maintains that there was no *purdah* (veil) system prevalent in those days. He expressed it so succinctly when he writes:

The fact that in the marriage ceremony, the bride was taken out of the house, when the stars appear, to do homage to the directions, to the polar and other stars, shows the absence of the *purdah* system. Pointing in the same direction are the indications such as for instance, the people being invited to have a look at the auspicious bride, etc.[19]

Dr. V.M. Apte has nowhere dwelt upon the *purdah* system in his book except in the above mentioned passage. Although a fact cannot be a matter of opinion, but in a case where a fact is deduced from other facts the deduction must undergo the test of sensible and impartial scrutiny. It is doubtful whether Dr. Apte's thought can stand the test of such investigation. Govind Mishra has made following objections against his thesis in his book:[20]

---

time feeding or in case the baby wakes up at night. Not a wise arrangement, warns psychiatrist Stuart Finch of the University of Arizona Medical School . . . Psychiatrists generally agree that regular sleeping in a parent's bed can impair the child's psycho-sexual development. An infant who remains in his mother's bed upto a year may have trouble acquiring a sense of identity separate from his mother, cautions Dr. Sugar. The child may develop anxiety, even panic, when separating from his mother. As a boy gets older, sleeping in his parents bed may promote an unconscious wish to possess his mother and remove his father. A little girl can develop similar feelings for her father and against her mother. R. Howard and E. Lewis Martha, "Bedrooms", *Sexology Today*, September 1980, pp. 41-42.

18. V.M. Apte, *op. cit.* pp. 86-87.
19. *Id.* at 42.
20. Govind Mishra, Right to Privacy in India 50-51, (1994).

- The absence of *purdah* system in those days is deduced solely from a single ceremony. He has not substantiated it either by pre or post marital situations.
- The ritual of taking the bride out of the house to pay homage to the polar or other stars was and is limited to a small section of Brahmins called *'Chhandogya'* only. Moreover, during the night visibility being poor, there would be less chance of the bride being seen by strangers.
- He maintains the fact that the people were invited to have look at the auspicious bride signifies the absence of *purdah* system. The fact that the people needed invitation to have a look at the bride might signify just the contrary to what he maintains. It may be inferred that but for such invitation a look at the auspicious bride was not permissible. Further, he has not clarified the real position whether or not it was open to all to have a look at the bride even without such invitation.
- To maintain that there was no telecommunication facility in the Vedic society purports to inform nothing about the Vedic society. Hence, to apply contemporary standards to judge the primitive society may lead to misleading conclusions. It is axiomatic that the anxious efforts of Dr. V.M. Apte to establish that there was no *purdah* system in those days is neither warranted nor well substantiated by facts, for he is trying to give the impression that was seeing India of Griha Sutras through the Indian glass of nineteen thirties.

(ii) Privacy in the Epic Period

(A) Privacy in Ramayana

Since privacy is the essence of human being its history begins with the history of human beings. Historical evidences show that it was prevailing as a social value in every civilization. The rule, that a woman ought not to be seen by a male stranger seems to be well established in the society as described in the Ramayan. The exception to the above rule as found in the following texts illustrate and prove the rule.

व्यसनेषू न कृच्छेषु न युद्धेषु स्वयंवरे।
न क्रत्तौ नो विवाहे वा दर्शनं दुष्यते स्त्रियाः।।[21]

(At the time of calamity, during physical and mental ailment, during war, in Swayambar, during performance of religious rites during marriage ceremony if a woman is seen by strangers, no wrong is said to have been committed).

A further category (i.e. when a woman is accompanied by her husband) has been added as revealed in the dialogue of Lord Rama wherein he says:

सैषां विपद्गताचैव कृच्छेण च समन्विता।
दर्शनं नास्ति दोषोऽस्या मतृसंमीचे विशेषतः।।[22]

(Sita is in distress and mentally ill when she is with me—under these circumstances she may give her audience to all. And it may not amount to any wrong).

The dialogue been Lakshman and Sita supports and illustrates the above view when Lakshman says:

दृष्टपूवं नतेस्पं पादौ दृष्टौ तवाघने।
कथमत्रहि पश्यामि रामेण रहिता वने।।[23]

(I have never seen your whole body before I have seen your feet only. How can I see you here in the forest, specially in the absence of Ram).

But mere glance was not considered a wrong. The practice of putting veil while stirring out of the house for ladies is also described in the epic. It is evidenced in the following texts when Ravan, the demon king, was killed in

21. Ramanarayan Dutta Shastri Ram (translated by) Valmiki Ramayan, Yudha Kand, p. 1412.
22. *Ibid.*
23. *Ibid.* Uttar Kand, 1576.

the battlefield. His wife, Mandodari, comes out of the palace without putting any veil and using any conveyance, addresses her deceased husband:

दृष्टवा न खल्वभिक्रुद्धो मामिहानवगुण्ठिताम्।
निर्गता नगर द्वारात् पद्भ्यामेवागतां प्रभो।।[24]

(I do not have veil on my face. I have come all the way from the city-gate on foot. Under these circumstances, why don't you get angry?)

पश्येष्टदार दारांस्ते भ्रष्टलज्जावगुण्ठनान्।
बहिर्निष्पतितान् सर्वान् कथं दृष्ट्वा न कुप्यसि।।[25]

(Discarding their veils and thereby disregarding shame, all your wives have come out. See all these why don't you get angry?)

The analysis of the following texts reveals yet another norm of the society that seeing a sleeping woman (other than one's wife) was also prohibited. When Hanuman reached Lanka, he started inspecting the inner section of the palace in course of searching Sita. He entertained a doubt about the propriety of his action.

निरीक्षमाणश्च ततसताः स्त्रियः स महाकपिः।
जगाम महतीं शंका धार्मसाधवसशंकितः।।[26]

(Hanuman, having inspected the inner apartment of the palace and having seen several sleeping women, entertained a great doubt regarding the propriety of his action).

परदारोवरोधस्य प्रसुप्तस्य निरीक्षणम्।
इदं खलु ममात्यर्थं धार्मलोपं करिष्यति।।[27]

(To behold other women while sleeping causes evil consequences and diminises one's acquired merit)

---

24. *Ibid.*, Yuddha Kand, p. 1401.
25. *Ibid.*, p. 1402.
26. *Ibid.*, Sundar Kand, p. 891.
27. *Ibid.*

Not only to see other women but to touch them was also prohibited as illustrated and exemplified in the following texts:

परस्पर्शात् तु वैदेहया न दुःखतरमस्तिमे।
पितुर्विनाशत् सौमित्रे स्वराज्य हरणात् तथा।।[28]

(The fact that some one else may touch my wife is a matter of greatest unhappiness for me. Even my father's death or losing my kingdom would not give me that sorrow what I am subjected to by the above fact.)

कथं राजा स्थितो धार्मे परदारान् परामृशेत।
रक्षणीया विशेषेण राजदारा महाबल।
निवर्तय गतिं नीचां परदाराभिमर्शनात।।[29]

(How a king, who follows the righteous duties, can touch other woman? Ladies from royal family are specially to be protected. One must avoid the evil consequences that may result out of such touch).

एवं चैवमकामां त्वा न च स्प्रक्ष्यामि मैथिली।
कामं कामः शरीरे में यथा कामं प्रवर्तताम्।।[30]

(O, Sita ! even when you are in my captive, I will not touch you if you do not like. Let my lust for sex attack me!)

We also find references that one ought not to touch voluntarily the body of other man except her husband. The following texts prove and explain that to disturb one's meditation was considered a wrong and as such punishable.

यन्मां लोभयसे रम्भे काम क्रोधजयषिणम्।
दश वर्ष सहस्त्राणि शैली स्थास्यसि दुर्भगे।।[31]

(In order to win over sex and anger I was meditating, you have disturbed my meditation as punishment for which you turn to be stone for ten thousand years).

28. *Ibid.*, Aranya Kand, p. 496.
29. *Ibid.*, p. 606.
30. *Ibid.*, Sunder Kand, p. 915.
31. *Ibid.*, Bal Kand, p. 154.

In the description of palaces and other houses, secret apartment for ladies, bedrooms and drawing rooms are mentioned. The following text indicates that an attempt to see or over hear any confidential deliberations between two persons, was considered a wrong for which capital punishment used to be awarded.

यः श्रृणोति निरीक्षेद्वा सवधयो भवितातव।
भवेद वै मुनि मुरव्यस्य वचनं यद्यवेक्षसे।।[32]

(Regard being had to be the words of the sage, let others know that anybody who will overhear our conversations or see us talking shall be killed).

It so happened that Lakshman the younger brother of Ram, himself had to violate the order for certain pressing reasons, and consequently had to undergo the punishment awarded by the royal committee headed by the sage, Vasistha. The capital punishment was, however, commuted to as his banishment.

Further impersonation was considered a wrong and was punishable. Once Indra, the king of gods, made himself to appear as a sage, Gautam and entered his cottage in his absence and had sexual intercourse with his wife, Ahalya. Gautam, on his return to his cottage, saw Indra posing himself as Gautam and said:

मम रूपं सामास्थाय कृतवानसि दुर्मते।
अकर्त्तव्य मिदं यस्माद विफल स्त्वं भविष्यसि।।[33]

(You impersonated me and did what ought not to have been done. As a punishment for which you will be deprived of your testicles)

महापार्श्व निवोधत्वं रहस्यं किंचिदात्मनः।
चिरवृतं तदारव्यास्ये यदवाप्तं पुरामया।।[34]

32. *Ibid.*, Uttar Kand, p. 1666.
33. *Ibid.*, Bal Kand, p. 126.
34. *Ibid.*, Yuddha Kand, p. 1081.

(Ravan addressing to Mahaparshwa: Long long ago, there happened a secret even when I was cursed. I will let you know that secret event of my life today).

The above text exemplifies a voluntary disclosure of an event which no one knew except Ravan.

(B) Privacy in the Mahabharata

It is a well known fact that Draupadi was the common wife of all the five brothers of Pandavas. To avoid embarrassment to Draupadi a rule was made (and accepted by all brothers) which runs as under:

द्रौपद्या नः सहासीनमन्योऽन्यं योऽभिदर्शयेत्।
स नो द्वादश वर्षाणि ब्रह्मचारी वने वसेत्।।[35]

(If any one of us happen to see Draupadi while she is in company of one of us, he will have to undergo the punishment of banishment for twelve years in the forest as *Brahmacharin*).

Once it so happened that while Draupadi was with Yudhishthir (the eldest brother of the Pandavas) in the room, Arjun (the younger brother) urgently need to collect his weapon kept in that very room. Seeing no other way to collect his weapon, Arjun had to violate the rule by intruding upon their privacy. Thereafter, he presented himself for undergoing the prescribed punishment.

Mahabharata prohibited killing of a person while sleeping.[36] A woman was not supposed to be seen by any male (stranger). This is amply supported by both the epics Ramayan and Mahabharat. But mere glance was not considered a wrong. It was the mental approach revealed through such glance that was the determining factor to establish whether a wrong was committed.[37] The practice of putting veil while stirring out of the house for ladies is also

35. Shreepad Damodar Satavalekar (ed.) Mahabharat, Adi Parva, p. 1000.
36. *Ibid.*, at pp. 34 and 424.
37. Ramayaraan Duta Shashtri (ed.) Valmiki Ramayan, p. 775..

described in the epic.[38] Further, not only to see other women but to touch them was also considered a wrong.[39] Overhearing confidential talks and seeing others involved in such talks was meted out with rigorous punishment.[40] Impersonation was prohibited and penalized.[41] One who used to divulge the misdeeds of another when confidentially informed in a lonely place for keeping it secret was to be punished.[42] Once the king Pandu, killed a he-deer while it was enjoying sex with a she-deer. The deer was none else but a transmigrated sage named Kindam, who made his dying declaration as under:

अहं हि किंदमोनाम तपसा प्रतिमो मुनिः।
व्यपत्र पन्मनुष्याणां मृग्यां मैथुन माचरम।।[43]

(I am a sage named Kindam. To avoid the feeling of shame I became a deer and was enjoying sex with a she-deer)

The above text establishes that the feeling of shame is a peculiar property of human nature which distinguishes human sex from animal sex. It is the feeling of shame that derives human beings to a lonely place for the enjoyment of sex. The sage, Parasara, desired to have sexual intercourse with the girl known as Matsyagandha and signified his desire to her. This all happened near a river on both sides of which several people were having their bath. Matsyagandha replied:

साब्रवीत्पश्य भगवन्पारा वारे ऋषीन्स्तिान्।
आवर्योदृश्य तोरेभिः कथं तुस्यात्समागमः।।[44]

(Don't you see many sages standing on both sides of river ! How can I have sexual intercourse with you within the reach of their sight. Thereafter, the sage, by virtue of his

38. *Id.* at 1401-02.
39. *Id.* at 496, 606, 915 and 963.
40. *Id.* at 1666.
41. *Id.* at 126.
42. *Id.* at 392.
43. *Supra* n. 35 at p. 595.
44. *Ibid.* at p. 301.

supernatural power, produced mist bringing the visibility to an extremely poor and enjoyed sex with her.)

In those days of *kaliyug* women of bad character, dodging their husbands, shall clandestinely enjoy sex with servants and animals. Further, the following texts contain the prohibition of the meeting of a woman and a man in a lonely place.

मदं प्रमादं पुरुषेषु हित्वा संयच्छभावं प्रतिगृह्य मौनम।
प्रद्युम्न साम्बावपिते कुमारौ नोपासितव्यौ रहितेकदाचित्।।[45]

(With care and modesty, do not express your desire to another man. Although Pradumna and Samba are your sons yet never sit with them in a lonely place).

We also find reference in Mahabharata that who do not even think to have sex with other women in lonely place, go to heaven.[46] Further, the seeing of a naked woman seemed to have also been prohibited. This is evident from when Ganga reached near Brahma, her dress was blown up by the air. All gods and sages present there got their heads down except one Mahabhikh who kept looking on. For such an unwarranted act of Mahabhikh, Brahma cursed him to take birth in Martyalok as a measure of punishment.[47] There were many more instances where secret affairs of the sages must not be divulged.

(iii) Privacy in Manusmriti

Since privacy is the essence of human beings its history begins with the history of human beings. Historical evidences show that it was prevailing as a social value in every civilization. Manusmriti proves the prevalence of rules respecting the privacy of individuals in ancient Indian society. A person was not to be disturbed while meditating, sleeping or studying. The following text support the above view:

---

45. *Ibid.*, Aranyak Parva at p. 1197.
46. *Ibid.*, Anushasan Parva at p. 850.
47. *Ibid.*, Adi Parva at p. 499.

एकाकी चिन्तयेन्नित्यं विविक्ते हितमात्मनः।
एकाकी चिन्तयानो हि परं श्रेयोऽधिगच्छति।।[48]

(One should meditate alone in a lonely place for only by meditating alone he will attain salvation).

We also find references in Manusmriti that a learned and wise person should not see a naked woman, except at the time of sexual intercourse, a naked woman ought to be seen. He should avoid talking to a woman (other than his family member) in a lonely place.[49] It is also revealed from the text that if a person, not ill-famed for adulterous act, is said to commit the crime of *"strisangrahana"* if he talks to another woman at the bank of a river, in a forest and in a lonely place and shall be fined one thousand panas.[50] Further, enjoyment of sex and food were recommended in a secluded place, away from the sight of other persons. Even to attend the call of nature was required to be in a secluded place where one may not be observed by others.[51]

(iv) Privacy in Arthashastra

Our ancient law in Dharmashastras also recognised the concept of privacy. The law of privacy has been well-expounded in the commentaries of the old law.[52] Kautilya in his Arthashastra written around 321-296 B.C. has prescribed a detailed procedure to ensure right to privacy while ministers were consulted.[53] The sole purpose of the detailed procedure prescribed for consulting the ministers is to ward-off possible

---

48. Hargovind Sastri (ed.) Manusmriti, 276.
49. *Id.* at 188 and 190.
50. *Id.* at 463.
51. *Id.* at 189.
52. Shrinivas Gupta, Right to Privacy Is An Aspect of Human Dignity, *Lawyer (Journal Section)*, Vol. 17, p. 69; Shrinivas Gupta, Right to Privacy: A Kind of Personal Autonomy, *Lex Et Juris* 39 (August 1988); Richard P. Claude (ed.) Comparative Human Rights, 151 (1976).
53. R. Shama Shastri, Kautila's Arthasastra (1961) at p. 19; Shinivas Gupta, *op. cit.*, p. 69; also see Dilbir Kaur Bajwa, Right to Privacy—Its Origin and Ramifications, *Civil and Military Law Journal*, 1990, Vol. 26, pp. 51-52.

leakage or divulgence of the State policies in the statecraft the legacy of which is to be found even today in the provisions of the Indian Official Secrets Act, 1923. On the subject of citizen's privacy and kings obligation to know about 'national security risks', while advocating the employment of spies, he did not recommend to them the role of eavesdroppers. On the other hand, he urged the loyal spies of the king to infiltrate congregations of people in pairs and stir a debate on the affairs on the State. The people were thereby encouraged to join the debate, and their views could be publicly elicited. Although aspects of privacy in ancient Indian law cannot absorb our attention further, suffice it to say that a high degree of awareness of the need for privacy, as a basic human value, existed in ancient India.[54]

In Kautilya's Arthashastra, also, elaborate rules regulating the construction of houses are prescribed. The rules prescribed run thus:

The owner of houses may construct their houses in any other way they collectively like, but they shall avoid whatever is injurious. With a view to ward-off the evil consequences of rain, the top of the roof shall be covered with a broad mat, not blowable by the wind. Neither shall the roof to be such as will easily bend or break. Violation of this rule shall be punished with the first amercement. The same punishment shall be meted out for causing annoyance by constructing doors or windows facing those of other's houses, except when these houses are separated by the king's road or high road . . . [55]

With the exception of private rooms and parlours (*angana*) all other parts of houses as well as apartments where fire is ever kindled for worship or a mortar is situated shall be thrown open for common use.[56]

It is evident from the above excerpts that the house used to be divided into two main parts, viz., (a) private

54. E. Jeremy Hutton *et. al.* The Right to Privacy in The United States, Great Britain and India in Richard P. Claude (ed.) Comparative Human Rights 151 (1976).

55. R. Shama Shastri, *op. cit.*, pp. 189-90.

56. *Id.* at 190.

rooms and parlours meant for exclusive use of ladies, and (b) the rest of the house open for common use for the family members alone. The sanctity of the family house was secured by prohibiting persons to enter another's house (without the owner's consent) either during the day or night. The punishment prescribed for violation of such prohibition was the first amercement and the middle most amercement respectively.[57] Further, anyone who used to construct doors and windows facing other's houses causing annoyance to his neighbours was to be punished. One among the factors causing annoyance was the exposure of private rooms and parlours meant for exclusive use of ladies, or they were not supposed either to be seen by male (stranger) or go out of their houses.[58]

A review of Hindu scriptures abundantly proves the prevalence of rules respecting the privacy of individuals in ancient Indian society. A person was not to be disturbed while meditating, sleeping or studying. Enjoyment of sex and food were recommended in a secluded place, where one may not be observed by others.[59] Similarly, a male was enjoined not to see, touch or meet other woman in a lonely place. Visits to others' house without the owner's consent at odd hours and nights were prohibited.[60] Although, aspects of privacy in ancient Indian law cannot absorb our attention further, suffice it to say that a high degree of awareness of the need for privacy, as a basic human value, existed in ancient India.[61]

III. RIGHT TO PRIVACY UNDER ISLAMIC LAW

Islamic law is a divinely ordained comprehensive system regulating public and personal matters as well.[62] It is

57. *Id.* at 261.
58. *Ibid.*, see also Govind Mishra, Privacy and the Indian Legal System, 12 *Delhi L. Rev.* 62 (1990).
59. Govind Mishra, *op. cit.* at p. 63.
60. *Id.* at 64.
61. E. Jeremy Hutton *et. al., op. cit.* at p. 151.
62. Medani Abdel Rahman Tageldin, Right to Privacy And Abortion: A Comparative Study of Islamic and Western Jurisprudence, 12 *Aligarh Law Journal*, 140 (1997).

called *Shariah* which means the right path. The word Islam itself means total submission and surrender to God alone. The Quran, the holy book of God revealed to the Prophet Mohammed and traditions of Prophet Mohammed are the principal sources of Islamic law. Prophet Mohammed was not only the transmitter of the Quran but he also interpreted it. The tradition of Prophet which are technically called *Sunnah*: is the second source of law and it comprises what the Prophet said, did, and agreed to. "*Hadith*" is the index and recorded compilations of the *sunnah* by the companions of the Prophet. The third source of *sharia* is "*ijma*" which is the consensus of opinion of Muslim jurists on cases not directly provided by the two principal sources of Islamic law. In addition, Muslim jurists use "*qayas*" which is reasoning by analogy to derive a rule of law from the *Quran* or the *Sunnah* in order to regulate new cases by applying to them the principles, upon which the divine revelation had regulated similar cases.[63]

Islamic law has developed by the immense, rich researches of the qualified Muslim scholars and jurists based on the fundamental sources so as to keep with the requirement of the society. The different views of the jurists according to the different methods adopted in their investigations led to the foundation of a number of schools of law in the Islamic jurisprudence. There are four major schools of law within the Islamic jurisprudence, derived their names from the founder-scholars. These schools are: The *Hanafiyyah,* the *Malikiyyah,* the *Shafiyyah* and the *Hanabilah.*[64]

Islamic law explicitly protects privacy of home a fundamental human right. The home derives its importance as a sanctuary for the family and carries with it associations and meanings which make it particularly important. The peculiar immunity that the law has thrown around the dwelling house is explicitly expressed in the famous maxim "a man's home is his castle,"[65] is a supreme and valid truth

63. *Ibid.*
64. *Id.* at 140-141.
65. I.P. Massey, Constitutionalization of the Right of Privacy in India in B.P.S. Sehgal (ed.) Human Rights in India, 311 (1995).

which is valued in all cultures and civilizations. We find references in verses of Quran where the privacy of the home is explicitly guaranteed.

In this context Quran states:

> O ye who believe, enter not houses other than your own without first announcing your presence and invoking peace upon the people therein. That is better for you, that you will be heedful . . . and if you find no one therein, still enter not until permission hath been given, and if it to said unto; go away, for its is purer for you, Allah knoweth what you do.[66]

The Prophet Mohammed also emphasized the right of people to be protected against unreasonable intrusions into their privacy. He stated:

If a person looks at you, (referring here to a man's home where he expects privacy) without your permission and you pelt with a stone and put out his eye, no guilt will be on you.[67]

The morality of Islam based on the concept of *Haya* aims at inculcating the feeling of shyness in human nature and tries to develop it as a part of man's mental make-up so that it may serve as a strong moral deterrent against all evil inclinations. As an Islamic term, *Haya* implies shyness which a wrong-doer feels before his God and conscience. This is the force that prevents man from indulging in indecency and obscenity. If the man commits a wrong under the impulse of his animal nature, it is this shyness that makes him feel the pangs of conscience. To counter act "*munkar*"[68] the Divine

---

66. Quran xxiv: 27, 28 quoted in Medani Abdel Rahman Tageldin, *op. cit.*, p. 141.
67. See Sahih Muslim (authenticated traditions of the Prophet reported by Muslims) (1930).
68. Adultery, theft, lying and all other sins which man commits under the impulse of his animal nature, run counter to his human nature. All such acts have been described by the Quran by the comprehensive word, "*Munkar*" which is unknown or little known in its literal sense. These acts have been called "*Munkar*" because they are unknown and repugnant to human nature. (Vide, S. Abul A'la Maududi, Purdah and the Status of Woman in Islam, Translated and edited by Al Ash'ari, 4th ed. (1979) 161.

Law giver has specified. The Holy Prophet said:

> When you do not *Haya*,
> you may do whatever you please.[69]

The Quran asserts that the urge to clothe oneself and conceal one's shameful parts is innate within man.[70] Sense of modesty is a part of human nature. The feeling of *Haya* is inherent in man though in a crude form. Islam aims to educate *Haya* by refincing it.[71]

The following excerpts bring out prohibition to look at other women and a duty to cover shameful parts of the body. The holy Quran says:

O Prophet, tell the believing men to restrain their eyes (from looking at other women) and guard their shameful parts; this is a pure way for them; surely, Allah knows full well what they do. And (O Prophet), tell the believing women to restrain their eyes (from looking at the other men) and guard their shameful parts (24: 30-31).[72]

Hazrat Jabir asked the Prophet what he should do it he happened to cast a look by chance. The Prophet instructed him that he should turn his eyes away forthwith.[73]

Al-Ghazzali, a distinguished Muslim jurist, has pointed out that the right to freedom from unreasonable intrusions extends under the Islamic law to one's clothing is that no one is authorized to inspect the clothing of another person to determine what they be concealed therein without a reasonable cause.[74] A person's correspondence is also inviolate. The Prophet Mohammed says: 'He who reads a

69. *Id.* at 162.
70. *Id.* at 1.
71. *Id.* at 162.
72. *Id.* at 163 (The first command that the males and females have been given is to observe *Gaddi-i-Basar* which means "restraining the eyes" in its literal sense. As glossed, it indicates that casting of the eyes, which does not serve any social purpose but is charged with sexual motive instead, is prohibited).
73. *Id.* at 161.
74. Al-Gazzali, V. Ishya Ulum al-Din, Science of Religion, 34, quoted in Medani Abdel Rahman Tageldin.

letter of his brother without his permission, will read it in hell.'[75] The Islamic law guarantees of freedom of opinion, expression and intellectual liberties. The rule that privacy of home as core value is immune from unreasonable infringement is clearly illustrated by Omer Ibn-al-Khattab (a prominent companion of the Prophet Mohammed and the second ruler of Islamic State after the death of the Prophet).

The Prophet said:

> When a ruler begins to search for wrongs among his people he wrongs them.[76]

A ruler was prohibited to intervene in the private affairs of the citizens. Caliph Umar once heard a man singing inside a house. Sensing some mischief, he started peering into the house where he saw a woman and some wine along with the man. On being reminded that he was violating their right to privacy, he gave up his idea of punishing the man and let the man free after taking oath from him that he would live a pious life in future.[77]

The Holy Quran further enjoins:

> " . . . And spy not each other."[78]

Thus, it is revealed from the foregoing study that the privacy of home is guaranteed under Islamic law as a core value and fundamental human right, yet the privacy of home is not absolute, and can be regulated and restricted when it interferes with a compelling state interest. Privacy of the home is fundamental, but this does not mean that a person may do anything at any time as long as the activity takes place within a person's home. The privacy of the home can be restricted, restricted when it interferes in a serious manner

---

75. See Jalal Al-din Al-Suyuti, Al Jami Al-Saghir, 165 (manual report of the Prophet's traditions), Egypt, 1964.
76. Sheikh Showkat Hussain, Right to Privacy, *Journal of Islamic and Comparative Law Quarterly*, Vol. III, No. 2 (June 1983), p. 107.
77. *Ibid.*
78. *Ibid.*

with health, safety, rights and privileges of others or with the public affairs. Further, the Muslims always maintained the distinction between "public and private" and a high level of consciousness about privacy is reflected in their language, culture, architecture and other aspects of everyday life.[79]

IV. PRIVACY IN BRITISH AND POST-BRITISH PERIOD

While Britain has few laws specifically concerned with privacy, there have been continuing legislative debate and discussion in scholarly journals and public discussion promoting active formulation of laws to counteract recently perceived challenges. In the most technologically and economically advanced society considered, the United States, the courts have declared the existence of privacy rights implied in the Constitution and the national legislature has approved several laws dealing with specific privacy problems. India is far behind both Britain and the United States in active judicial enforcement, or even public discussion, of privacy laws. The lack of demands for judicial enforcement of the laws safeguarding privacy, may mislead a casual observer to believe that there are no laws safeguarding this human right in India. Nevertheless, research in Indian law on the subject reveals propositions which are somewhat startling.[80]

With the urbanization, industrialization, literacy and education the scope of privacy extended in both respects, i.e., intrusion and maintaining of privacy. Various legislations of 19th century also acknowledge the concept of privacy in India. The Indian Penal Code, 1860 under Section 509 provides for protection of privacy interest.[81] Similarly, Sections 26, 164 (3) and 165 of Code of Criminal Procedure, 1898 also provide for protection of privacy interest. Certain provisions of the Indian Evidence Act, 1872 also defend one's privacy interests. Under Section 122 of the Indian Evidence Act, a

79. E. Jeremy Hutton, *et. al., op. cit.,* p. 151.

80. *Ibid.*

81. Section 509 specifically makes it a crime to intrude upon the privacy of a woman intending to insult her modesty.

married person shall not be compelled to disclose any communication made to him by the spouse during the marriage.[82] Further the Banker's Book Evidence Act, 1891 protects a customer from dissemination of the transaction details. However, under Section 6 of the Act, an inspection may be made under an order of the court. The Indian Easement Act, 1882 under Section 18 provides the right of person to prevent his neighbour from constructing on his land in such a manner to be able to overlook the female apartment of his house thus interfering with their seclusion. The purpose of this provision was to protect the privacy interests of the women folk. Again the Income Tax Act, 1961 under Section 137 protect the financial interest of an assessee. Further Section 15 of the Census Act, 1948, the personal details coming to the hands of the Government are protected from disclosure.

There are also provisions in certain statutes which pose threat to the right to privacy. The Indian Post Act, 1898 confers power[83] on the State and Central Governments to intercept postal articles on the occurrence of any public emergency or in the interest of the public safety or tranquillity by an order in writing. As many as six private member's bills seeking to amend the Telegraph Act, 1885 and the Post Office Act, 1898, so as to debar telephone tapping and postal censorship were pending in the Lok Sabha for two years.[84] Considering the need for recognition of the right to privacy the Law Commission of India recommended insertion of a new section in the Penal Code making unauthorised

82. This section also creates a disability that no such person shall be permitted to disclose any communications. The marital privacy, to an extent, is thus protected. Under Section 130, a witness shall not be compelled to produce document regarding the property he holds a pledge or mortgage. He may also not be compelled to produce documents, the disclosure of which may incriminate him. This section protects privacy of a witness regarding his financial details. The privacy interests of clients are protected under Section 126 where the lawyers are not permitted to disclose communications made by clients to them. Under Section 129 confidential communications placed with the legal advisors are also protected from disclosure.
83. See Section 26 of the Act.
84. A.G. Noorani, Parliament and Privacy, *Economic and Political Weekly*, 239, February 11, 1984.

photography and use of artificial listening or recording apparatus, and publishing such information listened or recorded as offences.[85]

The Second Press Commission recommended an amendment to the Press Council's Act, 1978 to protect the right to privacy by making it one of the functions of the Press Council, in furtherance of its objects, to ensure on the part of the newspapers, news agencies and journalists, the maintenance of high standards of public taste including respect for privacy.[86]

The post-independence period in India witnessed the emergence of many constitutional rights including, the right to clean environment, right to education, etc. The right to privacy is one of such right which has of late been accorded constitutional recognition in this period. The right of privacy is a new comer when compared with other right like due process of law and *habeas corpus* as it is not found in any of the classic texts of the eighteenth century. In the Constituent Assembly Mr. Karimuddin as proposed addition to the clause to the draft Article 14[87] which was in substance similar to right to privacy and against search and seizure as guaranteed in the Fourth Amendment of the U.S. Constitution. Dr. B.R. Ambedkar also supported the move. However, Dr. Ambedkar's support was a little reserved one and not forceful enough to secure incorporation of right to privacy in the Constitution. Possibly the Constituent Assembly members did not visualize the importance of the right of privacy as an aspect of personal liberty.[88] After independence in 1950, India adopted its own written Constitution. Unfortunately, the right to privacy does not find place in the part of fundamental rights specifically provided under the Constitution of India. Inherently our courts were not ready to recognize the right to privacy due to the influence of the English law. But the constitutional provisions are potential enough to introduce the

---

85. Law Commission of India, 42nd Report on Indian Penal Code, 1971, pp. 339-40
86. Report of the Second Press Commission (1982) as quoted in E.S. Venkataramiah, Freedom of Press: Some Recent Trends, 117 (1987).
87. Now Article 20.
88. Constituent Assembly Debates (1948-49), Vol. VII, p. 794.

right to privacy by an active judiciary. Frankly speaking, the privacy right in India is still in the stage of evolution. It has to go through a case to case development. The technological developments or discoveries in modern times pose a serious threat to citizen's privacy. The traditional remedies fail to protect the privacy right in this scenario, this right has been recognised in India in the Information Technology Act, 2000. The Act provides for freedom of every citizen to secure access to information under the control of public authorities consistent with public interest, in order to promote openness, transparency and accountability in administration.[89]

V. SUM-UP

A close analysis of the concept of privacy abundantly proves that prevalence of rules respecting the privacy of individuals in ancient Hindu society. A person was not to be disturbed while he was sleeping, meditating or studying. Enjoyment of sex and food were recommended in a secluded place, away from the sight of other persons. Even a call of the nature was attended in a secluded place where one may not be observed by others. Further a male was enjoined not to see, touch or meet other woman in lonely place. Visits of others' house without the owner's consent at odd hours and during nights were prohibited. The practice of veiling eyes among a section of women was also in existence. Information given in confidence was not to be divulged. The Mitakshara enjoins that one who wears other's garments shall be punished.[90] It has been observed that "*purdah*" has been no part of Hindu religion and civilization. There is not even a trace of its existence in the Ramayana, Mahabharat and the dramas of Kalidas or in any other Sanskrit literature, epic or classical, "*purdah*" is the legacy of the Mohammadan influence in India. Unveiling the veiling system, one cannot but reach the conclusion that the regulation of sexual life in the society was the main objective for its introduction ever since the institution of marriage originated and came to stay

89. See, The Information Technology Act, 2000.
90. J.R. Gharpure (Trans.), The Mitakshara, verse 238, p. 364.

with human population. Much before the advent of Islam in India, seclusion of women from a male-stranger's gaze was a well established social norm in the Hindu society. The texts of the epics, that is, the Ramayana and the Mahabharat quoted in the foregoing study establish it beyond any doubt. Moreover, Islam did not introduce the veiling system, it only approved of the pre-existing custom of veiling in Arabia. Islam only perpetuated it as a means of separation between the sexes rather than introducing it as a custom.[91] The more focus under Islamic law was the privacy of home is guaranteed as a core value and fundamental human right. Yet, the privacy of home is not absolute, and can be regulated and restricted when it interferes with a compelling State interest. Privacy of the home is fundamental, but this does not mean that a person may do anything at anytime as long as the activity takes place within a person's home. Privacy of home can be restricted when it interferes in a serious manner with health, safety, rights and privileges of others or with the public welfare.

It is also revealed from the foregoing study that various legislations of 19th century also acknowledge the concept of privacy in India. The British Indian rulers used to shadow freedom fighters, and the methodology of secret watch and domiciliary visits became part of police exercise. The relevant rules found their way into police manuals. The post-independence period witnessed the emergence of new constitutional rights. When the Constitution of India was framed these anti-privacy strategies came to be challenged although interception of postal and telegraph communication and telephone tapes, also part of the police kit, have escaped judicial review. In the beginning of 21st century due to scientific and technological advancements it is very difficult to identify the infringement of this right for the purpose of taking legal action. On the other hand, in this computer age, we have to strike a balance between the interest of the individual in keeping his affairs to himself and his affairs to others so that he enjoy the fruits of the society also.

91. Robert Roberts, The Social Laws of the Quran at p. 19.

4

Legal Framework of Right to Privacy in India

I. INTRODUCTION

Right to privacy in India is a peculiar blend of constitutional, customary and common law right scattered over various legal fields. As a customary right it is treated as an easement forming part of statutory law. As a part of our constitutional rights to life and liberty, it is considered to be the illustration of progressive development of human rights and basic freedoms. Though it has so far not developed as a separate independent tort, its need is being felt by all, as without its development, emergence of an orderly social order may be delayed. It is, therefore, the recognition of a right of special significance and potentiality, adding a totally new dimension to our democratic and welfare-oriented jurisprudence. Emergence, development and recognition of this right proves that our jurisprudence is dynamic and is constantly evolving and bringing the law closer to the lives of the people. Developing new concepts, ideas, like privacy right is the sure proof that our law is organic, alive and kicking and not dead or static.

There are several customary rules prevailing in India

which protect privacy interest of an individual. Similarly, constitutional provisions have provided protective umbrella to this right. Besides customary rules and constitutional provisions several other statutes recognize right to privacy directly or indirectly. Hence, an endeavour is being made by the author to discuss these provisions separately in the succeeding pages.

II. PRIVACY AS A CUSTOMARY RIGHT

Custom has been recognized as one of the important sources of law of India. It takes its birth in some need felt by the society; and satisfaction of such need might have been obtained in the beginning, through some transitory and isolated acts gradually giving rise to general conviction of the necessity of such satisfaction. The acts would develop into a customary law of people. There are so many rights derived from customary rules. Not all of the customs but few of them are codified as the law of the nation. It is not only Acts of the legislature or subordinate legislation but also customs and usages having the force of law. This is made clear by the definition of the expression "law" in clause (3)(a) of Article 13 of the Constitution of India. The term "law" includes "customs" and "usages" having the force of law.

Indian judicial history indicates that privacy as a right, was recognised as a part of custom from ancient times, and received statutory recognition in Section 18 of the Indian Easement Act, 1882. Illustration (b) is said to be providing legitimacy to this customary right and ensures its continuous enjoyment in accordance with custom. There exists in some parts of India a principle, based upon Hindu customary law, that a property owner, to insure his privacy, may acquire an easement over the property of a neighbour preventing him from erecting a window, overlooking the window of his own house. This principle in a codified form has existed since 1773 and, in some States of India, it is judicially enforced under Indian Easements Act, 1882,

It is, however, clear that there is no general recognition of this right as such and the courts before they could grant relief in a complaint of invasion of privacy, insisted on proof of custom. So when it is generally known that in a particular town or State, the privacy was customary, the courts took judicial notice of the custom under Section 57 of the Evidence Act. In such cases the plaintiff was absolved of this responsibility of proving the custom as a fact. Illustration (b) to the Section 18 of the Easement Act makes it clear that such a right can be acquired as a customary easement. Inspite of it, the judicial trend does not appear to be either permitting its acquisition otherwise or extending the ambit and scope of this right.

In *C. Krishna Murthy* v. *Rajlingam,*[1] it was held that the courts in India, however, do not recognise any natural right of privacy and believe that such a right can be acquired only as a customary easement. In the instant case it was held that a custom in order to be valid should be ancient, certain and reasonable besides being enjoyed openly and peaceably. So where a person alleges that another has infringed his right of privacy, he has to establish that a customary right of privacy existed in the neighbourhood in which he lives and that he is individually or as a member of a particular class entitled to claim such a right on the basis of the custom before he can be heard to complain that it is infringed. In other words, the courts insisted on plaintiff showing that the customary right of privacy not only existed in a locality, but also that the plaintiff had been actually enjoying the right.[2]

In *Bhulanlal* v. *Altaf Hussain,*[3] the court held that the basic difference between right of privacy as an easement and a common law right in Tort, is that the right is attached to land and not to a person. The customary right is usually claimed in respect of houses of apartments generally occupied by females and does not extend to apartments ordinarily used by males. The customary right is, therefore, available only in respect of premises, which are secluded from observation and cannot be claimed in respect of a garden, a courtyard or a *varandah* not intended to be so secluded from observation. It was, therefore, held that a person cannot claim privacy in

1. AIR 1980 Andhra Pradesh 69, para 8.
2. Padumadas *v*. Smt. Parwati, AIR 1985 All. 648.
3. AIR 1945 All. 335.

respect of an extensive vacant site, which is used as an open air privy and bath.[4]

In *Keshav Sahu* v. *Dashrath Sahu*,[5] it was held by the court that the easementary right of privacy cannot stretched to oppressive lengths. It protects only those parts of a house, which are usually utilised by females such as latrines, open bathing places for females, etc. and is extension to cover other parts of the house which are not generally used by females is not to be countenanced.

Section 509 of the Indian Penal Code specifically makes it a crime to intrude upon the privacy of a woman, intending to insult her modesty. It was neither land or otherwise obstructed the appertures.[6] It was neither imported from England nor a creation of the genius of Thomas Babingtom Macauley but only a codification of a long established tradition of the Indian people. In England no action would lie for the loss of privacy or amenity by the opening of windows in a neighbouring house.[7] A right of privacy cannot be acquired under Section 26 of the Limitation Act but may arise by express grant or local usages.[8]

Where a person alleges that another infringed upon his right of privacy he must prove that the customary right of privacy exists in the neighbourhood in which he lives and further that he is individually or as member of his particular class entitled to take advantage of such custom.[9] In this case the court curtly observed "but for circumstances which we shall presently state, we might then have felt compelled to reconsider whether the decision *Gokul Prashad* v. *Radho*,[10] should still retain its full force after nearly half a century as passed, when it is manifested that the force of custom especially the custom of *purdah*, may be largely varied in the

4. Givraj *v.* Keshavji, AIR 1952 Kutch 22.
5. AIR 1961 Orissa 154.
6. Kashi Nath *v.* Ram Jiwan, AIR 1933 Lah 847.
7. Chandller *v.* Thomson (1811) 3 Champ 80.
8. Srinarain *v.* Jadu Nath 5 CWN 147; Kesho Saha *v.* Mt. Muktakimn, AIR 1931 Pat 212.
9. Bhagwan Das *v.* Zamarred, AIR 1929 All 676.
10. ILR 10 All (1888) 358.

course of so long period. It was held by the Allahabad High Court that a right of privacy being a customary right, it is always open to the court to see whether the custom is, in all circumstances, reasonable and whether it has ceased to be enforceable by desuetude. The court, therefore, held that the customary right of privacy can be said to be existing only in respect of the inner courtyard of the house.[11] It consequently, held that where the window of the defendant's house overlooked the outer courtyard of the plaintiff's house and not the inner courtyard and that the outer courtyard opened on a wide lane between the houses of the parties, and even before the construction of the first floor of the defendant's house, it was overlooked completely from the open roof of his house, there can be no right of privacy in respect of an outer courtyard of one's house.

Existence of this right in India recognises the prevalent truth that no one irrespective of the caste and creed likes to countenance his ladies while in their homes busy in the domestic routine of life being watched, observed or stealthily stared by strangers. In *Ganeshilal* v. *Smt. Rasool Fatima,*[12] the court noticed that the Indian women have always been jealous of intrusion of their privacy in their homes. It is not always that the women inside their houses are clothed with the attire which they normally use while appearing in public. Therefore, privacy inside the house is a right of every woman and much more so far a woman who has inhibitions by custom or religious notions to appear in public and keeps herself in seclusion by observing *purdah*. The court, therefore, held that the defendant had infringed the right of privacy of the plaintiff, who was a *pardanashin* lady by opening new windows in his house. In fact, *purdah* having religious sanctity has formed the corner stone of this customary right.

In 1963, in *Basai* v. *Hasan Raza Khan,*[13] the court through Justice S.S. Dhawan recognised *purdah* as the basis of this right and held that it entitled the owner of one property to

11. See, *supra* n. 1.
12. AIR 1977 All. 118. This case was subsequently followed by the same High Court in Diwan Singh *v.* Inderjeet, AIR 1981 All 342.
13. AIR 1963 All. 340.

compel the owner of the another to modify the design or architecture of his property so that the woman residing in the dominant tenements could be kept in *purdah*. According to the court, the right is not based on "natural modesty or human morality." The Jammu and Kashmir High Court in *Gulam Hussain* v. *Aziz Sheikh*[14] has, however held that this right can be claimed on the basis of "natural modesty and human morality" apart from any custom in the locality.

Inspite of the aforesaid, the judicial process has not recognised the customary right of privacy all over the country. Though such a right is accepted as existing in Uttar Pradesh, a part of Gujarat and Orissa, it has been found not existing in Bengal, Bihar and Madhya Pradesh.

Gokul Prashad v. *Radho*[15] is the leading decision on the subject establishing the customary right of privacy in Uttar Pradesh. The court after a review of various older authorities,[16] laid down that in India, the court should not *ab initio* rule out the right of privacy, but could recognize its existence in proper cases. The court took judicial notice of prevalence of *purdah* system in the country and held that it is reasonable that a neighbour should not be allowed to erect new buildings or to open or extend doors or windows in old buildings in such a way as would substantially interfere with those parts of the neighbour's house of primes, which are used by the *purdanashin* women. The court, therefore, ruled that substantial interference with the right of privacy affords a good cause of action entitling the plaintiff to an injunction. Rajasthan High Court recognised the existence of such a right in Jaipur in *Saiyad Habib* v. *Kamalchand*.[17]

In *Maniklal* v. *Mohanlal*,[18] it was recognised that privacy as a custom existed in Gujarat and its invasion was an

---

14. AIR 1966 JK 49.
15. See, *supra* n. 10.
16. Nath Mall *v.* Zuka-Oolha Beg, S.D.A., N.W.P. Rep. 92 (1855); Goor Dass *v.* Manohar Dass, N.W.P.H.C. Rep. 1867, 269; Ram Baksh *v.* Ram Sukh, N.W.P.H.C. rep. 1868, 253; Mata Prasad *v.* Bihari Lal, Unreported S.A. No. 8 of 1886; and Lachman Prasad *v.* Jamna Prasad, Weekly Notes, 1887, 295 (Cawnpore case)
17. AIR 1969 Raj 31
18. AIR 1920 Bom. 141.

actionable wrong. Further in *Bhai Govind* v. *Harilal,*[19] the court held the right of privacy existed not merely in some parts of Gujarat, but in the whole Gujarat, Orissa High Court, however, recognised existence of such a right in only those houses, which are utilised by females.

In *Keshav* v. *Gampet Hirachand,*[20] the court decided that the opening by defendant of a window which looked not into the plaintiff's private apartments, but into an open courtyard outside his house, was not an invasion of the plaintiff's privacy which would entitle him to have the window closed. In *Kamathi* v. *Gurandan,* [21] the Madras High Court held that there was no right of privacy in Madras. But in Punjab it has been held that with regard to the usages and habits of natives, the right of privacy in a dwelling house may be a cause of action when the defendants opened a new door in an upper storey so as to invade the right of privacy of plaintiff and the court could make a special order directing the close of the door.[22] No right of privacy can exist in respect of a sitting room appropriated to males.[23] Where the defendant opened certain apertures towards the plaintiffs house which was already overlooked by the defendant's house in several places, the court held that there was substantial and material invasion of the right of privacy.[24] A right of privacy is assumed to exist in all Indian towns. Each case must be governed by its particular facts but the question in each case is whether the construction amounts to a substantial interference with the right of privacy, where it was found that the window was useless and that it was set in the wall merely to infringe the right of privacy of the adjacent owner. The court held that its removal should be directed.

---

19. AIR 1942 Bom 217.
20. 8 BHCR, ACJ 67.
21. S. 3 M.H.C.R. 141.
22. Nanuck Chand *v.* Lolla, 21 P.R. 1169; See also Gohree *v.* Jaintee, 91 P.R. 1899; Shibdayal *v.* Golab 96 P.R. 1876.
23. Sital Ojhu *v.* Rekha, A.W.N. 1892, 159.
24. Abdul *v.* Bhawan, 4 A.L.J. 445.

In *Abhirchand* v. *Manik Ramnarayan*,[25] the Madhya Pradesh High Court insisted on strict proof of the custom of privacy in the State and refused to judicially recognise it unless proved. However, in *Gulab Chand* v. *Manikchand*,[26] the court was of the opinion that the right based on *purdah* entitled the owner of one property to compel the owner of another to modify the design and architecture of his property so that the women residing in the dominant tenement could be protected. According to the court, the right is based on natural modesty of human morality. The court, however, held that the customary right of privacy can be claimed only in respect of apartments, which are generally occupied and used by females and does not extend to apartments ordinarily used by males, the basis of the customary right of privacy being the *purdah* system, which was confined to the protection of *purdahnashin* women and those parts of a house, which were ordinarily occupied by females. The court ruled that new constructions cannot be made to overlook apartments, which are generally occupied and used by women and have been so occupied and used for a period sufficiently long to establish a right of privacy. It may be that the custom once established does not extened only to women, who are in the habit of observing *purdah*, because women of all races are entitled to a certain degree of privacy beginning on the custom of their class and even those who expose their faces in public expect to have their privacy respected in their more private apartment.

In *Sri Bhagwan Ramchandraji* v. *Babu Purshottamdas*,[27] the court considered this right in the erstwhile state of Bhopal where *purdah* among Muslims was observed to the extreme and to a great extent amongst the Hindu subjects as a part of their culture. The court was of the opinion that "so far as the right of privacy is concerned, that is a valuable right and no person can by his action violate the right of privacy of other persons. In this connection, the custom prevalent amongst a

---

25. 1978 MPLJ 204.
26. AIR 1960 MP 63.
27. Second Appeal No. 101 of 1959 decided on 25.11.1960 by P.K. Tare, J. (as he then was).

particular community, as also their way of life may have to be taken into consideration while deciding the right of privacy. No person has a right to act in a manner, which would violate the right of privacy of other persons, but it is equally true that the right of privacy cannot be extended to an oppressive length." The court, therefore, ruled that "it would have to be decided in each case whether the right of privacy violated is substantial or material or whether the right of privacy claimed by the plaintiff is to an oppressive extent." The court further opined that the "plaintiff's right of privacy was not violated merely because a person standing in the door or window of the plaintiff's house could be seen through the windows of the defendant's house."

In another case, that is, *Anupam Kumar* v. *Shantibai,*[28] the court held that the demand for legal protection of the right of privacy would emanate from an emotional disturbance in the user by the member of her family of the property on the ground that they are being watched by the neighbour. It has to be shown that this conduct would per se be offensive and calculated to annoy and cause emotional distress. Factors, such as, right of the family, the *purdah* observed by them, the faith that such intrusion affects the modesty, dignity, or decency of the person living in the neighbourhood may have a bearing on the question. The mere assumption that a view of their house was exposed from the windows would not in itself suffice to establish infringement of this right.

In 1974, in *Achhar Singh* v. *Pritoo,*[29] Justice D.B. Lal, granting relief to the plaintiff, observed that when in the plaint a specific plea was taken that right of privacy was infringed, which was not denied in the written statement, the plaintiff was not required to lead any evidence on this point. In other words, the defendant admitted that there was a right of privacy and that the same was infringed by the opening of the two windows. It was accordingly held that the plaintiff's right of privacy was infringed by the two windows. Further,

---

28. 1978 (1) M.P. Weekly Note, p. 369.
29. I.L.R. 1974 Him. 876.

the court was of the opinion that in India such a right has always been recognised as a valuable right arising out of a local custom.

It is evident that the customary right of privacy has been upheld by majority of the High Courts in India. It would, therefore appear that privacy right as a custom covers a part of common law wrong amounting to tort and would overlap Dean Prosser's first category of intrusion cases with the main difference that such cases in tort have a wide ambit and scope and include personal acts as well. It may, however, appear that with the modernisation of the society, rigour of 'purdah' system has been reduced and, therefore, not many cases of invasion of customary right of privacy now go to our law courts. Therefore, privacy as a customary right has come to stay in the Indian legal system and a invasion of privacy is an infraction of a right for which the person injured has remedy at law.

III. PRIVACY AS A STATUTORY RIGHT

The right to privacy is a socio-legal right in India. There is no single unifying legislation relating to right of privacy in India. There are several statutes, which directly or indirectly protect right of privacy. Various legislations of 19th century also acknowledge the concept of privacy in India but without its definition. The Indian Penal Code, 1860 under Section 509 provides for protection of privacy interests. Similarly, Sections 26, 164(3) and 165 of the Criminal Procedure Code, 1898 also provide for protection of privacy interest. The Indian Easement Act, 1882 under Section 18 provides the right of person to prevent his neighbour from constructing on his land in such a manner as to be able to overlook the female apartments of his house thus interfering their seclusion. The purpose of this provision was to protect the privacy interests of the women folk.

After independence in 1950, India adopted its own written Constitution. Part III of the Constitution of India contains a long list of fundamental rights. The inclusion of a chapter of Fundamental Rights in the Constitution of India is in accordance with the trend of modern democratic thought, the idea being to preserve that which is an indispensable condition of a free society. The aim of having a declaration of fundamental rights is that certain elementary rights, such as, right to life, liberty, freedom of speech, freedom of faith and so on, should be regarded as inviolable under all conditions and that the shifting majority in legislature of the country should not have a free hand in interfering with those fundamental rights. Unfortunately, the right to privacy does not find its place in the part of fundamental rights specifically provided under the Indian Constitution. The right of privacy attempts to preserve individuality by placing sanction upon outrageous or unreasonable violations of conditions for this sustenance. This then is the social value to be served by the law of privacy. It is served not only in the law of torts but in other areas. Protection of privacy is the central purpose of the privilege against self-incrimination in Article 20(3) of the Constitution of India. The privilege reflects the respect which we accord to the inviolability of human personality and the right of each individual to a private zone where he may have his private life. It reflects the private inner sanctions of the individual feeling and thought and prescribes state intrusion to extract self-condemnation. It is indeed a matter of great satisfaction that all the four Central Bills on Right to Information in our country, i.e. Press Council Bill, 1996; PCI-NIRD Bill, 1997; the Shourie Bill, 1997 and Freedom of Information Bill, 2000 have recognised right to privacy and have provided for an exemption from disclosure of purely personal information. In fact, the Freedom of Information Act, 2003 passed by the Parliament recently does incorporate this provision. The State legislations[30] on the right to information have also taken care of this issue and do protect an individual's right to privacy by prohibiting disclosure of information which would cause unwarranted invasion of privacy of any person. To reiterate, there are several statutes which directly or indirectly protect right of privacy. How and at what extent these statutes protect the right of privacy shall be discussed under the following heads:

---

30. See Section 5(b) of Goa Right to Information Act, 1997; Section 5(vi), Rajasthan Right to Information Act.

(i) Privacy and Person

The Indian legal system not only guarantees one's right to life[31] but also protects a person against infliction of any pain, disease or infirmity.[32] It does not allow criminal force against any person.[33] It protects one from injury, fear and annoyance.[34] In making an arrest, the police officer has been authorised actually to touch or confine the body of the person to be arrested,[35] but this provision does not make it mandatory that for effecting arrest, the police officer should actually touch or confine the body of the person to be arrested before a person can be said to be taken in custody; submission to the custody by word or action is sufficient.[36] Handcuffing and iron bar have been outlawed by the Supreme Court except in exceptional circumstances.[37] The apex Court has observed that "handcuffing is prima facie inhuman and, therefore, unreasonable, is over-harsh and at the first slush arbitrary. Absent fair procedure and objective monitoring, to inflict irons is to resort to zoological strategies repugnant to Article 21 . . ."[38]

It is implicit in Articles 14 and 19 of the Constitution of India that when there is no compulsive need to fetter a person's limbs, it is sadistic, capricious, despotic and demoralising to humble a man by menacling him. Such arbitrary conduct surely slaps Article 14 on the face. The minimal freedom of movement which even a detainee is entitled to under Article 19 cannot be cut down cruelly by application of handcuffs or other hoops. It will be unreasonable so to do unless the State is able to make out that no other practical way of forbidding escape is available, the prisoner being so dangerous and desperate and the circumstances so hostile to safe keeping. Even in cases where

---

31. The Indian Penal Code, 1860, Section 302.
32. *Id.*, Section 319 read with Section 321.
33. *Id.*, Section 352.
34. *Id.*, Section 350.
35. The Code of Criminal Procedure, 1973, Section 46.
36. AIR 1960 SC 1125 at 1131.
37. Prem Shankar *v.* Delhi Administration, AIR 1980 SC 1535.
38. *Ibid.*

in extreme circumstances, handcuffs have to be put on the prisoner, the escorting authority must record contemporaneously the reasons for doing so. Otherwise under Article 21 of the Constitution of India, the procedure will be unfair and bad in law.[39]

Even in the extreme cases, the escorting officer is required to get the approval of the presiding officer whenever he handcuffs a prisoner.[40] While arresting, the police officer should maintain good behaviour. If they act maliciously, they are liable to be punished.[41] Section 509 of the Indian Penal Code, 1860 makes it a crime to intrude upon the privacy of woman intending to insult her modesty. Further, Indian law does maintain privacy in jail also. Male and female prisoners are not to be kept in the same place.

There are other several statutes[42] which make a vexatious and unnecessary detention or arrest of an individual punishable if there exists no reasonable ground of suspicion. Indian criminal law has embodied some of the modern constitutional safeguards some 130 years back. This standard in United States of America only in 1960's. For example, *Miranda* v. *Arizona*[43] decided by the United States Supreme Court in 1966, is less stringent in some regards than the Indian Evidence Act, 1872. The latter prohibits the admissibility of any confession of guilt made to a police officer, unless it be made in the immediate presence of a magistrate.[44] Moreover, under Indian law an accused person has the privilege of protection of privacy against an arbitrary search. According to Section 165 of the Criminal Procedure Code, the power of a police officer to conduct a search is

39. *Id.* at 1541-1543.
40. *Id.*
41. The Indian Penal Code, 1860, Section 220.
42. The Customs Act, 1962, Section 136; The Foreign Exchange Regulation Act, 1973, Section 58; The Gold Control Act, 1968, Section 94; The Medicinal and Toilet Preparations (Excise Duties) Act, 1955, Section 17; The Central Excise and Salt Act, 1944, Section 22; and The Opium Act, 1878, Section 18.
43. The Indian Evidence Act, 1872, Section 25.
44. *Ibid.*

limited to quests pursuant to the investigation of an offence.[45] While conducting a search, the officer must enlist two respectable residents of the locality to join him as witnesses. Therefore, to protect a citizen's privacy, magistrate must comply with conditions for warranting a search according to Section 94 of the Code. These conditions are mandatory and not merely directory.[46]

The Indian legal system further ensures that the consent of an individual, as and when required to be exercised must be free. The decisional aspect of 'consent' is wanting in 'will' though both pertain to an individual's volition. There are several statutes[47] which require the consent of the owner or occupier, to be obtained prior to any entry is made into any dwelling house, building or the like premises. The wife is not permitted to disclose any communication made by the husband during marriage unless the husband, who made it, consents and similarly, the husband also cannot disclose such communication unless the wife consents.[48] An advocate is not permitted to disclose any communication made to him in the course and for the purpose of professional employment without his client's express consent.[49] The contents or condition of any document with which he has become acquainted in the course of his professional employment or any advice given are also not to be disclosed by him. The obligation thus imposed on him continues even after his employment has ceased. The interpreters and the clerks or servants of such advocates are also under the same obligation. Further, no one is to be compelled to disclose to the court any confidential communication which has taken place between him and his

---

45. The Code of Criminal Procedure, Section 165.
46. *Id.*, Section 94; See also The New Swadeshi Mills *v.* S.K. Rattan, AIR 1968 Guj. 117.
47. The Indian Works and Defence Act, 1903, Section 4; The Slum Areas (Improvement and Clearance) Act, 1956, Section 27; The Cantonment Act, 1924, Section 247; The National Waterways Act, 1982, Section 10; The Oriental Gas Company Act, 1857, Section 2 and the Road Transport Corporation Act, 1950, Section 42.
48. The Indian Evidence Act, 1872, Section 122.
49. *Id.*, Section 126.

legal professional advisor unless he offers himself as a witness, in which case he may be compelled to disclose any such communications as may appear to the court necessary to be known in order to explain any evidence which he has given, but no others.[50]

Article 8 of the European Convention on Human Rights guarantees the right to respect for private life, the text provides little material to assist in determining the scope of the right. In recent years various writers, a considerable number of legal societies and several international organizations have made studies in this field, all of them arriving at the conclusion that the individual has a right to the protection of his privacy.

(ii) Privacy and Right to Die

Whether right to privacy include right to die also is a newly emerging notion of privacy in United States of America. The current law in Untied States allow patients to refuse life saving care in order to "permit to die with dignity[51] and to protect the patient's status as a human being."[52] The right to die is essentially a right to self-determination.[53] The court describes it as the right of a person to control his own body. Cases recognising this right have attempted to create a sphere of autonomy in which patients—not their physicians or the State—decide whether and under what conditions they live or die.

Unlike United States, Indian legal system do not accept a person's right to die. A person's dignity in relation to his right to die cannot be connected to various reasons. The State has moral obligation to support every individual's right to life not right to destroy his life. The dignity clause of right to privacy does not support destroying life. A patient has to get support to survive not to die. Indian Penal Code, 1860 under

---

50. *Id.*, Section 129.
51. Rasmussen *v.* Fleming, 741 P. ed. 674, 678 (Ariz. 1987).
52. Superintendent of Belcher Town State *v.* Saikewiez, 370 N.E. 2d 417, 424 (Mass. 1977).
53. Mc Connel *v.* Beverly Enters Conn. Inc. 553 A 2d 596, 601 (Conn. 1989).

Section 309 makes attempt to commit suicide punishable.[54] Hence, right to privacy cannot protect right to die in Indian jurisprudence.

(iii) Privacy and Exposure to Medical Examination

The right to privacy includes right to control over one's body; whether any interference with it should be allowed or tolerated or not, depends on his desire or consent, express or implied. The question, however, has arisen in a catena of cases whether the court can order medical examination of a person. There is a close relationship between medicine and law. The physician as an expert witness is a common feature in courts. But there is no uniformity of opinion among the courts. In the case of *Birindra Kumar* v. *Hemlata,*[55] the Calcutta High Court held that the court can order medical examination of a person, where there is an allegation of impotency, etc. Similar view was also expressed by the Madras High Court in *George* v. *Sundari Edward.*[56] But the court in *Ranganathan* v. *Lakshmi*[57] took a different stand and held that except in case of lunacy, there is no other provision empowering the court to compel medical examination. Of course, in case of refusal by a party, the court may draw adverse inference. In *Bipin Chandra* v. *Madhuriben,*[58] the Gujarat High Court has held that compulsion for medical examination is an interference with the personal liberty of an individual. Similar view was followed by Mysore High Court in the case of *Revamma* v. *Shansappa.*[59] In *G. Venkatanarayana* v. *K. Lakshmi Devi,*[60] the Andhra Pradesh High Court, after reviewing all case law, held that the exposure to medical examination aided by scientific data cannot be construed as deprivation of personal liberty and breach of Article 21 of the Constitution of India.

---

54. In a Bombay High Court case, however, the court held the provision of Indian Penal Code 309 *ultra vires.*
55. AIR 1921 Cal. 459.
56. (1954) 67 Mad. Law 676.
57. AIR 1955 Mad. 546.
58. AIR 1963 Guj. 250.
59. AIR 1972 Mys. 157.
60. AIR 1985 A.P. 1.

The right to privacy is not absolute when this right is in conflict with the other rights of person. The right to privacy of AIDS infected people has received judicial attention during the recent times. The question here arises is whether AIDS infected people have a right to privacy or not. The question as acquired immense importance in the present time. It will not be an exaggeration to say that the whole community is sitting on AIDS bomb ready to explode anytime. In *Mr. 'X'* v. *Hospital 'Z'*,[61] the Supreme Court was seized on an issue concerning the AIDS patient and his right to privacy and confidentiality regarding his medical condition, and the right of the lady to whom he was engaged to lead a healthy life. The Supreme Court held that the life of the fiancee would be endangered by her marriage and consequently she was entitled to information regarding the medical condition of the person she was to marry.

In a recent case of *Sharda* v. *Dharampal*,[62] the Supreme Court was confronted with the issue whether subjecting a person to a medical test be in violation of Article 21 of the Constitution. The court outlined the concept of the law of privacy in India and was of the opinion that the right to privacy in terms of Article 21 of the Constitution is not absolute.

It is submitted that the correct view seems to be that the court may order medical examination whenever it is essential in a case to determine disputed questions of fact, but a person may not be compelled to undergo such examination, if he refused to do so. However, the court may be justified in drawing an adverse inference, in case of such refusal.

In United States, also, courts are empowered to order medical test as in India. As we know right of privacy is not an absolute right. The well-ordered society subjects the individual to varying kinds of invasion of the person.[63] Some

---

61. AIR 1999 SC 495.
62. MANU/SC/0260/2003; See also M. Vijaya *v.* The Chairman and Managing Director, Singareni Collieries Company Ltd., AIR 2001 AP 502.
63. Rochin *v.* California, 342 US 165 (1952).

of them concern the public safety and others the general health of the community.[64]

(iv) Privacy and Defamation

Protection against breach of privacy and protection against defamation cover two different areas of a person's life. The law of defamation protects the reputation of an individual. The law of privacy protects the feelings of an individual. The same statement may injure a person's reputation and also hurt his feelings. At the same time one can conceive statements that injure one's feelings, without causing any harm to reputation where the statement is true. In such situations no action for defamation would lie, because the information that is disclosed is merely embarrassing, not false. Here exactly is the need to evolve a new cause of action—the tort of privacy.

Section 499 of the Indian Penal Code, 1860 defines defamation as "whoever, by words, either spoken or intended to be read, or by signs or by visible representation, makes or publishes any imputation concerning any person intending to harm or knowing or having reason to believe that such imputation will harm, the reputation of such person, is said, except in the cases hereinafter excepted to defame that person." This definition also protects a deceased person from being defamed. It covers artificial person as well. Further the definition embraces innuendo too.

The extent and concern for human dignity in the Indian legal system may well be imagined by its intolerance of any indignity even to any human corpse.[65] The dignity, in this context, outlives an individual's life and takes care of his decent burial. This right, it is said, is in existence since very ancient times as customary right.[66] Further, the law of defamation protects the reputation of a dead person by prohibiting an imputation of anything which would harm the reputation of that person, if living, and is made with the intention to hurt the feeling of his family and other

---

64. Adam Carlyle Breckenridge, The Right to Privacy 88 (1971).
65. Indian Penal Code, 1860, Section 297.
66. B.B. Katiar, Law of Easements and Licence, p. 337.

relatives.[67] In protecting one's reputation, the law of defamation does not make any distinction between a minor or a major, a sane or insane, a wise or an idiot, a healthy or an infirm and a male or a female.[68]

There are certain exceptions with regard to defamation. Imputation of the truth which public good requires to be made or published cannot amount to defamation. Similarly, public conduct of public servants can be published or expressed which does not constitute defamation. Further, it is not defamation to express in good faith any opinion whatsoever respecting the conduct of any person touching any public question, and respecting his character, so far as his character appears in that conduct and no further. Publication of a substantially true report of the proceedings does not amount to defamation. Similarly, the merits of the case decide in the court or the conduct of witnesses and other concerned can be published or expressed. It does not constitute defamation.

In English law, defamation is divided into libel and slander. Libel is representation made in some permanent form, for example, writing, printing, picture, effigy or statute. Slander is the publication of defamatory statement in a transient form, for example, it may be spoken words or gestures. Under Indian law libel and slander are not clearly demarcated. There is no such distinction. The Indian law of defamation protects privacy of an individual. If a person injures the reputation of another, he is liable to be punished under Indian law.

Although closely related, invasion of privacy is distinct from libel, slander or defamation. An action for invasion of privacy differs from a libel action in that in the former truth is not a defence,[69] and it is not necessary to the cause of action to allege or prove special damages.[70] Another significant difference between the two types of actions is that a libel may arise from publication of a defamatory statement

---

67. Indian Penal Code, 1860; Section 499.
68. Code of Criminal Procedure, 1973; Section 199.
69. Smith *v.* Das, 251 Ala 250, 37 SO 2d 118.
70. *Ibid.*

to only one person, whereas invasion of privacy, at least by false light publicity, by definition requires publicity of falsehood to a substantial number of people.[71]

There is a distinction between causes of action or invasion of privacy and defamation with regard to respective interest protected and compensated by each. The gist of the cause of action in privacy cases is not injury to one's public reputation or status as in defamation cases, but injury to emotions and mental sufferings.[72] In right to privacy cases, the primary damage is the mental distress from having been exposed to public view, although injury to reputation may be an element bearing upon such damage. The published matter need not be defamatory, on its face or otherwise. In fact, it might even be laudatory and still warrant recover.[73]

Where false statements are made about an individual he or she may bring an action for defamation. However, as well as taking on the stress and cost of litigation and the risk of losing the case, a libel action keeps the issue in the public eye for longer than it might otherwise have been and can lead to further media intrusion into the claimant's family and private life.

Two actors, from the Australian soap opera 'neighbours', failed in a libel action against a newspaper which had altered and used their images without their consent.[74] The newspaper had published a photograph of the claimants' faces superimposed onto the near-naked bodies of models in pornographic poses. The accompanying text made it clear that the photographs had been produced without the consent of the claimants. The House of Lords held that a claim for libel could not be founded on the headline or photograph in isolation from the related text. On the facts of the case the ordinary and reasonable reader would not have formed the opinion that the claimants were involved in

71. Fellows *v.* National Enquirer, Inc. 2nd Dist. 165 Cal. App. 3d 512, 211 Cal. Reptr 809.
72. Wade, Defamation and the Right to Privacy, 15 *Vand. L. Rev.* 1093 (Oct. 1962).
73. Time, Inc. *v.* Hill, 385 US 374.
74. Charleston *v.* News Group Newspaper Ltd. (1995) 2 AC 65.

making pornographic films. Hence, there can be no libel where the statements made are true.

(v) Privacy and Home

Home is a place of shelter and a retreat from the outside world. It is a presumption of common law that a man should be safe in his own house; his house is commonly called his castle, which the law will not permit even sheriff to enter into, but by his consent unless in criminal cases. He is well guarded as a prince in his castle. The security of one's privacy against arbitrary intrusion by the police is basic for a free society and is implicit in the concept of ordered liberty. From the earliest days, the English common law drastically limited the authority of law-officers to break the doors of a house to effect an arrest. Such action invades the precious interest of privacy summed up in the ancient adage that a man's house is his castle. As early as the Thirteenth Year Book of Edward IV (1461-1473), at folio 9, there is a recorded holding that it was unlawful for the Sheriff to break the doors of a man's house to arrest him in a civil suit in debt or trespass, for the arrest was then only for the private interests of a party. Remarks attributed to William Pitt, Earl of Chatham, on the occasion of a enforcement of an excise on cinder, eloquently expressed the principle: "the poorest man may in his cottage bid defiance to all the forces of the Crown. It may be frail; its roof may shake; the wind may blow through it; the storm may enter; all his forces dare not cross the threshold of the ruined tenement."[75]

The sanctity of home[76] is a right which has long been expressly recognised in most national Constitutions. Nevertheless, the provisions governing the subject in domestic

---

75. David H. Flaherty, Privacy in Colonial New England, 87-88 (1972); 15 Hansard, Parliamentary History of England 1753-1765, p. 1307; see also Jagdish Swarup, Tagore Law Lectures: Human Rights and Fundamental Freedoms, 172 (1975).
76. The concept of home has varied at different times and in different places. It should be noted that the Council of Europe has set-up a Committee of experts with instructions to prepare whatever instruments are most suitable for harmonizing fundamental legal concepts in Europe. The Committee is dealing *inter alia*, with the concept of 'residence' and 'domicile'.

law do not always provide sufficient protection for the individual's interests. According to the conclusions of the Nordic Conference of Jurists in May 1967, "the criminal provisions in this field may not provide adequate protection for individual interests. Similarly, civil remedies designed primarily to protect ownership or possession may not extend protection to individuals who have the mere use of premises or other property without possession.[77] Unauthorised entry into a person's home for the purpose of learning the secrets of his private life can amount to a violation of Article 8 of the European Convention on Human Rights (which the United Kingdom has recently implemented in the Human Rights Act, 1998), even if the national law the essential conditions for the offence of violation of domestic privacy have not been met. Apart from the Greek case, the right to respect for the home has not so far raised any difficult problems for the European bodies responsible for enforcing undertakings under the Convention.

It is an age old tradition of Indian which teaches us not to enter any home without knocking the door first. In the case of In *re-Ratanmala*,[78] where a police officer and others proceeded to the bed room of a girl and pushed open the door, as the court observed ". . . without even the civility of a knock or warning to her to prepare for the intrusion. Thus, even a prostitute is entitled to be informed before entering into her bedroom.[79] Similarly, a man can command the view of the interior of his neighbour's house does not entitle him to gaze at his neighbour's home at all times. Indian Easement Act, 1882 covers protection of a home's privacy. Further Indian Penal Code, 1860 under Section 460 makes house trespass punishable. The section includes building, tent or vessel used as a human dwelling or used as a place for worship or as a place for the custody of property.[80] It ensures

77. Conclusions of the Nordic Conference of Jurists on the Right to Privacy, May 1967, point 12(a).
78. AIR 1962 Mad. 31.
79. State of Maharashtra *v.* Madhukar Narayan Mardikar, AIR 1991 SC 207.
80. Indian Penal Code, 1860; Sections 442 and 448.

every man to enjoy complete freedom within his house. House trespass may be justified by the authority of law. Even where law authorises to enter a dwelling house, consent of the house occupier or owner is to be taken before entering the house.[81] Some Acts[82] provide seven days previous notice to the occupier for the purpose and some other Acts[83] prescribes a reasonable notice to the concerned owner or occupier. Most of the entries are required to be made during the daytime,[84] or reasonable time[85] or in a reasonable hour in the day time.[86] While entering into the dwelling house, due regard ought to be paid to the social and religious customs and usages of the occupants.[87] Similarly, due regard ought to be paid to the women members of the family.[88]

One question may arise here, privacy of home is sacrosanct and it is protected. But there are thousands of people who are homeless or shelterless. Can they enjoy privacy of home? Michael D. Granston has discussed this question and has gone through the cases decided by United States Supreme Court for the purpose of his study.[89] The United States law exalts the home above other locations. The Fourth Amendment to the United States Constitution, for example, protects people from unreasonable searches of their houses. The term 'houses' of fourth amendment has been discussed in several cases. In *Katz* v. *U.S.*,[90] the Supreme

81. The Cantonments Act, 1924, Section 247; The Orient Gas Company Act, 1857, Section 2; and The Road Transport Corporation Act, 1950, Section 42.
82. The Northern India Canal and Drainage Act, 1873, Section 14; The Indian Works of Defence Act, 1903, Section 4.
83. The Electricity Supply Act, 1948, Section 74; The Metro Railways (Construction of Works) Act, 1978, Section 24.
84. The Code of Civil Procedure, 1908, Sections 55 and 62; The Slum Areas (Improvement and Clearance) Act, 1956, Section 26, etc.
85. The Electricity Supply Act, 1948, Section 74.
86. The Metro Railways (Construction of Works) Act, 1978, Section 24.
87. The Cantonment Act, 1924, Section 248.
88. The Income Tax Act, 1974, Section 46.
89. Michael D. Granston, From Private Places to Private Activities: Toward A New Fourth Amendment House For the Shelterless, 101 *The Yale L.J.* 1305 (April 1992).
90. 389 US 347 (1967).

Court rejected earlier concept of house as protected areas. Justice Stewart declared that "The fourth amendment protects people not places. The special protection conferred upon houses has been extended to other residential dwellings. These dwellings have included apartment buildings,[91] boarding houses,[92] motel rooms,[93] and dormitories.[94]

The home also provides a limited sanctuary from obscenity laws. As a result of this approach, a home is one of the riskiest places for a journalist to gather news. The media generally cannot enter a home without the consent of the owner or occupant. Exceptions to this general rule have been made in the event of natural disasters. In one case, a photographer who accompanied a fire marshal into a home destroyed by fire was not liable for intrusion, because the court found implied consent based on common custom and practice.[95] Authorised police activity at a home, however, normally does not authorise media presence as well. Recent years have seen a proliferation of reality-based television shows in which journalists follow police, emergency medical teams, and similar government agents to document high drama for the audience. To the extent these officials carry on their business in public, journalists generally are free to record what transpires. That freedom, however, essentially stops at private homes, even when law enforcement officials have a valid search warrant and invite the media to join them inside. In *Wilsen* v. *Layne*,[96] the Supreme Court held that "it is a violation of the Fourth Amendment for police to bring members of the media or other third parties into a home during the execution of a warrant when the presence of the third parties in the home was not in aid of the execution of the warrant."

Michael D. Granston's conclusion is worthwhile to point out. He says:[97]

91. US *v.* Carriger 541, F 2d 545.
92. State *v.* Person 298 NE 2d 922 (Ohio).
93. Pate *v.* Municipal Court, 89 Cal. Reptr. 893.
94. Smith *v.* Lubbers, 398 F. Supp. 777 (W.D. Mich. 1975).
95. Florida Publishing Co. *v.* Fletcher, 340 SO 2d 914 (Fla Sup Ct 1976)
96. 526 US 603 (1999).
97. Michael D. Granston, *op. cit.*, at 1330.

> The burgeoning shelterless population has rendered the courts understanding of fourth amendment 'houses' obsolete. The post Katz shift from private property to private places as the defining criterion of fourth amendment 'houses' though responsive to advances in governmental surveillance—inadequately protects the rights of those forced to inhabit areas exposed to the public. To protect the rights of those individuals, the courts need to alter their understanding of fourth amendment 'houses' once again its time by shifting their focus from private places to private activities.

From this observation, Indian courts, towards the interpretation of house, would take due consideration for the sake of protecting privacy. There are two possible theories for protecting privacy at home. The first is that activities in the home harm others only to the extent that they cause offence resulting from the mere thought that individuals might be engaging in such activities and that such harm is not constitutionally protectable by the State. The second is that individuals need a place of sanctuary where they can be free from societal control. The importance of such a sanctuary is that individuals can drop the mask, desist for a while from projecting on the world the image they want to be accepted as themselves, an image that may reflect the values of their peers rather than the realities of their natures.[98] Thus, the sanctity of man's house and the privacies of life still remain protected from uninvited intrusion of physical means by which words within the house are secretly communicated to a person on the outside. It is, therefore summed up that if privacy has any physical locale in modern society, it is the home, properly renowned as a haven in the heartless world.

(vi) Privacy and Family

If privacy has any social focus, it is in the family, a set of intimate relationships that can flourish when sufficiently

---

98. Upendra Baxi, K.K. Mathew on Democracy, Equality and Freedom, 305 (1978).

protected from public scrutiny.[99] The protection of the institution of family life and its inviolability is considered as indispensable in any orderly society.[100] And the Indian legal system is no exception to it. Family is the primary institution from where early socialization begins. Family gives support to a person's potential capability. Family life lies in the mutual confidence, rights and obligations and sexual fidelity between husband and wife. It can be conducive only when family privacy is given due regard. The family is prior to State both in order of time or existence and in order of thought. It has special claim upon civil authority for protection against public dangers. Therefore, Will Durant[101] has rightly stated that:

> The family has been the ultimate foundation of every civilization known to history. It was the economic and productive unit of society, tilling the land together; it was the political unit of society, with parental authority as the supporting microcosm of the State. It was the cultural unity transmitting letters and arts, rearing and teaching the young; and it was the moral unit, inculcating through cooperative work and discipline, those social dispositions which are the psychological basis and cement of civilized society. In many ways it was more essential than the State; government might break up and order yet survive, if the family remained; whereas it seemed to sociologists that if the family should dissolve, civilization itself would disappear.

The family is not beyond regulation and it would be an absurdity to suggest either that offences may not be committed in bosom of the family or that the home can be

---

99. Franklin E. Zimring, Legal Perspective on Family Violence, 75 *Cali. L.R.* 521 (Jan. 1987).

100. Govind Mishra, Privacy and the Indian Legal System, 12 *Del. L. Rev.* 68 (1990).

101. Will Durant, The Mansions of the Philosophy quoted in Augustine J. Osgniach, O.S.B., The Philosophical Roots of Law and Order, 280 (1970).

made a sanctuary for crime. The right of privacy most manifestly is not an absolute. Adultery, homosexuality, fornication and incest are not immune from criminal enquiry, however, privately practised. Adultery, homosexuality and the like are sexual intimacies which the state forbids altogether but the intimacy of husband and wife is necessarily and essential and accepted feature of the institution of marriage, an institution which the state not only must allow, but which always and in every age it has fostered and protected. It is one thing when the state exerts its power either to forbid extra-marital sexuality altogether, or to say who may marry, but it is quite another when, having acknowledged a marriage and the intimacies inherent in it, it undertakes to regulate by means of the criminal law and details of that intimacy.

The Indian Penal Code, 1860, penalizes bigamy under Sections 494 and 495. Whoever by deceitful means cause any woman, not lawfully married to him, to believe that she is lawfully married to him and to cohabit or have sexual intercourse with her is liable for punishment. The crime of adultery is also punishable under Section 497 of the Indian Penal Code. To be brief, the main thrust of Chapter XX of the Indian Penal Code is to penalize extra-marital sex. Further, the inviolability of the family life is protected under the Indian Evidence Act which provides that no person shall be compelled to disclose any communication between husband and wife.[102] The rationale of the above provisions is that admission of such testimony would have a powerful tendency to disturb the peace of families and to weaken, if not to destroy, the mutual confidence upon which the happiness of the married life depends. The prohibition rests on no technicality that can be waived at will, but is founded on a principle of high import which no court is entitled to relax.[103] The protection is not confined to cases where the communication sought to be given in evidence is of a strictly confidential character, but the seal of law is placed on all communications of whatever nature which pass between the

102. The Indian Evidence Act, 1872, Section 122.

103. Ram Chandra *v.* Emperor, 1933 Bom. 153.

husband and wife. It continues even after the marriage has been dissolved by death or divorce.[104] If the rule were otherwise but benefit of such privacy-confidence in the marriage—would be undermind by the fear of disclosure in the uncertain future.

Further, Article 17 of the International Covenant on Civil and Political Rights, 1966 *inter alia* provides right of privacy of family. This covenant is equally applicable in India because India is party to the Covenant. This provision bar 'arbitrary interference' or 'arbitrary or unlawful interference' with a person's family. In addition, both the Universal Declaration {Article 16(3)} and the Covenant on Civil and Political Rights {Article 23(1)} provides that the family is the natural and fundamental group unit of society and is entitled to protection by society and the State.

(vii) Privacy and Sex

Sex has been a natural urge of all the creatures of the world. Nature has imbibed this instinct so that the process of procreation is continued, and this would have been the reason for addition of element of pleasure with sexual intercourse.[105] According to Indian culture, the union of man and woman is treated as a pious union. Nearly all societies, primitive as well as modern have sought privacy for sexual relations. Even where there is crowed quarters and the lack of insulation in traditional homes, no doubt, challenged the imagination of couples, but the expectation of sexual privacy was always present. Sexual activities are supposed to be made in a private place. Even in brothel sexual activities are performed in a separate room. Thus, even a prostitute is entitled to sexual decencies. If anybody enters into room without knocking the door or without warning that violates privacy of a person.[106] Even a woman of easy virtue is entitled to right of privacy and no one can invade her

---

104. Woodroff and Ameer Ali, Law of Evidence, Vol. 3, p. 2402 (1968).
105. Surender Kumar Singh, Human Rights of AIDS Infected People *vis-à-vis* Healthy People, 199 *AIR Journal Section* (2000).
106. *In re* Ratanmala, AIR 1962 Mad. 31 at p. 52.

privacy.[107] For this reason also privacy of family and home is considered a fundamental rights.

The notion of sexual privacy, however, is changing day by day. In modern society there is neither any norm nor any discipline for sex. Today sex players are totally socialist, secular, democratic and universal. They have one permanent partner (wife) at home and search other new bed-partner whenever they go out of home.[108] In United Kingdom, a couple was travelling from Margate to London by train. The train was fairly crowded but the couple engaged in oral sex in front of the passengers. Subsequently, they had sex of a more conventional kind. After having such relation they each lit a cigarette in no smoking compartment. For this they were apprehended and punished for smoking but the court did not punish them for performing sexual activities in public.[109]

The life style of Western culture and that of eastern culture particularly Indian culture is totally different. The concept of sexual privacy is also different. In India, Islam has allowed for polygamy. A Muslim can have as many as four wives at a time, provided all are treated as equals. Similarly, we find the customary law of the tribals in general has not forbidden polygamy. Polygamy is more widespread among the tribes of north and central India. They themselves make understanding of sexual privacy. Wives or husbands maintain sexual privacy while making intercourse. Other partner does not intervene in their course.

The right of privacy has also come to fore in recent years in United States of America. While deeply ingrained in United States constitutional and legal history, much of the development of this right in the recent years has taken place in the context of the issues dealing with sexual freedom and women's rights. Technological advances of the twentieth century have contributed troubling dimensions to the problem of protecting privacy. However, the technological advances

---

107. State of Maharashtra *v.* Madhukar Narayan Mardikar, AIR 1991 SC 207; State *v.* Gurmit Singh, AIR 1996 SC 1393; See also State *v.* Gangula, AIR 1997 SC 1588.
108. *Supra* n. 105 at 199-200.
109. *The Pioneer*, 13 (August 13, 1992).

and other pressures on privacy have led to a more explicit recognition in United States public law of the importance of safeguarding the right of privacy as against competing interests such as public morality and law enforcement.

(viii) Privacy and Unnatural Offences

Privacy is not an absolute right. In the name of privacy immoral acts or illegal acts are not protected in India. Indian law do not ignore morality. There are statutes which directly protect private as well as public morality. Under Section 377 of the Indian Penal Code unnatural offences are liable to be punished. The Section reads—"whoever voluntarily has carnal intercourse against the order of nature with any man, woman or animal shall be punished . . ." This section does not protect unnatural offences in the name of privacy. Even if a husband practices sodomy with his wife, he will come under the grip of law.

Wolfenden Committee was constituted in United Kingdom to consider the matter of homosexual activities conducted in private. The Committee in its report in 1957, recommended that law should not regulate sexual conduct in private between two consenting adults. In United Kingdom, when Sexual Offences Act, 1967 was enacted, it did not make homosexual offences conducted in private between consenting males as a crime. If homosexuality cannot amount to crime, naturally lesbianism is also exempted. Lord Devlin opposed Wolfenden Committee's view and was of the opinion that law should take account of private morality also.

(ix) Privacy and Conjugal Rights

The conjugal right is not the creature of any statute. But it is inherent in the very institution of marriage itself. The Law Commission of India in its 71st Report stated that the essence of marriage is a sharing of a common life, a sharing of all the happiness that life has to offer and all the miseries that has to be faced in life, an experience of the joy that comes from enjoying the common things of the matter and of the spirit and from showering love and affection of one's offspring.

The remedy of restitution of conjugal rights had its

origin in the ecclesiastical law of England. But now it has been abolished in England by the Matrimonial Proceedings Act, 1970. In India, it was applied as a part of justice, equity, and good conscience. However, the Hindu Marriage Act, 1955, enacted it as a statutory remedy. The purpose of the remedy is to preserve and not to disrupt the marriage. Cohabiting means the husband and wife living together as husband and wife.[110] They must live together not merely as two people, living in one house but as husband and wife.[111] Through the decree of restitution of conjugal rights, the withdrawing parties is ordered to return to the conjugal fold, so that consortium is not broken. Consortium means, "companionship, love, affection, comfort, mutual services, sexual intercourse."[112] The question of relation between the right to privacy and conjugal rights arose for the first time in *T. Sareetha* v. *T.V. Subbaiah*.[113] The court has extended the concept of sexual autonomy to Hindu women by striking down Section 9 of the Hindu Marriage Act, 1956 providing for restitution of conjugal rights. Justice Chaudhary extended the protection of privacy to inhuman and degrading treatment of forcible sexual cohabitation.[114] Relying on Western sexologists the court held that the sexual autonomy was necessary for the enjoyment of life. The freedom to choose partner for sexual act was included into enjoyment of life. The court further observed that by this matrimonial remedy, "during a moment's duration the entire life style would be altered and would even be destroyed" without her consent. This situation was treated as a violation of individual dignity and right to privacy.

However, in *Harvinder Kaur* v. *Harmander Singh Chaudhary*,[115] Justice Avadh Bihari Rohtagi of Delhi High Court has expressed a contrary view and upheld the validity of Section 9 of the Hindu Marriage Act. The court held that

110. Thomas *v.* Thomas (1948) 2 KB 294.
111. Wheatley *v.* Wheatley (1950) 1 KC 39.
112. V.K. Bansal, Right to Life and Personal Liberty in India, 109 (1978)
113. AIR 1983 Andhra Pradesh 356.
114. *Ibid.*, para 35.
115. AIR 1984 Delhi 66.

though sexual relations constitute most important attribute of concept of marriage but they do not cosntitute its whole content. Sexual intercourse is one of the elements which goes to make up the marriage but it is not the summum borum. According to Rohtagi, J. one great defect of Andhra High Court is that it regards marriage as a legalised means of sexual satisfaction and not as a partnership for life. The Andhra High Court decision is based on misconception of the true end of marriage.

The Supreme Court finally set the controversy at rest in *Saroj Rani* v. *Sudershan Kumar*[116] by approving the judgment of Delhi High Court in Harvinder Kaur's case. Justice Mukharji speaking on behalf of the court declared that court prefer to accept the view of the learned single Judge of the Delhi High Court. The court ruled that Section 9 serves social purpose as an aid to the preservation of marriage and therefore satisfies Articles 14 and 21 of the Constitution. However, unfortunately, the Supreme Court did not consider the question of wife's right to privacy. The court was influenced by the method of execution of the decree of restitution of conjugal rights.

(x) Privacy and Nuisance

Unlawful interference with a person's use or enjoyment of land or some right over, or in connection with it is called nuisance.[117] It is the wrong done to a person by unlawfully disturbing him in the enjoyment of his property or, in some cases, in the exercise of common right, for example, noise, vibrations, heat, smoke, smell, fumes, water, gas, electricity, excavations or disease producing germs. Nuisance is similar to trespass in so far as in either case the plaintiff has to show his possession of land. In India, there is no comprehensive enactment in relation to nuisance which cover all aspects of nuisance. However, Indian Easement Act, 1882 and The Limitation Act, 1963 have made some provisions in this regard.

---

116. AIR 1984 SC 1526.
117. Bhanwarlal *v.* Dhan Raj, AIR 1973 Raj. 212.

The tort of nuisance is underdeveloped in India. It does not protect sufficient privacy interest. It is also limited as trespass. For example, spying on one's neighbour is probably not in itself a private nuisance although watching and besetting a man's house with a view to compelling him to pursue and particular course of conduct has been said to be nuisance in common law.[118] Further, persistent telephone calling is a nuisance[119] which invades a person's privacy but the use of a telephoto lens to look into the private bedroom would not. Similarly, playing loudspeakers in the street may violate a person's privacy.

(xi) Privacy and Trespass to Land

The concept of trespass is one of the oldest principles in United Kingdom law. Trespass to land is a tort in English law. Mistakes, such as the defendant mistakenly believing that the land belongs to him, is no defence. There is no liability if the act is involuntary[120] and if the act is unintentional an action may only lie in negligence.[121] The right to bring an action in trespass belongs to the person in possession of the land at the time of the trespass. If a trespasser peaceably enters the land the person in possession of the land may request him to leave and if he refuses to do so may remove him from the land by his own acts or by instructing another to do so, using no more force than is reasonably necessary. If the trespasser enters forcibly the person in possession does not need to request him to leave before removing him from the land. The court can grant an injunction to prevent continued or threatened repetition of a trespass.

The law of trespass is recongised in India. Trespass of the others land is prohibited. However, in practice only forcible entries are brought into the court as a trespass. Entering peacefully to others land, though a trespass, is not brought into the court of law. Trespass to the land and

118. Lyons and Sons *v.* Wilkins, (1899) 1 Ch. 255 CA.
119. Motherwell *v.* Motherwick, (1976) 73 DLR 93 do 62 (Atla App. Div.).
120. Smith *v.* Stone (1647) Stry 65.
121. Letang *v.* Cooper (1965) 1 QB 232.

dwelling house is prohibited by some Public Offences and Punishment Act, 1970.

The action of trespass is of limited purpose. It protects from physical interference only. It does not protect photography, bugging, tapping, snooping from the distance without entering to other's land. Prying neighbour with binoculars, electronic eavesdropping and spying by electronic devices do not amount trespass.

Thus, trespass protects privacy of a person in certain respect. It restricts, physical intervention so its scope is limited to protect privacy. Indian legal system protect such types of privacy which is devised out of trespass law.

(xii) Privacy and Trespass to Person

The concept of trespass is one of the oldest concept in United Kingdom law: 'The house of everyone is to him as is his castle and fortress, as well as his defence against injury and violence, as for his repose,'[122] The Indian legal system ensures that every man to enjoy complete freedom within his house. Trespass may be justified either by the authority or consent of the person concerned or the authority of law.[123] Even where entry into a dwelling house is authorised by or under an Act, such entry is not made without the consent of its occupier or owner.[124] In some Acts, seven days previous notice to the owner or occupier is required to be given before the intended entry into the dwelling house. Further the law of assault and battery are closely connected with right to life and personal liberty and both the offences are punishable under Section 352 of the Indian Penal Code.

(xiii) Privacy and Press

Freedom of Press has been acclaimed as the cornerstone of modern democratic state. It is often described

---

122. Seymayne's case (1603) 5 Co. Rep. 91, 916.
123. B. S. Sinha, An Introduction to Law of Torts Through Indian Cases, 155.
124. The Orient Gas Company Act, 1857, Section 2; The Cantonments Act, 1924, Section 247; The Road Transport Corporation Act, 1950, Section 42; and The Slum Areas (Improvement and Clearance) Act, 1956, Section 57.

as fourth estate.[125] The press enjoys a prestigious position in democratic countries where constitutions guarantees freedom of press. The freedom, like all other liberties, cannot be absolute and is subjected to restrictions in public interest. Privacy of individual is a right to be protected even from the gaze of the press. Invasion of privacy by press may arise when information about private affairs of a person is published by newspaper. India have neither popular press nor there is a practice to pay handsomely to freelancers. According to Justice V.R. Krishna Iyer, Press has the public duty to inform or expose even the private life of public persons, which affects the people's interest. Where a reputed journal devoted to the dissemination of information on public matters or personalities for democratic edification comes with important discoveries bearing on a high functionary's private sexual deviance impacting on his image and activities as a public servant, exposure of such delinquency is the public duty of the Press in a democratic polity. Moreover, where officers "perverting and polluting by stink an office of trust or seat of authority won by the franchise of citizens or sworn in by the highest executive of the nation." Justice Iyer adds, "the jurisprudence of public office in a democratic republic demands that the purity, even sex purity of public power is invigorated by a fearless Press unmasking violators and not abdicate its sacred function of informing the public whose right to know is fundamental to fundamental rights."[126]

As for privacy, Justice Iyer said, [127] the Press should not intrude into the personal lives of people. "At the same time, some amount of exposure of the privacy of public men, which affects public good, is needed," he added.

Right to privacy has been accorded judicial recognition in the United States of America. But the role of press as an invader of privacy is less prominent in the Untied States and the law does not display any uniformity. The tort law appears to cover following four kinds of invasion of privacy;

---

125. Lucas A. Powe Jr., The Fourth Estate and the Constitution 261 (1992).
126. Justice V.R. Krishna Iyer quoted by Faizan Mustafa, Constitutional Issues in Freedom of Information, 79 (2003).

intrusion into an individual's physical solitude; publication of private matter violating ordinary decency; putting some one in false light; and appropriation of an individual name or likeness (normally for commercial purposes).

One of the most distinctive new developments in United States culture in the second half of the nineteenth century was the pervasive sense that what were once private matters were being discussed in public and given wide and scandalous exposure. The modern media—with all its voyeurism and sensationalism—was really born in the late nineteenth century as the result of the rise of inexpensive, mass-circulation newspapers and of the emergence of a political and journalistic culture in which the revelation of public scandal was seen as a necessary precondition to justice and emancipation. Technological change and the rise of big cities enabled the cheap "penny press" to exert greater and greater influence on United States society. The new sensational press broke down old mores and conventions, all the while appealing to the democratic justification that it was simply "giving the people what they want" (while making hefty profits). It was in this context that the old order concerning freedom of the speech came to an end and modern world of free speech was poised to be born.[128]

The right to freedom of speech and expression and the right to privacy are two sides of the same coin. One person's right to know and be informed may violate another's right to be let alone. Just as the freedom of speech and expression is vital for dissemination of information on matters of public interest, it is equally important to safeguard the private life of an individual to the extent that it is unrelated to public duties or matters of public interest. The law of privacy endeavours a balance of these competing freedoms.

The development of media in modern times has a special relevance to the evolution to bring the private life of an individual into the public domain, thus exposing him to

---

127. *Ibid.*

128. Rochelle Gurstein, The Repeal of Reticence: A History of America's Cultural and Legal Struggles over Free Speech, Obscenity, Sexual Liberation and Modern Art, 52 & 62 (1996).

the risk of an invasion of his space and his privacy. In India, newspapers were, for many years, the primary source of information to the public. A study of the freedom of expression is incomplete and unbalanced without a reference to the counter-value of the right to privacy. Just freedom of speech and expression is vital for the dissemination of information on matters of public interest, it is equally important to safeguard the private life of an individual. The question that arises whether Tehelka acted in derogation of the right to privacy of the public officials exposed what is the extent of privacy legally enjoyed by a person when he functions in a public capacity? While some scholars have cautioned against the indiscriminate use of methods adopted by Tehelka, and have suggested that the yardsticks of necessity and proportionality be adopted, the author submits that while the requirement of regulation of press freedom cannot be denied, such restraint ought to be exercised by journalists themselves in the larger interest of the media as a whole, and the same cannot be imposed on the press by law as that would contravene Article 19(2) as it stands today. The only restrictions which can be legally imposed on the freedom of the press to adopt various means of obtaining information, is by the press itself, by way of self-regulatory framework. The prevalent situation of Indian polity signified by absolute lack of accountability of various public functionaries and an immense void as far as information to the masses is concerned, can not be ignored. The relevance of an exercise like Tehelka must be examined in the context of democratic governance in India.

Tehelka has been incapacitated by the events following publication of its tapes—its assets have been frozen, various cases have been lodged against the Tehelka personnel/ executives post the expose, regarding alleged Income Tax and Fera violations. While there has been no clear legal adjudication of Tehelka's liability under the law, in actual fact, it has been penalized over the last many years. Its freedom has been curtailed, though by means which are entirely extra-constitutional. Tehelka and the like, are essential to maintain free flow of information which is absolutely imperative for a healthy and vital democracy, and it is towards its end that such freedom cannot be pruned, directly or indirectly.

The press and right to privacy came for the first time under notice in *R. Rajagopal* v. *State of Tamil Nadu*.[129] In this case, the facts shows that the prison authorities attempted to prevent *Nakkheeran*, a Tamil Weekly from publishing the autobiography of Auto Shankar, who had been convicted for six murders and was sentenced to death. The announcement that the weekly was about to publish the autobiography sent shock waves among senior I.A.S., I.P.S. and several other officers and politicians, as it was expected to uncover the close nexus between the prisoner and such officers and politicians. The editor preferred a writ petition under Article 32 of the Constitution of India asserting the freedom of press and their right to publish the book. The respondents contended that the intended publication was likely to be defamatory and their required to be restrained. The issue of the right to privacy came up in this context. The Supreme Court held that the press had the right to publish what they claimed was the autobiography of Auto Shankar insofar as it appeared from the public records, even without his consent or authorisation. However, if the press items went beyond the public record and published his life story, that might amount to an invasion of his right to privacy. Similarly, the government and prison officials who sought to protect themselves against possible defamation (by ostensibly seeking to protect the privacy of the incarcerated prisoner), did not have the right to impose a prior restraint on the publication of the autobiography; their remedy, if at all, could arise only after the publication.

The court recognized two aspects of right to privacy: (1) the tortuous law of privacy which affords an action for damages resulting from an unlawful invasion of privacy, and (2) the constitutional right "to be let alone" implicit in the right to life and personal liberty under Article 21. A citizen has the right to safeguard his own privacy, that of his family, marriage, procreation, motherhood, child bearing, education, etc. and no person can publish anything relating to such

129. AIR 1995 SC 264.

matters without the consent of the person concerned. The court acknowledged two exceptions to this rule: First, where the matter has become a matter of public record, the right to privacy no longer subsists.[130] Second, public officials are not entitled to claim privacy when the act or conduct in question relates to the discharge of their official duties. Even where the publication is based upon facts found to be untrue, the public official is not entitled to protection unless it is shown that the publication was made with reckless disregard for truth. It is sufficient for the publisher to show that he acted after a reasonable verification of facts. The Press Council of India was first set-up in the year 1966 by the Parliament on the recommendations of the First Press Commission with the object of preserving the freedom of the press and of maintaining and improving the standards of press in India. The present Council functions under the Press Council Act, 1978. In 2005, certain norms of journalistic conduct were made which are as follows:

> 13. The Press shall not intrude or invade the privacy of an individual unless outweighed by genuine overriding public interest, not being a prurient or morbid curiosity. So, however, that once a matter becomes a matter of public record, the right of privacy no longer subsists and it becomes a legitimate subject for comment by Press and media among others. Explanation: Things concerning a person's home, family, religion, health, sexuality, person life and private affairs are covered by the concept of privacy excepting where any of these intrude upon the public or public interest.
> 14. Caution against identification: While reporting crime involving rape, abduction or kidnap of women/females or sexual assault on children, or raising doubts and questions touching the chastity, personal character and privacy of women, the names, photographs of the victims or other

130. Except in the interests of decency.

particulars leading to their identity shall not be published.

15. Minor children and infants who are the offspring of sexual abuse or 'forcible marriage' or illicit sexual union shall not be identified or photographed.
16. The Press shall not tape-record anyone's conversation without that person's knowledge or consent, except where the recording is necessary to protect the journalist in a legal action, or for other compelling good reason.
17. The Press shall, prior to publication, delete offensive epithets used by an interviewer in conversation with the Press person.
18. Intrusion through photography into moments of personal grief shall be avoided. However, photography of victims of accidents or natural calamity may be in a larger public interest.
45. Investigative reporting has three basic elements:
    (a) It has to be the work of the reporter, not of others he is reporting;
    (b) The subject should be of public importance for the reader to know;
    (c) An attempt is being made to hide the truth from the people;
    (ii) There being a conflict between the factors which require openness and those which necessitate secrecy, the investigative journalist should strike and maintain in his report a proper balance between openness on the one hand and secrecy on the other, placing the public good above everything;
    (viii) The private life, even of a public figure, is his own. Exposition or invasion of his personal privacy or private life is not permissible unless there is clear evidence that the wrong doings in question have a reasonable nexus with the misuse of his public position or power and has an adverse impact on public interest.

Media must as a role respect the right of privacy of AIDS patients and must not subject them to needless exposure and social stigma.

Right to privacy is an inviolable human right. However, the degree of privacy differs from person to person and from situation to situation. The public person who functions under public gaze as an emissary/representative of the public cannot expect to be afforded the same degree of privacy as a private person. His acts and conduct are of public interest ('public interest' being distinct and separate from 'of interest to the public') even if conducted in private may be brought to public knowledge through the medium of the press. The press has, however, a corresponding duty to ensure that the information about such acts and conduct of public interest of the public person is obtained through fair means, is property verified and then reported accurately. For obtaining the information in respect of acts done or conducted away from public gaze, the press is not expected to use surveill devices. For obtaining information about private talks and discussions, while the press is expected not to badger the public persons, the public persons are also expected to bring more openness in their functioning and cooperate with the press in its duty of informing the public about the acts of their representatives.

To keep the Press as a strong medium that can safeguard public interest it must observe self-censorship with a set of norms based on sound principles that offer due regard to both the freedom of expression and right to privacy. In this regard Press Council can play an effective role by giving proper direction to print media. The question here is whether all journals would view such guidelines with due respect or would they flout the norms for making space for spicy stories that would increase the circulation. The question may assume philosophic proportions if one asks whether ultimate motive of a paper is to educate the public or to entertain even at the expense of morality.

If the Press goes beyond the ethical limit, it may lead to unnecessary litigation in the realm of tort which labels separately defamation and violation of privacy.[131] Obviously, the government may even be led to think in terms of curbing the liberty that the press enjoys. On the other hand, if the press exhibits maturity by making itself subject of self-scrutiny, it can act as a bulwark of freedom.

In the United Kingdom in 1972 the Younger Committee Report on Privacy stated that since in complaints of invasion of privacy there might be conflict of interests between the need of the public to be informed and the need to respect individual's privacy, the balancing of these interests in each case was to be left to the judgment of the Press Council. It also recommended that the Council should try to codify its adjudications on privacy so that a ready guidance might be available to journalists and to the interested public. Further, the Calcutta Committee, 1989-90 emphasized that individual privacy should be considered along with freedom of speech and expression. The Committee pointed out that freedom of expression was subject to a number of exceptions, one of which being protecting individual privacy. The encroachment by press and other mass-media into privacy rights of individuals through the help of modern technology is the new threat. The concept of privacy is multidimensional and ever widening with every advancement in technology. Hence it seems that evolution of the concept step by step through judicial decisions would be prudent course. Here, judiciary can take note of the ever widening concept and use it as a parameter for deciding disputes that involve the question of privy rights.

(xiv) Privacy and Communication and Correspondence

Like the right to the sanctity of home, the right to respect for correspondence is proclaimed in the Constitution of the great majority of States. In the usual meaning of the term 'correspondence' covers all communications between different persons by means of letters. Article 8 of the European Convention on Human Rights refers to protection

131. David Bedigfield, Privacy of Publicity? The Enduring Confusion Surrounding The American Tort of Invasion of Privacy, 55 *M.L.R.* 111 (1992); see also Peter Prescott, Kaye *v.* Robertson—A Reply, 54 *M.L.R.* 451 (1991).

of correspondence only, not of communication in general. Broadly speaking, the Convention protects the right to respect for all communications, whatever their nature: telephone, telegraph, electrical, wireless, pneumatic, etc. Thus, the interception, suppression or disclosure of a message transmitted by these means of communication can constitute a violation of Article 8 of the Convention.

Human anxiety to protect mails and messages is as old as the institution of spying or secret service which is said to be the second oldest profession of the world. Interception of messages, signals and letters by postal censorship, monitoring, tapping telephones and breaking codes is the standard practice of modern intelligence agencies. In the ancient period, since intelligence was communicated through "gudha lekh", i.e. pre-determined signals, and with assistance of pigeons, secret agents must have made elaborate arrangements to intercept these messages. "Mudraraksasa," a Sanskrit classic, written by Vishakadutta, mentions the art of opening a sealed letter without damaging the seal.[132] Similar practice was being adhered to by the London Post Office. It has been alleged that in London, the Post office engages in the systematic opening of letters at the Investigating Division in Euston and at a 'special section' near St. Paul's. Sophisticated equipment such as long, thin pliers which enable letters to be rolled up and removed from envelopes via the corners, are apparently used. Still more advanced equipment is already in service . . . allowing some mail to be read un-opened. This is done by electronic scanning which can detect the carbon used in most kind of ink.[133]

Strong protection for privacy is given by a section of federal law, originally enacted in 1825 in U.S.A., which makes it a crime to take mail before delivery to the addressee with design to obstruct correspondence, or "to pry into the business or secrets of another", or to open, secret, embezzle or destroy. The United States Code makes it an offence for any postmaster or other postal employee to unlawfully detain, delay, or open any mail. Federal laws protecting

132. D.S. Trivedi, Secret Service in Ancient India, p. 49.
133. Raymond Wacks, The Protection of Privacy, 48 (1980).

telegraphic communications derive mainly from the Federal Communications Act of 1934. By its terms it prohibits anyone involved in transmitting or receiving the communication from divulging or publishing anything having to do with it (including the very fact of its existence) outside the regular channels of communication. The same section of Federal Communication Act relates to interference with telegraph communication is the basis of federal law restricting wiretapping of telephone communication. Further, eavesdropping has been recognised as a crime by the common law for centuries, and a number of States have provisions in their statutory law making of a crime.[134]

Indian Post Office Act, 1898 prescribe punishment to the personnel of post office if they are found guilty of carelessness endangering to safety of postal articles or causing delay in its conveyance or delivery.[135] Similarly, detaining the mails of postal articles or even opening the mail bag in course of transmission by post by any person without due authority is made punishable.[136] Similarly, the Indian Telegraph Act, 1885 prescribes additional punishment for one who unlawfully tries to learn the contents of any message given for transmission in the telegraph office.[137] The Indian Telegraph Act, 1885 was amended by the Parliament in 1972 which authorizes certain officers to intercept such message or stop their transmission if it was considered to be in the interest of the country or the public for maintenance of friendly relations with foreign states, etc.[138] Commenting upon the above amendment, it has observed[139] that the right of privacy in India suffered a set back in 1972. It is submitted that the amendment may be rationalized if it is thought of as imposing a reasonable restriction on the right in question keeping in view the paramount interest of national security risks and friendly relations with foreign countries. Thus, as

134. Hyman Gross, Privacy—Its Legal Protection, 32-53 (1976).
135. Section 2(1).
136. *Ibid.*, Section 67.
137. The Indian Telegraph Act, 1885, Section 24.
138. The Indian Telegraph (Amendment) Act, 1972, Section 2.
139. Richard P. Claude (ed.) Comparative Human Rights, 80 (1976).

the position stands today, subject to the overriding powers of the State during public emergency, inviolability of mails and messages is well protected in the Indian legal system in normal and general circumstances. In an age of revolutionized communication, privacy is clearly under seize but law-makers have shown scarce concern on the issue. While in many other countries, there are now a variety of statutes in place[140] that seek to protect these rights, Indian laws on the subject lag far behind.

(xv) Privacy and Privileged Communication

In law, a privilege is an immunity, or exemption conferred by special grant to a certain class or individual in derogation of a common right. Usually, a privilege is created by law on the ground of some consideration of public policy. The law excludes, or dispense with, some kinds of evidence on grounds of public policy, because it is thought that greater mischiefs would probably result from requiring or permitting their admission than from granting a privilege. By "public policy" we do not mean some merely political consideration. Public policy embraces considerations of paramount importance—be they political, social or any other—which the law deems it proper to take into account from the point of view of public welfare. In addition to public policy and public welfare we may add another element, namely that most, if not all, of the privileges recognized by the law are needed for the proper functioning of the particular relationship. It may be domestic—as husband and wife—or professional—attorney an client, or may be wider—e.g. government retention of certain information or it may consist in a particular character occupied by the person concerned, for example, the judge privileged under Section 121 of the Indian Evidence Act, 1872.

A privilege is granted because it is considered more important to keep certain information confidential than it is to require disclosure of all the information relevant to the issues in a pending proceeding. Although, in the field of the

140. Such as the Privacy Act, 1988 (Commonwealth) and the Data Protection Act, 1988 in the United Kingdom.

law of evidence, privilege operate merely as exclusionary rule, they also have a wider importance namely, that they represent a right to be let along, a right to unfettered freedom in certain narrowly prescribed relationships, from the coercive or supervisory powers of the state and from the nuisance of its eavesdropping.[141]

Two common rationales justify the existence of privileges. The first known as the utilitarian rationale, focuses on justifying confidential communications within the context of various professional relationships, for example, attorney and client, physician and patient, clergyman and penitent. This approach, espoused chiefly by Dean Wigmore, hold that these privileges are justified in order to encourage full communication within these relationships.[142] Wigmore believed that there are four essential conditions for the establishment of such privilege:

(i) The communication must originate in a confidence that they will not be disclosed.

(ii) The element of confidentiality must be essential to the full and satisfactory maintenance of the relation between the parties.

(iii) The relation must be one which in the opinion of the community ought to be sedulously fostered.

(iv) The injury that would injure to the relation by the disclosure of the communication must be greater than the benefit thereby gained for the correct disposal of litigation.[143]

Although these conditions might be interpreted quite broadly, Wigmore did not do so. Rather he construed them strictly, justifying traditional privileges such as that protecting attorney-client communications but refusing to recognise new ones. Courts have also strictly interpreted the conditions mandating privileges. In particular, most courts only consider

---

141. Louisell *et. al.*, Principle of Evidence and Proof, 467-8 (1972).

142. Michael F. Kelleher, The Confidentiality of Criminal Conversations on TDD Relay Systems, 79 *Cal. L. Rev.* 1362 (Oct. 1991).

143. J. Wigmore, Evidence in Trials at Common Law, 527 (1961).

systematic harms when evaluating Wigmore's injury requirement. Ignoring the harm to the individual in the specific case, courts instead attempt to balance the benefit of protecting the class of communications against the cost to the goal of truth-seeking.

Numerous commentators have criticized the assumptions underlying the utilitarian justification for privileges. The chief attack questions whether existing privileges actually encourage communications at all. No empirical data is available which will demonstrate whether the privilege actually encourages communications between attorneys and their clients. Critics argue that people typically do not know of or understand the privileges. Defenders of privileges counter that although the benefits of privileges are difficult to quantify, they are significant and outweigh the costs to the truth-seeking function. Defenders also point out that the costs involved are difficult to estimate and tend to be overstated.

The second justification for privileges is that they protect certain privacy interests. While the utilitarian justification looks only to prevent widespread systematic harms to a class. The privacy rationale is concerned with harm to the individual communicant. Thus, communication within certain relationships should not be pried into, not because the privileges promote communication but because the relationship is an essential private one.[144]

The Indian Evidence Act, 1872 provide privileges to certain relations.[145] Similarly, judicial privileges, state secrets and professional privileges are recognised under the Act. These privileges are recognized under the Act. These privileges undoubtedly protect privacy interest but are not adequate to protect privacy of all relations. The Indian legal system obligates the professionals not to reveal the confidential information obtained in course of their

144. Michael F. Kelleher, *op. cit.* at 1362-1363; Note, Development in Law: Privileged Communication, 98 *Harv. L. Rev.* 1473 (1985): Note, The Attorney—Client Privilege and the Corporation in Shareholder Litigation 50 S *Cal. L. Rev.* 303, 306 (1977).

145. See, Sections 122, 126, 127, 128 and 129.

professional functions. An advocate is not permitted to disclose any communication made to him in the course and for the purpose, of his employment as an advocate without the express consent of his client. The obligation, thus imposed on him continues even after the employment has ceased. Similarly, the respect for human dignity is the principal objective of the medical profession. Confidences concerning individual or domestic life entrusted by patients to the physician and defects in the disposition or character of the patient observed during medical attendance should never be revealed unless their revelation is required by the laws of the state. There may be so many private conversations between family members other than the spouse. Privacy interest is not limited to relations, but it extends with individual's own interaction to anyone whomsoever he interacts in a private affairs.

(xvi) Privacy and Camera Proceedings

Yet another but related aspect is the provision regarding in camera trial which stands as an admission on the part of the administration of justice of those qualities of individuals which inhibit them to speak out certain facts in front of general public coupled with a policy consideration that certain matters of intimate and personal nature or prejudicial to the safety of the State[146] ought not to be discussed in general public. Majority of the Acts which provide for in camera proceedings relate to, and deal with, the matrimonial causes.[147] In Indian legal system, there are four categories of cases where trial in camera is required viz. (i) cases involving safety of the State, (ii) cases involving trade secrets, (iii) matrimonial cases, and (iv) cases involving lunacy. The cases of matrimonial disputes and lunacy are entirely related to private and domestic life with which public has no legitimate concern. Matrimonial cases involve

146. The Official Secrets Act, 1923, Section 14.

147. The Converts' Marriage Dissolution Act, 1866, Section 14; The Indian Divorce Act, 1869, Section 53; The Parsi Marriage and Divorce Act, 1936, Section 43; The Special Marriage Act, 1954, Section 33 and the Hindu Marriage Act, 1955, Section 22.

sordid details of domestic life. They may create embarrassing situation to parties if they are disclosed. In some other cases,[148] proceedings may be conducted in camera if (a) either party so desires or (b) if the court thinks fit to do so. In case of former one, the court has no discretion to refuse it. Even when neither party so desires, it is open to the court in its discretion to hear and conduct such proceedings in camera.[149] Similarly, parties may request for camera proceedings under Section 43 of the Parsi Marriage and Divorce Act, 1936.[150]

The Code of Criminal Procedure, 1973 empowers the presiding judge or Magistrate to exclude the general public or any particular individual from any enquiry or trial of any case, at any stage at his discretion.[151] The Lunacy Act provides for the consideration of the petition in private in the presence of the petitioner or his or her representative and such other persons as thought fit.[152] The Monopolies and Restrictive Trade Practices Act, 1969 also provides that if the commission is satisfied of the confidential nature of any offence or for any reason, it may hear proceeding in private, give directions as to the persons who may be present there and prohibit any publication of evidence given before it.[153]

The trial in camera would be useless if the matter or proceedings and decision is allowed to publish. Public has no concern in such cases. The courts, therefore, have been empowered to prohibit any publication of such proceedings without obtaining their prior permission. The Hindu Marriage Act, 1955 prohibits to print or publish any matter in relation to the proceedings in camera without obtaining prior permission of the court.[154] Any publication of such proceedings in camera without obtaining prior permission of the court will amount to contempt of the court.[155]

---

148. The Hindu Marriage Act, 1955, Section 22; The Special Marriage Act, 1954, Section 33.
149. The Indian Divorce Act, 1869, Section 53; The Converts' Marriage Dissolution Act, 1866, Section 14.
150. The Parsi Marriage and Divorce Act, 1936, Section 43.
151. The Code of Criminal Procedure, 1973, Section 327.
152. The Indian Lunacy Act, 1912, Section 9.
153. See, Section 17.
154. See, Section 22.
155. The Contempt of Courts Act, 1971, Section 7.

(xvii) Privacy and Data Protection

Privacy has become an issue in modern democratic societies which are characterised by large-scale, sophisticated bureaucratic structures and advanced technology in communication and information systems. A major factor of the privacy problem is the absence of legislation and organized rules ensuring privacy, confidentiality and due process to the subjects of computerized information. Data banks have been established at all levels of Government, business and the military services without any real knowledge or concern for their potential impact over individual rights. The privacy issue is all the more urgent because of widespread use of information systems to administer services which many people may consider essential to their well being. Along with the values of a democratic system people have constantly rising expectations in terms of medical services, health, insurance, credit, family assistance and education. Those in search of jobs, credit, housing, welfare and other services must disclose extensive information of a particular nature, in order to obtain these benefits. The information further accumulates into the files maintained by various private and public institutions. If the facts about a person are freely disclosed with the knowledge and consent that they may be shared with others, there has been no violation of privacy.[156]

The privacy issue involves other concerns often emotionally associated with, but not actually included in the concept of privacy. People may feel threatened by the very existence of massive and efficient information systems even though the privacy has not actually been invaded. They are often concerned about the endless search for personal data by social scientists, market researchers, opinion pollsters and the institutions that use the data.

Concern for privacy is caught up in the more general debate regarding the effect of technology on society. Some contemporary thinkers share a pessimistic view of this relationship and conclude that what is technically feasible is

156. Hyman Gross, Privacy—Its Legal Protection, 21-25 (1976); see also A.H. Robertson, Privacy and Human Rights, 135-137 (1972).

allowed to occur without regard for the consequences. Hannab Arendt, Herbert Marcuse and Lewis Mumford share this attitude.[157] At the other end of the spectrum are those who argue with Alvin Toffler[158] that technology has allowed the individual a greater range of choice than he has ever enjoyed before, one that may further even be bewildering broad. They argue that problems resulting from modern technology can be solved by the use of more technology. The privacy issue, however, will suffer from being embroiled in this debate. Since technology is here to stay, the privacy discussion should not focus on its desirability, but rather on finding ways to protect humanistic values and goals. Given the ease and speed with which information passes from one organization to another, it could become the basis for unjust discrimination. But concomitantly with increasing legal recognition of privacy, there has developed a technological ability to invade it by a number of means heretofore not known. Data on individuals is easily collected and as easily stored. What is technologically possible will be done.

Professor Arthur R. Miller, identifies four recent developments that relate to the late twentieth century concern for privacy.[159] (1) Massive record-keeping; (2) decision-making by dossier; (3) unrestricted transfer of information from one context to another; and (4) surveillance conduct at one level or another. He further states that the modern concept of privacy does not relate to intrusion, misappropriation, embarrassing private facts or false light. These things constitute the work of lawyers in their quest to get things within rigid limits.[160] But record-keeping and data collection represent new and different ways of disrupting solitude and seclusion as more and more institutions collect more and more information about more aspects of our lives.[161]

---

157. Quoted in S.K. Sharma, Privacy Law—A Comparative Study, 171 (1994).
158. *Ibid.*
159. Richard F. Hixon, Privacy in Public Society, 183 (1987).
160. *Ibid.*
161. *Ibid.*

Professor Miller is right in believing that technology advances tend inexorably to narrow the defensible area. It is not only the Justice Department that has a compendium of data on private citizens. There is a Medical Information Bureau that dispenses data to insurance companies on the medical history of applicants for insurance. With the development of the computer, it has become possible to collect, instantly retrieve and analyse vast amounts of personal information. Access to this personal data has been expanded by the computer's ability to retrieve data access agency, institutional, governmental and geographic boundaries.

Attempts have been made to establish some form of regulation or control in respect of the use of data in United Kingdom. In 1961, Lord Mancroft introduced a Bill in the House of Lords "to protect a person from any unjustifiable publication relating to his private affairs and to give him right at law in the event of such publication." Bills concerned primarily with computerized information were introduced in 1969, and in 1972. During 1969 a private Member's Bill, the Data Surveillance Bill, was introduced in the House of Commons with the aim of providing legislation to prevent the invasion of privacy through the misuse of computer information. The Bill did not become law but nevertheless included interesting new proposals, such as registration of computer-operated data banks and the compulsory supply of print-outs which may well be embodied in future legislation. Most lawyers and computer specialists probably feel that it is too early to be sure exactly what legislative provisions are desirable, but nevertheless the Data Surveillance Bill was a valuable contribution to awakening public opinion to the type of measures that may eventually be necessary.

In 1975, the Home Secretary Mr. Roy Jenkins prescribed a white paper entitled Computers and Privacy in which the Government announced its intention to appoint a non-statutory body to be known as the Data Protection Committee. Owing to the death of the Chairman-designate, Sir Kenneth Younger, the Committee was eventually chaired by Sir Norman Lindop. It reported in 1978. Prior to this, the Younger Committee noted that the computer problem as it affects privacy in Great Britain is one of the apprehensions and fears and no so far, one of facts and figures. Unlike the Younger Committee which has preceded it the Lindop Committee was not concerned with those aspects of privacy which are not connected with the handling of personal data in information systems, such as intrusions into private premises, 'snooping' and so on. Also the Committee was aware that there were certain aspects of data protection which have no immediate connection with privacy—the use of inaccurate information as the basis of taking decisions affecting individuals, for instance. The Committee proposed a Data Protection Act which should apply to the "automatic" (computerized) handling in the United Kingdom of personal data by any use. A Data Protection Authority should be established, whose duties would be to ensure that the handling of such data would be carried out with adequate safeguards for the interests of the 'data subjects', and in particular their privacy.[162]

Some of the concerns felt about unauthorized use of personal information, and the invasions of privacy represented by personal data files finally achieved a level of redress in the Fair Credit Reporting Act, 1970. Until the Act was passed, the average citizen had no recourse against the agencies who compiled and disseminated information that may have been used against them. There are various provisions in the Act that seek to protect privacy to some degree.[163] Data Protection law ensures protection of living individuals with respect to the disclosure of personal data relating to them which is stored on computer. The current law, the Data Protection Act, 1998 implemented in March 2000, controls the compiling, and use of data relating to living individuals processed in the United Kingdom or elsewhere under the control of a United Kingdom established person or company, called a data controller. The Act limits the extent of data which may be stored, the processing of

---

162. S.K. Sharma, *op. cit.*, pp. 176-77; see also Hyman Gross, *op. cit.*, p. 25; G.B.F. Niblett, Computers and Privacy in A.H. Robertson (ed.) Privacy and Human Rights, 173-74 (1972).
163. Hyman Gross, *op. cit.*, pp. 26-27.

data and how it can be disclosed. Data must be fairly and lawfully processed, relevant and kept up-to-date. Limits are put on the transfer of data outside the European Economic Area.

The United States of America has passed its Freedom of Information Act in 1966, enacted a Privacy Act in 1974 in order secure individual from embarrassing situations. The Privacy Act of 1974 is based on the congressional finding that (a) the maintenance of personal information systems by federal agencies directly affects the individual privacy, (b) the proliferation of information systems, including computers, while necessary for the efficient and effective operation of the government presents a major potential for harm to individual privacy, and (c) it is necessary and proper for the Congress to control personal information systems operated by federal agencies in order to protect the privacy of individuals identified in their systems.[164]

The Act rests on the principle that:[165]

(a) There must be no personal data record keeping systems whose very existence is secret;
(b) There must be a way for an individual to find out what information about him is in a record and how it is used;
(c) There must be a way for an individual to prevent information about him obtained for one purpose from being used or made available for other purposes without his consent;
(d) There must be a way for an individual to correct or amend a record of identifiable information about himself; and
(e) Any organization creating, maintaining, using or disseminating records of identifiable personal data must assure the reliability of the data for their intended use and must take reasonable precautions to prevent misuse.

164. Hugh *v.* O'Neil: The Privacy Act of 1974: Introduction and Overview, 5 *Bureaucrat* 135 (July, 1976).
165. *Id.* at 145.

From this observation, the author can draw an inference about personal information. Personal information whatsoever it be should not be used for other than the purpose for which it is collected without consent of the concerned person.

In India, there are several statutes[166] which prohibit divulgence of information acquired. These statutes authorise collection of data for certain purposes. As regard State led initiatives, Andhra Pradesh has proposed a Data Processing (Special Contracts) Act in the line with global standards. Accordingly, the Andhra Pradesh Data Protection law seeks to:

(i) Protect sensitive consumer related information being processed or stored by the BPO/ITES companies or their business associates.

(ii) Provide a data protection and consumer privacy regime similar to the one in European Union, the United Kingdom and the United States.

(iii) Enable the companies outlocating to Andhra Pradesh to enforce their agreements with regard to privacy/protecting of sensitive information.

(iv) Provide an avenue for redressal of grievances and resolution of disputes.

(v) Enable the foreign companies to proceed against their partners/associates in case of violation of privacy rules.

The Andhra Pradesh led initiative is the first of its kind in the country, and a move that will comfort overseas clients as to the privacy concerns over the processing of private data by third party service players in the State. Most overseas clients protect the privacy of personal data being processed in

166. Section 44 read with second schedule of the State Bank of India Act, 1955; Sections 11 and 15 of the Census Act, 1948; Section 5 of Bankers' Book Evidence Act, 1891; Section 51 read with the first schedule of the National Bank of Agriculture and Rural Development, 1981; Section 20 read with the Schedule of the National Co-operative Development Corporation Act, 1962; Section 4(3) of the International Monetary Fund and Bank Act, 1945, etc.

India by their preferred providers through the traditional contract route.

Some of the information concerning privacy are not of such a serious nature. But some personal information are more sensational which need protection. When we talk about privacy of information, we should understand related concept of confidentiality and secrecy also. Because of some common features in privacy and, secrecy and confidentiality, the distinctive feature among them gets blurred. Privacy as a human right has got to be distinguished from 'secrecy' and 'confidentiality'. Secrecy is a means to an end and while privacy is an end in itself, confidentiality is reposed, secrecy is maintained and privacy is respected.[167] One of the reasons of secrecy is to foster right of privacy of an individual and the role of confidentiality is to preserve private life and information. In India, secrecy is the rule rather than the exception.[168] There are a number of reasons for maintaining secrecy in government. Secrecy is necessary in the interest of defence, national security, foreign relations, criminal law, personal privacy and trade secrets, etc.

The State in modern times collects a lot of information from citizens about their affairs. This information may relate to health, business secrets or financial status of an individual. This disclosure of this information may harm their reputation and act to their prejudice. But at times even access to this information may have to be allowed to determine whether the executive has been administering the law wrongly and with an unequal hand and giving benefit to those who were not lawfully entitled to them. But where the information is not relevant for this purpose, the accepted rule may be "non-disclosure", recognizing the inviolable right of privacy of an individual.[169]

When the individual has supplied information voluntarily to the government it may be necessary to keep the information secret to save him from harassment and

---

167. Govind Mishra, Privacy and the Indian Legal System, 12 *Del. L. Rev.* 54 (1990).
168. S.N. Jain, Official Secrecy and the Press, 4 (1982).
169. *Id.* at 5.

inconvenience. If voluntary information or its source is disclosed it may deprive the government of future information.[170] Information is confidential when it is entrusted to another, in the belief that it will go no further.[171] Circumstances frequently arise in which an individual communicates intimate facts on the understanding that access to it will be refused to all save the recipient or, in some cases, to those who have a clear interest in knowing of it. There has been an increased concern in India about the impact of data protection laws enacted in other countries. The National Task Force on Information Technology and Software Development had submitted an "Information Technology Action Plan" to the then Prime Minister in July 1998, calling for the creation of National Policy on Information Security, Privacy and Data Protection Act for handling of computerised data. It examined the U.K. Data Protection Act of 1998 as a model and recommended a number of cyber laws including one on privacy and encryption. It is disgusting that no legislative measure however, has been considered on this vital issue to date. Former NASSCOM President Dewang Mehta on September 20, 2000 announced that the government is likely to start work soon on framing data protection law in the country. Apart from the special case of the lawyer-client relationship the following are some of chief instances in which an obligation of confidence arises:

(A) Health

Health is a pre-condition for life while life is the pre-condition for the existence of the society. Society cannot be conceived without life. Therefore, life requires the first and the foremost place among the social values. There can be no second opinion that preservation of human life is of paramount importance. It is the obligation of those who are in charge of the health of the community to preserve life. Doctors have an onerous responsibility to the public. As required under the Indian Medical Council Act, 1956, the

170. *Ibid.*

171. J. Wigmore, *op. cit.* at 527; see also Michael F. Kelleher, *op. cit.* at 1362.

Medical Council of India has prescribed the Professional Standards and Code of Ethics for Medial Practitioners. The declaration that a medical practitioner as to make at the time of his registration, includes a pledge to respect the secrets which are confided in him by his patients. The confidential relationship between doctor and patient is enshrined in the hippocratic oath:[172]

Whatever in connection with my professional practice or not in connection with it, I see or hear, in the life of men, which ought not to be spoken of abroad, I will not divulge, as reckoning that all such should be kept secret.

But this duty of a doctor is not an unqualified one. This duty may have to succumb to the countervailing public interest in, for instance, the protection of third parties against infectious disease[173] or violence or in the administration of justice. But no Hippocrate's concept of confidentiality has to extend to whole organization within his profession. All functionaries of health department are expected to maintain confidentiality.

The seemingly inexorable drift, towards medical data banks has given rise to understandable fears about the confidentiality of the information held. The resolution to the growing problem of medical confidentiality is generally left to the ethics of the profession, but where a doctor, hospital or other repository of medical information discloses such information, without the patient's consent, to a party who has no legitimate interest in receiving it, an action for breach of confidence lies. The Code of Medical Ethics, Regulation 11 in India provides that doctor should not disclose the matter of medical concern which is confidential. Confidences concerning individual or domestic life entrusted by patients to a physician and defects in the disposition or character of the patient observed during medical attendance should never be revealed unless their revelation is required by the laws of

172. Dawson, The Duties of a Doctor as a Citizen, *Brit. Med. J.* 1474 (1954).

173. The European Convention on Human Rights, which came into force on 3 September, 1953 recognizes an exception to the protection of privacy in the interest of public safety, for the protection of health.

the State.[174] To publish without permission photographs or case reports of the patients in any medical or other journal in a manner by which their identity could be made out is prohibited.[175] Similarly, every dentist has a duty to keep all the information of a personal nature which he comes to know about a patient directly or indirectly in the course of professional practice in utmost confidence.[176]

The conduct prescribed by the Medical Council of India for medical practitioners is well in tune with Geneva Declaration which expects the doctor to respect the secrets of the patient which are confided in him. According to the International Code of Ethics, "A doctor shall preserve absolute secrecy on all he knows about his patient because of the confidence entrusted in him."[177]

(B) Employment

An applicant for employment normally submits information, some of which may be of a personal nature, on the assumption that it will be seen or heard only by those who have a manifest interest in knowing of it. There is also a legitimate expectation, which he shares with the others of any references, that such references will be in most cases be read only by those who are directly concerned in making the appointment and no one else, not even, of course, by the applicant himself. These considerations will apply also to the employee who applies for promotion, etc. There is an implied term in contracts of employment that an employee will not disclose his employer's secrets, or misuse his confidential information. But is there a reciprocal implied duty imposed on an employer to maintain the confidentiality? Indian law is silent in this respect.

174. The Code of Medical Ethics, Regulation 11 quoted in Govind Mishra, Privacy and the Indian Legal System, 12 *Del. L. Rev.* 70(1990).
175. *Ibid.*
176. The Dentists (Code of Ethics) Regulations, 1976, Reg. 4(g).
177. P.M. Bakshi, Doctor's Duty: Keeping Secrets, *The Hindustan Times*, September 20, 1984.

(C) Banking

Banks are primary among the kinds of business organizations whose records and functions would be significantly improved by automating their operations. Most banks, even small ones, now have computerized records and can produce information, about customers' transactions with much greater ease than in the more cumbersome manual days. Perhaps using this expanded record keeping capability as a starting point, the Federal Government in 1970 enacted into law the Bank Secrecy Act. The treasury regulations growing out of this Act, required extensive record-keeping and reporting on the part of all Banks. The putative reason for the Bank Secrecy Act was to supply federal agencies with information that would help them in "criminal, tax and regulatory investigations." There was particular emphasis on the foreign currency transactions in an effort to prevent large scale manipulations that deprived the United States government of large tax revenues. In theory the idea seems laudable; in practice, many bankers and other concerned people felt the provisions of the Act and implementing regulations were unconstitutional.[178]

The law of Banking in India recognizes a banker's contractual duty of confidences. Several statutes recognize this relationship and transaction and secrecy of banking documents should be observed. This provision extends to the protection of bank account and other banking transactions. Nobody other than the concerned account holder is entitled to get information relating to his account. This is the duty of whole employees of the Bank to maintain the secrecy of the same. However, this provision is subject to some exceptions. It does not amount disclosure when it is disclosed under the compulsion of law or for the purpose of legal proceedings. Similarly, any disclosure of such transaction to the auditor and inspector of the bank is allowed. Those who are entitled to inspect such records, have to maintain confidentiality of the same as the employer of the bank.[179] There are other

178. Hyman Gross, *op. cit.*, p. 30.

179. See The State Bank of India Act, 1955, Section 4; The National Bank for Agriculture and Rural Development Corporation Act, 1962, Section 20; The International Monetary Fund and Bank Act, 1945, Section 4(3), etc.

several statutes in India which prohibit divulgence of information acquired in the course of one's official capacity.[180]

In United Kingdom, there are four grounds under which a disclosure of information is justified:[181] (i) under compulsion of law; (ii) required in public interest; (iii) required in the protection of the banker's interest; and (iv) with the express or implied consent of the customer.

Most of the Banking Acts in India expressly provide provisions of secrecy of banking transactions. Further, employee's service rules also provide to swear an oath of secrecy and confidence.

(D) The Census

Census is the popular method of gathering personal information in different field of a person's life. Hence, people are always wondering whether their confidential information are being misused or cheated. Sometimes such fear created in the mind of people creates difficulty to collect data. Similar problem was faced by United States of America in the first census in 1790. Similar situation appeared in United Kingdom in 1971. A leader of the House, Mr. William Whitelaw, M.P. assured that "information about individual people and families under no circumstances be released to any authority outside the census organization itself."[182] Nevertheless, disquiet has been voiced about the adequacy of the measures adopted by the office for population census and surveys to maintain the anonymity of individuals. The white paper, computer and privacy declared: "Statistical works carry few risks for privacy because it gives information about groups of people, even though the original data related to identifiable individuals.[183] Sir Norman Lindop Committee was also convinced about this fact. In India, there is no clear legal protection of privacy while gathering the information. Only

180. The Industrial Disputes Act, 1947, Sections 21 and 30; The Export-Import Bank of India Act, 1981, Section 38; The Banking Regulation Act, 1949, Sections 34-A and 36 AD, etc.

181. Raymond Wacks, The Protection of Privacy (1980).

182. 815 Hansard, Cols. 814-821 (April 19, 1971).

183. *Supra* n. 181 at p. 129.

the employer's official duty to maintain confidentiality is there. The same rule applies to other institutions which collect personal information.[184] Provided that any personal information collected by statistics bureau or other authority institution is allowed to submit an evidence if the case falls under the same statute.[185]

(E) The Research

A distinguished scholar in social sciences has himself acknowledged that the accumulation of personal information by researchers constitutes a much greater invasion of privacy,[186] than the census. A developing body of literature is concerned with the question of ethics of social inquiry[187] and in particular, the question whether the individual's right to authority and the confidentiality of information about him is overridden "by the needs of the search for knowledge".[188] The Lindop Committee in United Kingdom was satisfied that the codes of practice established, for instance, by the British Sociological Association and the Medical Research Council, provided some assurance to the public that confidentiality and ethical practice are safeguarded.[189]

In India, no ethical code has been codified in relation to research work so far. However, a duty of confidentiality is always present to every researcher who is working in any institution. There is a dire need to develop a code of conduct to those all who practice in any research work. However, professional codes of conduct are available for Medical Researchers. Similarly, codes of conduct for chartered accounts and advocates are available in India.

(F) Credit Bureaus and Inspection Agencies

Outside of the federal government the largest information gathering systems are credit bureaus. The credit

184. See, The Census Act, 1948.
185. *Ibid.*
186. J.A. Barnes, Who Should Know What? 91 (1979).
187. *Id.* at 189-222.
188. *Id.* at 13.
189. Report of the Lindop Committee, para 26.29 (1978).

bureau performs a necessary function in highly fluid society such as the U.S. and does enable prospective employers, merchants or mortgage lenders to make judgments based on factual information about people of whose personal life they know nothing. The problems arise not in this honest, factual information that is dispensed by the credit bureaus but in the publication of facts that may be irrelevant to the particular investigation, may be misleading or been erroneous. Violation of the right of privacy is at the heart of the question of how much information is known about a person and how freely it is circulated to people who have no legitimate interest in knowing everything in a given file.[190]

Another investigative body that gathers and disseminates information about peoples; lives and habits as well as factual economic data is the inspection agency that delves into the backgrounds of applicants for insurance. This agency investigates very personal aspects of the applicant's life by talking to neighbours or associates, as well as gathering the factual material. In this way a great deal of subjective or openly biased information can find its way into a person's dossier. Since the investigators have neither the time nor the motivation to evaluate the material received, a good deal of conjecture and inaccuracy goes into the memory bank it can remain for years. Thousands of people have been refused employment, credit or insurance because of derogatory information in their dossiers of which they are totally ignorant.[191]

There are a number of credit agencies. They collect personal information which is susceptible to misuse. Lindop Committee recognised that "the growing number of agencies which sell information and the free circulation of information among firms in the consumer credit industry bring greater risk that information will become available to persons other than credit grantors."[192] The Consumer Credit Act, 1974 requires the grantor of credit to supply the consumer on request with the name and address of any credit reference

---

190. Hyman Gross, *op. cit.*, p. 26.
191. *Ibid.*
192. See, The Lindop Committee Report, para 13.33 (1978).

agency which has supplied information about him; on payment of a fee of 25p, the consumer must be issued with a copy of all information about him held by the agency. The Lindop Committee preferred to see the right of subject access as part of the detailed rules rather than the general principle to be declared in its proposed Data Act.[193]

The misuse of personal information obtained by credit agencies is not a serious problem in India. No cases are available in this respect. Since it has not emerged as a problem, the law relating to this area is not developed in our country. However, credit agencies are bound not to disclose such information. Because these agencies are created under the authority of law. As a legal creation they cannot do what the law does not permit expressly. And law does not expressly permit to disclose any information obtained in their official capacity if that information is personal one.

It may thus be summed up that several global standards exist relating to privacy and data protection. Chiefly among them are the European Union University (via Directive 95/96/EC the EU Data Protection Directive; Directive 96/96/EC that deals specifically with the protection of privacy in telecommunications in the EU; Regulation (EC)45/2001 of the European Parliament and of the Council of 18 December 2000 that deals with the protection of individuals with regard to the processing of personal data by the communication institutions and bodies and on the free movement of such data; Directive 2002/58/EC that seeks to respect the fundamental rights and observe the principles recognised in particular by the Charter of Fundamental Rights of European Union; and the Standard Contractual Clauses for Data Processors. The United Nations initiative (via Article XII of the Universal Declaration of Human Rights; Article 17 of the International Covenant on Civil and Political Rights of 16 December 1966; U.N. Guidelines concerning computerized personal data files. The OECD Guidelines for the security of information systems and networks: Towards a culture of security (flowing from 1980 OECD Guidelines

---

193. Ibid; paras 21.10 and 21.11; see also Raymond Wacks, The Poverty of Privacy, 96 *The Law Quarterly Review* 87 (Jan.-Oct. 1980).

Governing the Protection of Privacy and Trans-border Flows of Personal Data) and cryptography.

The protection afforded to personal data in India may not be considered adequate, as compared to the global standards set by various governments and institutions. However, there are distinct differences in the concept of privacy that we understand *vis-à-vis* the approach of the West. Generally, our society and culture is one of openness, and the concept of protecting one's identity from society is rather alien. This is not the position in western nations where personally identifiable data has been used to target minorities, fight war, telemarketing, financial fraud—the lot. However, some market players in India are misusing the general openness of Indian society to market credit cards, sell personal information, send spam, conduct illegal background checks on persons, etc. In this context, and in the background the various decisions of the Supreme Court, it would be necessary to balance the unique nature and needs of the Indian society with privacy and protection principles as expounded by the Constitution and the case law.

IV. PRIVACY: STATUS UNDER THE CONSTITUTION

The seminal idea of privacy as a 'right' originated in United States of America in 1888 when Justice Thomas Cooley, the American scholar named this then extremely nebulous concept as privacy, defining it simply as 'a right to be let alone.' The development of the concept has gone apace rapidly with the recent communication explosion and revolutionary advance in communication technology.[194] Today, all democratic societies have come to realize that privacy is at the heart of all human rights.[195] Privacy as a basic human right touches upon fundamental needs and values associated with man's gregarious nature.[196] Certainly, the level of

194. Justice R.S. Sarkaria, Freedom of Press: Defamation and Privacy, 15 *Press Council of India Review,* 11 (1994).

195. I. P. Massey, Costitutionalization of the Right to Privacy in India, in B.P.S. Sehgal (ed.) Human Rights in India, 310 (1995).

196. E. Jeremy Hutton, *et. al.* The Right of Privacy in the United States, Great Britain and India, in Richard P. Clause (ed.) Comparative Human Rights, 127 (1976).

technological and economic development creates pressures to protect these privacy values through legal enforcement techniques. Right to privacy in India is a peculiar blend of constitutional, customary and common law right scattered over various legal fields. As a part of our constitutional right to life and liberty, it is considered to be the illustration of progressive development of human rights and basic freedoms. Rights and freedoms of citizens are set forth in the Constitution in order to guarantee that the individual, his personality and those things stamped with his personality shall be free from official interference except where a reasonable basis of intrusion exists. In this sense, many of the fundamental rights of citizens can be described as contributing to the right to privacy.

India's Constitution does not cover right to privacy as one of the fundamental rights. The post-independence period in India witnessed the emergence of many constitutional rights including, the right to clean environment, right to education, etc. The right to privacy is one of such right which has been accorded constitutional recognition in this period. The Constituent Assembly Debates on 'Fraternity Clause' of the Preamble project the importance of the dignity of the individual. A few members, namely, B. Pattabhi Sitaramayya, Srimati Durga Bai, Thakurdas Bhargava, B.V. Keskar, T.T. Krishnamachari, M. Anathasayanam and K. Santhanam of the Constituent Assembly moved an amendment which sought to change the drafting of the clause to the following form: "fraternity assuring unity of Nation and the dignity of the individual." The proposed amendment was negatived. The reason for putting "dignity of the individual" first was that unless the dignity of the individual is assured, the nation cannot be united. Further, in the Constituent Assembly an amendment on the lines of the Fourth Amendment of the United States Constitution was moved by Kazi Karimuddin and it was also supported by Dr. B.R. Ambedkar.[197] Dr. Ambedkar said:

I am however, prepared to accept amendment No. 512 moved by Mr. Krimuddin. I think it is a useful provision and

197. Constituent Assembly Debates, Vol. VIII, pp. 794 and 796.

may find place in our Constitution. There is nothing novel in it because whole of the clause as suggested by him is to be found in Criminal Procedure Code so that it might be said in a sense that there is already the law of the land. It is perfectly possible that the legislatures of the future may abrogate the provisions specified in the amendment, but they are so important so far as personal liberty is concerned that it is very desirable to place these provisions beyond the reach of the legislatures and I am therefore, prepared to accept this amendment.

However, Dr. Ambedkar's support was a little reserved one and not forceful enough to secure incorporation of right to privacy in the Constitution. Possibly the Constituent Assembly members did not visualize the importance of the right to privacy as an aspect of personal liberty. But the Constituent Assembly after postponement of this question voted against the adoption of this amendment. Although the right of privacy akin to Fourth Amendment of the U.S. Constitution was denied, yet the Constitution guaranteed the second right as is available in the Fifth Amendment of the U.S. Constitution, that is, protection against self-incrimination vide clause (3) of Article 20 of the Constitution of India.

Privacy as one of the necessary ingredient of personal liberty suffered heavily on that account. Whereas the Constitution does not mention expressly the right to privacy, Article 21 miraculously has been playing a major role in the safeguard of privacy as an essential ingredient of personal liberty. It is again important to note that Article 21 by itself has not been a potent enough weapon in the defence of privacy until it is sharpened and made effective by judicial activism. Whether the word privacy implies positive or negative meaning depends upon the social and cultural background in which the concept of privacy has developed. It would be said that privacy is a dynamic concept and it takes its content from the culture it thrives in. It starts with life and protects human dignity. It is akin to the concept of natural justice which is in accordance with natural human law. One will agree to the privacy of a married couple in their conjugation. By granting this privacy in our intellectual perception what is in fact we are doing is we are granting the right to privacy to the couple. In other words, people unanimously recognize the right to privacy as inherent in human society.

Naturally such rights essential to decent and civilized living need not necessarily be defined or incorporated in the form of law or the legal constitutions and in such cases when the questions arise out of abrogation or appropriation of the inherent rights, they are left to the judicial wisdom for appropriate adjudication. The concept of privacy can either be interpreted in its absolute form or many a time when it is not possible to do so, it is to be construed in its relative form. In its absolute form it mainly manifests itself in terms of inherence. In its relative form the concept of privacy become opposed to that which is public. Hence, even in its relative aspect, it becomes inherent and in the terms of William Cohen and John Kaplan—'inalienable'. These rights to privacy which a government gives or takes away not only lose their element of inherence, but also make the concept of privacy void.

Therefore, in constitutional law the concept of right to privacy should be developed along with the concept of inherent right to privacy. This would be nothing new, because we have already made a beginning quite a long back around the blurred and nebulous concept of human law and its progress namely natural justice. Despite being nebulous in the consciousness of the people at large, every individual will feel strongly about his right to privacy and therefore, it can be generalized and accepted and nobody would object to this right. Thus, it becomes a universally accepted concept. It varies in its situational content which it takes from the culture in which it grows.[198]

Nothing can be more sacred to our democratic society than the security of the citizen in his home, and the privacy of the individual in the conduct of his personal affairs. The issue of the right of privacy is at crossroads.[199] The policy choices to be made in the next few years will determine

---

198. William Cohen and John Kaplan, Constitutional Law—Civil Liberty and Individual Rights, 516, 518-19 and 523-24 (1982).
199. S.K. Sharma, *op. cit.*, p. 116.

whether our nation will leash technology to prevent its stampede over the right to privacy or whether enormous interconnected data systems carrying information above all of us will grow unchecked. Until recently, the available technology made difficult the automatic transfer of information gathered by one agency for the purpose another without the knowledge of the individual. By living in a diffuse society certain rights to privacy are automatically surrendered by everyone. There are other rights to privacy that some citizens chooses to give up voluntarily. When a person wants a privilege that others do not have whether it is a government job, a credit card, or an educational scholarship—there is an implicit understanding that the goal is important enough to warrant giving out some relevant personal information. In that case, since it is a conscious decision made with the knowledge of how it will be used, the individual retains his or her free choice. Suddenly, people have become intensely aware that the situation has changed. Now they are faced with an erosion of their privacy, for which they will receive no benefit or right in exchange. In fact, the entire process of collection and transfer of information can and does occur without the individual's knowledge, yet alone his or her consent what is lost, as much as the right to privacy, is the right to control one's life.

Generally speaking, privacy as a positive right, is pregnant matter in India.[200] It is a new comer when compared with other rights like due process of law and *habeas corpus* and it is not found in any of the classic texts of the eighteenth century. It was comparatively easy to protect privacy at a time when encroachments thereupon could be identified and prosecuted or formed the subject of a civil action; but it is much more difficult in an age of scientific and technological development, when many encroachments cannot be perceived at the time when they are committed though their subsequent exploitation may have far-reaching consequences. At international level the right of privacy has been codified to some extent, in some Human Rights

---

200. Anirudh Prasad, New Dimensions of Right of Privacy under the Indian Constitution, 14 *JCPS* 258 (1980).

Instruments.[201] India as a member of the Untied Nations and as a signatory to the International Covenant, is under obligation to guarantee this right to its citizens. The State is directed to recognize and enforce international law as a matter of state policy. The Preamble of the Constitution of India assures the dignity of the individual. to live a dignified life is protected under Article 21 of the Constitution. In these commands of the Constitution lies the necessary basis for the protection of the right of privacy.

The Preamble of the Constitution of India assures the dignity of the individual. Dignity, here cannotes the intrinsic worthiness of every human being, without regard to his intelligence, skills, talents, rank, property or beliefs.[202] Dignity of an individual has been adjudged as an essential feature of the Constitution.[203] The assurance of dignity embraces right to privacy as well. Unfortunately, the right to privacy is not on of the "reasonable restrictions" to the right to freedom of speech and expression under Article 19(1)(a). Article 19 reads as follows:

> "19(1) All citizens shall have the right—
> (a) to freedom of speech and expression.
> . . . . .
> (2) Nothing in sub-clause (a) of clause (1) shall affect the operation of any existing law, or prevent the State from making any law, insofar as such law imposes reasonable restrictions on the exercise of the right conferred by the said sub-clause in the interests of the sovereignty and integrity of India, the security of the State, friendly relations with foreign states, public order, decency or morality or in relation to contempt of court, defamation or incitement to an offence."

The result of the restrictions being exhaustively enumerated is that unless a publication that invades the

---

201. Article 12 of The Universal Declaration of Human Rights, 1948; Article 17 of International Covenant on Civil and Political Rights, 1966; and at Regional level Article 8 of European Convention on Human Rights, 1953.
202. See, Williams Bernard, The Idea of Equality in H.A. Bedan (ed.) Justice and Equality, 116 (1971).
203. Kesavananda Bharti *v.* State of Kerala, AIR 1973 SC 1461.

individual's privacy is "immoral" or "indecent" it does not fall foul of Article 19(2).

However, this lacuna has not prevented the courts from carving out a constitutional right to privacy by the creative interpretation of right to life[204] and the right to freedom of movement.[205] In other words, in the absence of any express constitutional or statutory provisions recognizing right to privacy the Indian courts have seized the opportunities whenever they came and tried successfully to bring the privacy right within the purview of fundamental rights. Even though right to privacy is not enumerated as a fundamental right in our Constitution it has been inferred from Article 21. The right to privacy in India has derived itself from essentially two sources: the common law of torts and the constitutional law.[206] In common law, a private action for damages for unlawful invasion of privacy is maintainable. Under the constitutional law, the right to privacy is implicit in the fundamental right to life and liberty guaranteed by Article 21 of the Constitution.[207] This has been interpreted to include the right to be let alone. Article 21 miraculously has been playing a major role in the safeguard of privacy as an essential ingredient of personal liberty. It is again important to note that Article 21 by itself has not been potent enough weapon in defence of privacy until it is sharpened and made effective by judicial activism.

Similarly, Article 20 of the Constitution of India provides right against self-incrimination. This privilege against self-incrimination is one of the great landmarks in man's struggle to make himself civilized[208] which exempts a

---

204. Article 21.
205. Article 19(1)(g).
206. There are few statutory provisions contained in the Code of Criminal Procedure, 1973 {Section 327(1)}; The Indecent Representation of Women (Prohibition) Act, 1980 (Sections 3 and 4); The Medical Termination of Pregnancy Act, 1971 {Section 7(1)(c)}; The Hindu Marriage Act, 1955 (Section 22); The Special Marriage Act, 1954 (Section 33); The Children Act, 1960 (Section 36); and the Juvenile Justice Act, 1986 (Section 36), all of which seek to protect women and children from unwarranted publicity.
207. R. Rajagopal *v.* State of Tamil Nadu, (1994) 6 SCC 632.
208. Griswold *v.* Connecticut, 381 US 479 (1965).

person to speak against himself. It enables the maintenance of human privacy and observance of civilized standards in the enforcement of criminal justice.[209] Article 23 of the Constitution of India prohibits traffic in human being, begar and other similar forms of forced labour. It protects the person's autonomy and individuality. It recognizes the inviolate personality. Further, the Constitution guarantees freedom of conscience and right to profess, practice and propagate religion to all persons subject to public order, morality and health. Any religious privacy, if it exists, can be protected under Article 25 of the Constitution of India. Right to equality or equal protection of law under Article 14 of the Constitution provides everyone similar kinds of right of privacy.

All these rights are grouped in Part III of the Constitution as fundamental rights which can be remedied under Articles 32 and 226 of the Constitution. As a safeguard the Supreme Court of India and other High Courts exercise wide powers for enforcing these rights by issuing writs of *habeas corpus, certiorari, mandamus, quo warranto,* and the like under Articles 32, 226 and 228 of the Constitution. Article 13 of the Constitution forbids the State from making any law or regulation in contravention of these rights may be declared void. Constitutional right of privacy is emanated under these provisions of the Constitution.

Since the Constitution of India is silent on the subject of privacy, the Supreme Court has, in its determination to protect this fundamental personal right discovered in the provision of different articles or even outside them ample flexibility and scope for the development of implied "right to privacy". Once this right is declared to emanate from the totality of the constitutional scheme under which we live.[210] This is an excellent example of judicial creativity at its best level. Discovery of a new right is one aspect of creativity.[211]

---

209. M.P. Jain, Indian Constitutional Law, 568 (1987).

210. Poe *v.* Ullman, 367 US 497 (1960) quoted by Goldberg, J. in Griswold *v.* Connecticut, 381 US 479 (1965); see also Govind *v.* State of M.P., (1975) 2 SCC 148.

211. Upendra Baxi (ed.) K.K. Mathew on Democracy, Equality and Freedom, LXIII (1978).

Right to privacy is therefore not mentioned in the text of fundamental rights chapter of the Constitution. The right to privacy received the status of judicially created fundamental rights after the 25 years of the enforcement of the Constitution. The first case in which the right to privacy arose was *M.P. Sharma* v. *Satish Chandra*,[212] where the question was, whether state power of search and seizure under the Code of Criminal Procedure was violative of in individual's right to privacy. Then came in *Kharak Singh* v. *State of U.P.*[213] in which constitutional validity of Rule 236 of U.P. Police Regulations was challenged. The six judges Constitution Bench conceded the common law maxim that 'everyman's home is his castle' and relied on *Semayane's* case[214] where it was stated that, the house of everyone is to him a fortress. But the court upheld the U.P. Regulations except the clause dealing with domiciliary visits at night. The majority thus showed no awareness of attempt to reconcile the competing interest of the right to privacy and public good through surveillance over suspected character. Then in *Govind* v. *State of M.P.*[215] the minority opinion of Kharak Singh's case became the majority opinion. Methew, Krishna Iyer and Goswami, JJ. accepted the view that there exists a right of privacy in India.

In the recent years, the judiciary has protected the right to privacy of: rape victims;[216] press;[217] phone-tapping of individuals, politicians, professionals, officials and others;[218]

---

212. AIR 1954 SC 300; also see Board of Revenue, Madras *v.* R.S. Jhavar, AIR 1968 SC 59; Pooran Mal *v.* Director of Inspection, AIR 1974 SC 348; Deena *v.* Union of India, AIR 1983 SC 1155; V.S. Kuttan Pillai *v.* Ramakrishan, AIR 1980 SC 185.

213. AIR 1963 SC 1295.

214. (1604) 5 Coke 91.

215. AIR 1975 SC 1378.

216. State of Andhra Pradesh *v.* Gangula Satya Murthy, AIR 1997 SC 1588.

217. R. Rajagopal *v.* State of Tamil Nadu, AIR 1995 SC 264; Himachal *v.* Umed Ram, AIR 1986 SC 847; P. Rathinam *v.* Union of India, AIR 1984 SC 1844.

218. R.M. Malkani *v.* State of Maharashtra, AIR 1973 SC 157; see also Yusuf Ali Ismail Nagree *v.* State of Maharashtra, AIR 1968 SC 147; Rama Reddy *v.* V.V. Giri (1971) 1 SCR 399; Megraj Patodia *v.* R.K. Birla, AIR 1971 SC 1295; Peoples Union for Civil Liberties *v.* Union of India, AIR 1997 SC 568.

conjugal rights;[219] AIDS infected people;[220] sexual autonomy of women[221], etc. (For more details kindly see Chapter 6 of the study).

V. SUM-UP

It can thus be concluded that right to privacy in India is a peculiar blend of constitutional, customary and common law right scattered over various legal fields. As a customary right, it is treated as an easement forming part of statutory law. As a part of our constitutional right to life and liberty, it is considered to be the illustration of progressive development of human rights and basic freedoms. Though, it has so far not developed as a separate tort, its need is being felt by all, as without its development, emergence of an orderly social order may be delayed. Hence, it is the recognition of a right of special significance and potentiality, adding a totally new dimension to our democratic and welfare-oriented jurisprudence. Emergence, development and recognition of this right proves beyond doubt that our jurisprudence is dynamic and is constantly evolving and bringing the law closer to the lives of the people. Developing new concepts, ideas, like privacy right is the sure proof that our law is organic, alive and kicking and not dead or static.

---

219. T. Sareetha *v.* T. Venkata Subbaiah, AIR 1983 AP 356; see also Harvinder Kaur *v.* Harminder Singh, AIR 1984 Delhi 66; Saroj Rani *v.* Sudarshan Kumar, AIR 1984 SC 1526.

220. Mr 'X' *v.* Hospital 'Z', AIR 1999 SC 495; see also MX of Bombay Indian Inhabitant *v.* M/S ZY, AIR 1997 Bom. 406; M. Vijaya *v.* Chairman and Managing Director, S.C.C. Ltd., AIR 2001 AP 502; Sharda *v.* Dharampal (2003) 4 SCC 493.

221. Re-Ratanmala, AIR 1962 Mad. 31; see also State of Maharashtra *v.* Madhukar Narayan Mardikar, AIR 1991 SC 207; State of Punjab *v.* Gurmit Singh, AIR 1996 SC 1393.

5

Limitations on Right to Privacy

Privacy is not an absolute right. It is subject to some limitations like other rights. Though there is no express provision of right to privacy in the Constitution of India, yet it is recognised as a fundamental right emanated from various fundamental rights, indeed from the totality of the Constitution. For this reason, this right is limited in the same manner as other fundamental rights are limited. It cannot go beyond those rights under which it emanates. In every rights reasonable restrictions are allowed. But what are reasonable restrictions? The Constitution of India nowhere defines the expression "reasonable restrictions." The test of reasonableness has to be applied to each individual statute impugned and no abstract standard or general pattern of reasonableness can be laid down as applicable to all classes. The test of reasonableness varies from case to case depending upon the circumstances.[1] Generally, those restrictions are justifiable which are in the interests of general public, security of the State, public order, decency or morality, etc. The principle on which the power of the State to impose restriction is based, is that all individual rights of a person are held subject to such reasonable limitations and regulations

1. Golak Nath *v.* State of Punjab, AIR 1967 SC 1643 and 1655; Olga Tellis *v.* Bombay Municipal Corporation (1985) 3 SCC 545 and 579.

as may be necessary or expedient for the protection of the general welfare. Liberty has got to be limited in order to be effectively possessed. For liberty of one must not offend the liberty of others. In the words of Patanjali Shastri, J., "man as a rational being desires to do many things, but in a civil society his desires have to be controlled, regulated and reconciled with the exercise of similar desires by other individuals.[2] Further, in the words of Das, J., "Social interest in individual liberty may well have to be subordinate to other greater social interests."[3] General limitations of right to privacy which are recognised by the courts, jurists and scholars in the field are as follows:

I. PUBLIC INTEREST

This covers one of the most important aspects of an action for infringement of privacy. As in defamation, it is necessary in the public interest for people to know and comment about others. The Press has the duty to seek out information, to inform and comment. The risks which the Press and other purveyors of news and comment run in defamation are reduced by the defences of justification, fair comment, absolute and qualified privilege, and we consider that a defendant, whether the Press or not, should be entitled to plead to a claim for infringement of privacy that the publication, whether of fact or comment, was in the public interest.[4]

Right of privacy does not prohibit the publication of any matter of public or general interest, as where the plaintiff has become a public personage and has to that extent, waived the right, or in connection with the life of any person in whom the public has a rightful interest.[5] The same rule applies where the information would be of public benefit or

2. A.K. Gopalan *v.* State of Madras, AIR 1951 SC 27.
3. *Ibid.*
4. Mark Littman and Peter Carter-Ruck, A Report by Justice: Privacy and The Law, 37(1970).
5. Abernathy *v.* Thornton, 263 Ala 496, 83 SO 2d. 235; Cason *v.* Baskin, 159 Fla. 31, 30 SO 2d. 635, 638 (1947).

of legitimate concern to the public.[6] Even private facts may be published if they are matters of public interest or are news worthy,[7] because the right of privacy is not absolute. In other words, at some point, the public interest in obtaining information become dominant over the individual's desire for privacy. This is an important dimension of the philosophy of both the Younger Committee[8] and the Press Council[9] of United Kingdom.

Frankly speaking that where the subject-matter of the statement published is a public interest, plaintiff must prove the existence of a knowing reckless falsehood. Thus, a cause of action may be stated for a false light invasion of privacy even where the subject-matter is of legitimate public interest insofar as plaintiff can point to specific inaccuracies, placing him in a false light before the public, which are an offensive invasion of his privacy, and which were made without the exercise of ordinary care to determine their accuracy. However, it has also been held that a false light action will not lie when the matter purportedly publicized is of legitimate public interest, and if the operation of laws and activities of the police or other public bodies are involved, the matter is within the public interest. Similarly, the possible commission of a crime and the reporting of such a suspicion to the appropriate authorities are matters of legitimate public interest. It has been broadly stated that a false light invasion of privacy claim will not lie if a person is a public official and the publication relates to performance of public life or duties. Under some authorities, neither the non-private nature of published material nor public interest in the disclosure of the material are relevant factors in a false light claim.

---

6. Cox Broadcasting Corporation *v.* Cohn 420 US 469 (1975).
7. Although, there is no universally accepted test to determine whether a particular fact or incident is newsworthy. Most of the American courts have adopted a three part test focussing on—(i) the social value of the facts published, (ii) the depth of the intrusion into ostensibly private affairs, and (iii) the extent to which the party voluntarily acceded to a position of public notoriety, Forsher *v.* Bugliosi 6 Media L.R. 1097.
8. See Report of Younger Committee on Privacy, 1972, Paras 156-157.
9. Press Council Declaration of Principle on Privacy (23rd Press Council Report) 150 (1976).

In a landmark judgment delivered on May 31, 2001, the United States Supreme Court ruled that the media can disclose an illegally intercepted cellular telephone conversation about a public issue provided that it was not itself privy to the illegal interception.[10] The code of conduct drawn up by the British Press Complaints Commission refers to as: (i) Journalists should not generally obtain or seek to obtain information or pictures through misrepresentation or subterfuge; (ii) Unless the public interest, documents or photographs should be removed only with the express consent of the owner; (iii) Subterfuge can be justified only in the public interest and only when material cannot be obtained by any other means.[11] The expression "public interest" is defined precisely "for the purpose of this code as (i) detecting or exposing crime or a serious misdemeanour; (ii) protecting public health and safety; (iii) preventing the public from being misled by some statement or action of an individual or organisation". Relying on the Code, the Commission upheld The Sunday Times, sting operation in 1994 which exposed MPs who accepted money to ask questions in Parliament.[12]

The public interest relied on as the jurisdiction for publication or inquiries which conflict with a claim to privacy must be a legitimate and proper public interest and not only a prurient or morbid curiosity "of interest to the public" is not synonymous with "in the public interest."[13] The concept is rarely assigned only specific meaning and little guidance is to be found in deciding what considerations ought to be relevant in determining whether a publication satisfies the test. Younger Committee was of the opinion that the invasion of privacy is justified only at the point where the importance of the news exceeds the importance of the privacy. But where does point lie? The question has not been answered. It depends on the circumstances of each case.[14]

---

10. A.G. Noorani, Privacy *v.* Public Interest, *The Hindustan Times*, New Delhi, June 19, 2001.
11. A. G. Noorani, Privacy *v.* Public Interest, 22 *Press Council of India Review*, 44 (July 2001).
12. *Id.* at 44-45.
13. *Supra* n. 10 at 150.
14. *Supra* n. 8, para 187.

The public interest is widely construed to permit fair comment on a variety of matters.[15] But if privacy is to be protected by Statute, some formulation will be necessary. In 1979, a Bill proposed by the Australian Law Reform Commission provides a useful model:[16]

"(3) . . . The publication of private facts shall be regarded as being relevant to a topic of public interest where the matter in the statement or comment or the private facts, as the case may be—(a) related to public, commercial or professional activities, including proposed activities of a person for public, commercial or professional office; (c) was or were relevant to a decision taken, or then likely to be taken, on a public, commercial or professional question by any person who occupied, or was a candidate for election or appointment to an office; (d) related to any property or services offered to the public; (e) was or were facts the publication of which were necessary or desirable for—

(i) the apprehension of offenders;
(ii) the enforcement of the law;
(iii) public health or public safety; or
(iv) discussion on a matter relating to public administration or the administration of justice.
(v) was or were otherwise of legitimate concern to the general public or to any section of the public.

(4) The publication of matter or of private facts that are merely for the purpose of arousing prurient or morbid curiosity shall not be regarded for the purposes of this Act as being on a topic of public interest."

In *Time, Inc.* v. *Hill*,[17] The United States Supreme Court held that the opening of a new play linked to an actual incident was a matter of public interest. The first amendment

---

15. London Artists *v.* Littler (1969) 2 Q.B. 375; Slim *v.* Daily Telegraph Ltd., (1968) 2 Q.B. 157.
16. The Australian Law Reform Commission Report, Unfair Publication: Defamation and Privacy, 1979, published in the *Australian Law Journal*, 1979, Vol. 53, pp. 604-605.
17. 385 US 374 (1967).

protected disclosure concerning "all issues about which information is needed or appropriate to enable the members of society to cope with the exigencies of their period.[18] The instant case was criticised on the count that it permits the press to define matters of public interest as whatever the news media decide to report. Similarly, the decision is criticised also because it enables the court to define what are matters of legitimate public interest resulting in the possibility of censorship by judges. However, the Supreme Court now appears to have retreated from this position, at least in defamation cases.[19] The dissenting opinion of Fortas, J. is worth mentioning here which enables us to understand the limitation of the test of public interest:

The court may not and must not permit either public or private action that censors or inhibits the press. But part of this responsibility is to preserve values and procedures which assure the ordinary citizen that the press is not above the reach of the law—that its special prerogatives, granted because of its special and vital functions, are reasonable equated with its needs in the performance of these functions. For this court totally to immunise the press—whether forthrightly or by subtle indirection—in areas far beyond the needs of news, comment on public persons and events, discussions of public issues and the like would be no service to freedom of press, but an invitation to public hostility of that freedom.[20]

In *Govind* v. *State of M.P.*,[21] Mathew, J. observed that the fundamental rights explicitly guaranteed to a citizen have penumbral zones and that the right to privacy is itself a fundamental right, that fundamental right must be subjected to restriction on the basis of compelling public interest. But he did not define what was public interest.

---

18. *Ibid.*
19. Gertz *v.* Robert Welch, Inc. 418 US 323 (1974); Time Inc. *v.* Firestone, 424 US 374 (1967).
20. *Supra* n. 17 at 485.
21. (1975) 2 SCC 148.

II. PUBLIC FIGURE

A Public figure has been defined as a person who, by his accomplishments, fame, or mode of living, or by adopting a profession or calling which gives the public a legitimate interest in doing, his affairs, and his character, has become a "public personage".[22] In other words, he is a celebrity—one who by his voluntary efforts has succeeded in placing himself in the public eye. Obviously to be included in this category are those who have achieved at least some degree of reputation by appearing before the public, as in the case of an actor,[23] a professional baseball player,[24] a pugilist,[25] public officer,[26] famous inventors,[27] explorers,[28] war heroes,[29] and even ordinary soldiers[30] and no less a personage than the Grand Exalted Ruler of a lodge.[31] It includes, in short, any one who has arrived at a position where public attention is focused upon him as a person.

In innumerable judicial decisions in the United States such public figures are held to have lost, to some extent at least, their right of privacy. Three reasons are given, more or less indiscriminately, in these decisions:(i) that they have sought publicity and consented to it, and so cannot complain of it; (ii) that their personalities and their affairs already have

22. Cason *v.* Baskin, 159 Fla. 31, 30 SO Sd 635, 638 (1947); Hem Lata Jain, Right to Privacy: Where Does One Stop? *Lex Et Juris* 40 (October 1980).
23. Paramount Pictures *v.* Leader Press, 24 F. Supp. 1004 (W.D. Okl.1938); Chaplin *v.* National Broadcasting Co., 15 F.R.D. 134 (S.D.N.Y. 1953).
24. Ruth *v.* Educational Films, 194 App. Div. 893, 184 N.Y.S. 948 (1920)
25. Cohen *v.* Marx., 94 Cal. App. 2d 704, 211 p. 2d 320 (1950).
26. Martin *v.* Dorton, 210 Miss 668, 50 SO 2d 391 (1951) (Seriff); Hull *v.* Curtis Pub. Co., 182 Pa. Super. 86, 125 A. 2d 644 (1956) (arrest by policeman).
27. Corliss *v.* E.W. Walker Co., 64 Fed. 280 (D. Mass. 1894).
28. Smith *v.* Suratt, 7 Alaska 416 (1926).
29. Stryker *v.* Republic Picture Corp., 108 Cal. App. 2d 191, 238 p. 2d 670 (1951).
30. Continental Optical Co. *v.* Reed, 119 Ind. App. 643, 86 N.E. 2d 306 (1949).
31. Wilson *v.* Brown, 189 Misc. 79, 73 N.Y.S. 2d 587 (Sup. ct. 1947).

become public, and can no longer be regarded as their own private business; and (iii) that the press has a privilege, guaranteed by the Constitution, to inform the public about those who have become legitimate matters of public interest. On one or another of these grounds, and sometimes all, it is held that there is no liability when they are given additional publicity, as to matters reasonably within the scope of public interest which they have aroused.[32] However, the public figure loses his right of privacy only to a limited extent and the privilege of reporting news and matters of public interest is likewise limited. An illustration of the privacy of a public figure is a case in a trial court in Los Angeles, not officially reported, in which the actor Kirk Douglas, after engaging in some undignified antics before a home motion picture camera for his friends, was held to have a cause of action when the film was put up for public exhibition.

Right to privacy protects only those persons in whose affairs the community has no legitimate concern. It is unwarranted invasion of privacy which is reprehended. The general object of this right it to protect the privacy to private life. Those who enter into public life forfeit a degree of the privacy to which they might otherwise consider themselves entitled—a principle accepted by Samuel D. Warren and Louis D. Brandeis,[33] the Younger Committee,[34] the Press Council of United Kingdom[35] and the United States law.[36] It is generally recongised that the existence of such waiver carries with it the right to invade the privacy of the individual only to the extent legitimately necessary and proper in dealing with the matter which gave rise to the waiver,[37] that is to say, the waiver is limited to those matters which may be legitimately necessary or appropriate for the information of the public.

---

32. See cases cited *supra* notes, 24-31.
33. Samuel D. Warren and Louis D. Brandeis, The Right to Privacy 4 *Harv. L. Rev.* 193 (1890).
34. Younger Committee. *op. cit.*, Para 156.
35. *Supra* n. 9 at 151.
36. William L. Prosser, Privacy 48 *Calif L.R.* 383-423 (August 1960).
37. Time Inc. *v.* Hill, 385 US 374 (1967).

In this light the fact of *Time Inc.* v. *Hill*[38] are worth mentioning to elucidate and illustrate the point. The Hill family were residing in Florida when one day they were taken hostage in their own house by a group of escaped convicts. After a holdout that lasted for over two odd days the convicts fled. The Hill family were immediately raised to super star status and received continuous calls from the press and were questioned about their period of captivity. The family time and again re-affirmed that they were not ill-treated, threatened or humiliated by the convicts. After a point of time unable to take the growing media pressure, they moved west to Colorado. Time Inc. made out a story as to how the family was tormented and threatened by their captors and where the family for their own defence attacked the captors as well. The story was later made into a play (Screened at Broadway) and subsequently made into a movie (the movie was indecently shot in the home of the Hill family). The Hill family enraged at the violation of privacy filed a suit for damages, which was decided in their favour till the United States Supreme Court took the view that in light of the incidents that had occurred, they had become public figures and therefore they were not entitled to damages as long as the incident that they were complaining of dealt with the hostage drama (as that was what raised them to 'cult superstar' status).

A simple example to explicate this case would be the life of many of the Gujarat riot victims. They have stood up against the unfairness of the trial that has been thrust upon them and have approached the Supreme Court to transfer their cases. There is no doubt that they have become 'public figures' as per the definition of the various courts. Would one call it legitimate in splashing their already tormented life all on the claim 'public interest'?

An equally downside ruling was that again from the United States Supreme Court in *Hustler Magazine and Larry C. Flynt* v. *Jerry Falwell*,[39] wherein the respondent, a noted political critic was shown to have had an 'incestuous drunken

38. *Ibid.*
39. 485 US 46 (1988).

parody' with his mother. The lower Courts had granted the respondent damage for his loss of reputation, which was negated by the Supreme Court in its verdict. The Court in its verdict relied on the dissenting view of Justice Oliver Wendell Holmes (as the learned Justice then was) in *Abrams* v. *U.S.*[40]

> "When men have realized that time has upset many fighting faiths, they may come to believe even more than they believe the very foundations of their own conduct that the ultimate good desired is better reached by free trade in ideas—that the best test of truth is the power of the thought to get itself accepted in the competition of the market."

Of course, this does not mean that any speech about a public figure is immune from sanction in the form of damages. Since *New York Times Co.* v. *Sullivan*,[41] the Courts have consistently ruled that a public figure may hold a speaker liable for the damage to reputation caused by publication of a defamatory falsehood, but only if the statement was made.

". . . with knowledge that it was false or with reckless disregard of whether it was false or not."

Yet there are no parameters as what would be 'false and reckless disregard of the truth,' so, much of the matter remains unresolved.

The Indian Supreme Court has also carved out though an exception to this 'public figure rule' in the following words:

> The rule aforesaid is subject to the exception, that any publication concerning the aforesaid aspects becomes unobjectionable if such publication is based upon public records including Court records. This is for the reason that once a matter becomes a matter of public record, the right to privacy no longer subsists and it becomes a legitimate subject for comment by press and media

40. 250 US 616 (1919).
41. 367 US 254 (1964).

> among others. We are, however, of the opinion that in the interest of decency {Article 19(2)} an exception must be carved out to this rule, viz., a female who is the victim of a sexual assault, kidnap, abduction or a like offence should not further be subjected to the indignity of her name and the incident being published in press/ media.[42]

There is no doubt that this is a valid classification as the Constitution does permit the enactment of special laws for women and children under Article 15(4). Yet what is the fate of those who are not benefited by this exception?.

It is no secret that today, television is a money-making medium (true, there is dispersion of knowledge as well). Today's modern media is exactly what Justice Holmes in 1919 referred to as a 'market of free trade of ideas'. Should these unfortunate victims be the pawn in the success game of media barons? Or should it be assumed that merely because these people have entered the scope of 'public figures' would it be deemed that their right to privacy 'waived'?

This analysis would create a grave legal inconsistency, as the Indian Constitution does not permit the waiving of a Fundamental Right, and the right to privacy has been accepted as a Fundamental Right.

The Supreme Court in *Basheshar Nath* v. *C.I.T.*,[43] was of the view that a fundamental right being in the nature of prohibition addressed to the State, none of the fundamental rights under the Constitution can be waived. The same view has been reaffirmed in the later ruling of *Olga Tellis* v. *Bombay Municipal Corporation*,[44] where the Court re-affirmed that there cannot be any estoppel against the Constitution, the paramount law of the land, and that a person cannot waive any of the fundamental Rights conferred upon him by the Constitution in Part III, by any act of his.

---

42. R. Rajagopal *v.* State of Tamil Nadu, AIR 1995 SC 264 at p. 276.
43. AIR 1959 SC 149.
44. AIR 1986 SC 180 at paras 28-29.

A public figure is entitled to less protection by the law of defamation than a private person.[45] It equally applies to privacy cases. Here the question may arise, who is public figure? And how he became public figure? A public figure has been defined earlier to cover those who have assumed roles of special prominence in the affairs of the society. In this way, public figure includes not only great personality but also others who are catapulated into public prominence for a short period. For example, victims of an offence, accused, pardoned, rehabilitated civil litigants and other person whose acts are matters of public record, etc.

Legitimate public interest in one who has become a public figure, whether voluntarily or involuntarily, is not necessarily limited to the individual himself. It may, to some extent, include the members of his family or even others who have been closely associated with him, although there is nothing else about them to attract public attention.[46] The mere fact that some one is a public figure does not, of course, determine the extent to which his private life may legitimately be exposed. Where the information is of public benefit or of legitimate concern to the public private facts may be justified to be published.

The fact that a person is a public character or legitimate subject of news comment does not justify misleading publicity or misrepresentation.[47] Further, the privilege available to publisher in regard to a news worthy person does not protect the publisher if he or she fictionalises the matter. Similarly, a person who commercially exploits the name or likeness of a well known person without the latter's consent, is liable to invasion of privacy.[48] Public figure exemption does not protect lurid and indecent publications because it outrages the community's notion of decency.[49] It is, however, that the public figure loses his right of privacy only to a limited extent, and that the privilege of reporting news

45. New York Times *v.* Sullivan, 367 US 254 (1964).
46. See, Privacy, 62 *Am. Jur.* 2d (1990) Para 197.
47. Bell *v.* Birmingham Broadcasting Co. 266 Ala 266, 96 SO 2d 263.
48. Sharman *v.* C. Schmidt and Sons, Inc. (EDPa) 216 F Supp. 401.
49. Sidis *v.* F.R. Pub. Corp. 138 ALR 15.

and matters of public interest is likewise limited. The decisions indicate very definitely that both privileges apply only to one branch of the tort, that of disclosure of private facts about the individual. But even as to the disclosure of private facts, it appears that there must be some rather undefined limits upon these privileges. Justice V.R. Krishna Iyer has rightly pointed out that the jurisprudence of public office demands that even a sex purity of people in high places be initiated by a fearless press. The people who hold public offices wield power and are responsible to the people of the Republic. Their private lives to some extent at least do influence their public actions and decisions. In such a situation further discrimination become necessary than to class facts or deeds as public or private and circumstances in a particular situation, balancing the right of privacy and the right of information as a matter of public interest.

In order to recover a false light action, a public official or a public figure must show that defendant published a statement with actual malice. However, this showing is not required in the case of a limited public figure. Although, it is not necessary for an individual to seek publicity actively in order to be in the public eye, so as to limit his right of privacy, an individual cannot be deemed public merely because of the broadcast or publication alone. Moreover, determining whether a false light plaintiff is a public official is a matter of federal constitutional law, and State law standards are not determinative. In any event, plaintiff cannot sue for false light invasion of privacy if he is a public official and the publication relates to the performance of his public life or duties.

III. PUBLIC PLACE

The reporting or photographing of events which occur in a public place will, in most cases, be rightly untrammelled. This view has been endorsed by William L. Prosser, but not entirely in accordance with some of the decisions which he cited in its support. On the public street, or in any other public place, the plaintiff has no right to be alone, and it is no invasion of his privacy to do no more than follow him about.[50] Neither is it such an invasion, to take his photograph in such a place,[51] since this amounts to nothing more than making a record, not differing essentially from a full written description, of a public sight which anyone present would be free to see. On the other hand, when he is confined to a hospital bed[52] and in all probability when he is merely in a seclusion of his home, the making of a photograph without his consent is an invasion of a private right, of which he is entitled to complain. In *Gill* v. *Hearst Publishing Co's case,* where a couple's photograph was taken in a embracing position in market place. The photograph was published by a newspaper to illustrate an article on the subject of love. The plaintiff sued alleging that their right of privacy was invaded. The Court refused for a recovery of damage.

IV PUBLIC RECORD

The right of privacy is held not to be infringed by the publication of matters of public records. However, public records may not be forever privileged. There can be no liability for publishing matters of public record, as it has been recongised that the interest in privacy fades when the information involved already appears on the public record. However, matter which was once of public record may be protected as private facts where disclosure of that information would not be newsworthy of concerns purely private matters. If the record is a confidential one, not open to public inspection, as in the case of income tax returns,[53] it is not public, and there can be no doubt that there is an invasion of privacy. But it has been held that no one is entitled to complain when there is publication of his recorded date of

---

50. Chappell *v.* Stewart, 82 Md. 323, 33 Atl. 542 (1896); Mckinzie *v.* Huckaby 112 F. Supp. 642 (W.D. Okl. 1953).
51. Gill *v.* Hearst Pub. Co., 40 Cal. 2d 224, 253 P. 2d 441 (1953); Berg *v.* Minneapolis Star and Tribune Co., 79 F. Supp. 957 (D. Minn. 1948); United States *v.* Gugel, 119 F. Supp 897 (E.D.Ky. 1954).
52. Barber *v.* Time Inc., 348 Mo. 1199, 159 S.W. 2d 291 (1942).
53. Munzer *v.* Balaisdell, 183 Misc. 773, 49 N.Y.S. 2d 915 (Sup. Ct. 1944); Sellers *v.* Herry, 329 S.W. 2d (Ky. 1959).

birth or his marriage,[54] or his military service record,[55] and the same must certainly be true of his admission to the bar or to the practice of medicine, or the fact that he is driving a taxi-cab. The difficult question is as to the effect of lapse of time, and the extent to which forgotten records, as for example of a criminal conviction, may be dredged up in after years and given more general publicity. As in the case of news,[56] with which the problem may be inextricably interwoven, it has been held that the memory of the events covered by the records, such as a criminal trial,[57] can be revived as still the matter of legitimate public interest. But there is a leading case of *Melvin* v. *Reid*,[58] which held that the unnecessary use of the plaintiff's name, and the revelation of her history to new friends and associates, introduced an element which was in itself a transgression of her right to privacy. The answer may be that the existence of a public record is a factor of a good deal of importance, which will normally prevent the matter from being private, but that under some special circumstances it is not necessarily conclusive.

To reiterate, a matter that was once of public record may be protected as private fact where disclosure of the information would not be newsworthy.[59] The disclosure of the victim's identity in a rape trial was held by the Supreme Court to be justified because the first and fourteenth amendments prohibit a civil action for invasion of privacy.[60] Even if the court is correct in its view that "there are privacy interests to be protected in judicial proceedings,"[61] the application of the public record test will invariably demolish the plaintiff's claim.

---

54. Meetze *v.* Associated Press, 230 S. C. 330, 95 S. E. 2d 606 (1956).
55. Stryker *v.* Republic Pictures Corp., 108 Cal. App. 643, 86 N.E. 2d 306 (1949).
56. See, *supra* n. 25 and 49.
57. Bernstein *v.* National Broadcasting Co., 129 F Supp. (D.D.C. 1955).
58. 112 Cal. App. 285, 297 Pac. 91 (1931).
59. Diaz *v.* Oakland Tribune, Inc. (1st Dist) 139(a) App 3d 118, 188.
60. Cox Broadcasting Corporation *v.* Cohn, 420 US 460 (1975).
61. *Id.* at 495.

However, where there is express provision in law which prohibits publication of any record of judicial proceeding or trial in camera the public record standard would not apply.[62] In this case privacy interest would prevail. The practice of keeping records about individuals in has undergone dramatic changes during the last fifty years. This is mainly due to rapid urbanization, industrialization and recent technological advancements, especially in the field of electronics and computers. The Privacy Act, 1974 was enacted with a view to ensure that the records a federal agency maintains about an individual are as accurate, timely, complete and relevant as is necessary to assure that they are not the cause of unfairness on any decision about the individual made on the basis of them. Proper management of records about individuals is the key to this objective, and the Privacy Act seeks to enlist the individual's help in achieving it by giving him a right to see, copy and correct or amend the records about himself. The Fair Credit Reporting Act, 1970 and the Fair Credit Billing Act, 1974 also focus on fairness in record keeping, though their scope of application and their specific requirements differ from those of the Privacy Act.

V. PUBLIC DISCLOSURE

It is generally accepted that the requirement of public disclosure or publicity connotes publicity in the sense of communication to the public or general or to a large number of persons; as distinguished from one individual or a few.[63] The simple disclosure of private information to one other person is not sufficient to state a claim for the public disclosure of private facts.[64] However, there is no magic formula or body count that can measure it. It depends on the circumstances of particular case.

Although a few courts held in the past that the right of privacy could be violated by printing, writings, pictures or

62. See, Code of Criminal Procedure, 1973, Section 327.
63. Wood *v.* National Computer Systems, Inc. (CA8Ark) 814 F 2d 544.
64. Carcoran *v.* South Western Bell Tel. Co. (No. App) SW 2d 212.

other permanent publications, but not by word of mouth only,[65] now it is almost unanimously recongised that the right of privacy can be violated by publicly disclosing private facts about the plaintiff by any means whatsoever. This includes oral communications,[66] radio broadcasts,[67] motion picture,[68] television programme[69] and still photographs.[70] Some limits at least, of this branch of right of privacy appear to be fairly well marked out, as follows:

First, the disclosure of the private facts must be public disclosure and not private one. There must be in other words, publicity. It is an invasion of the right to publish in a newspaper that the plaintiff does not pay his debts,[71] or to post a notice to that effect in a window on the public street[72] or cry it aloud in a highway;[73] but, except for one decision of a lower Georgia Court which was reversed on the grounds,[74] it has been agreed that it is no invasion to communicate that fact to the plaintiff's employer,[75] or to any other individual, or even to a small group,[76] unless there is some breach of contract, trust or confidential relation which will afford an independent basis for relief.[77] Warren and Brandeis[78] thought that the publication would have to be written or printed

65. Grimes *v.* Carter (5th Dist.) 241 Cal. App. 2d 694.
66. Carr *v.* Watkins, 277 Md 578, 177 A 2d 841.
67. Mau *v.* Rio Grade Oil Inc. (DC Cal.) 28F Supp. 845.
68. Donahue *v.* Warner Bros. (CA 10 Utah) 194 Fed. 6.
69. Taylor *v.* K.T.V.B. Inc. 96 Idaho 202, 525 F 2d 984.
70. Democrat *v.* Graham 276 Ala 380, 162 SO 2d 474
71. Trammell *v.* Citizens News Co., 285 Ky. 529, 148 S.W. 2d 708 (1941).
72. Brents *v.* Morgan, 221 Ky. 765, 299 S.W. 967 (1927).
73. Bennet *v.* Norban, 396 Pa. 94, 151 A 2d 476 (1959).
74. Gouldman-Taber Pontiac, Inc. *v.* Zerbst, 96 Ga. App. 48, 99 S.E. 2d 475 (1957), reversed in 213 Ga. 682, 100 S.E. 881 (1957), on the ground that the communication was privileged.
75. Patton *v.* Jacobs, 118 Ind. App. 358, 78 N.E. 2d 789 (1948).
76. Gregory *v.* Bryan-Hunt Co., 295 Ky. 345, 174 S.W. 2d 510 (1943) (oral accusation of theft). On the other hand, in Kerby *v.* Hal Roach Studios, 53 Cal. App. 2d 207, 127 P. 2d 577 (1942), the distribution of a letter to a thousand persons was held, without discussion, to make it public.
77. Berry *v.* Moench, 8 Utah 2d 191, 331 P. 2d 814 (1958)
78. *Supra* n. 33 at 217.

unless special damage could be shown; and there have been decisions[79] that the action will not lie for oral publicity; but the growth of radio alone has been enough to make this obsolete,[80] and there now can be little doubt that writing is not required.[81]

Second, the facts disclosed to the public must be private facts, and not public ones. Certainly no one can complain when publicity is given to information about him which he himself leaves open to the public eye, such as the appearance of the house in which he lives, or to the business in which he is engaged. Thus, it has been held that the public school teacher has no action for a compulsory disclosure of her war work and other outside activities.[82]

In its traditional formulation, this public disclosures of private torts involves the "publicity" of "highly offensive," albeit true, private facts about someone that are "not legitimate concern to the public." To fulfil the publicity requirement, the disclosure must reach many people that the information effective becomes public knowledge. At the first blush, this tort looks like the natural home for privacy suits against credit bureaus. However, even though courts impose public disclosure liability upon store owners who "publicize" the names of debtors in their stores, courts generally refuse to hold credit bureaus liable for disseminating this and much more information to their subscribers. Three factors seem to ground this disparate judicial treatment.

First, credit bureaus enjoy the same qualified privilege with respect to the disclosure tort as they do wish respect to the intrusion tort, provided the report recipient has a legitimate need for the information that the credit report provides.[83] If not, the credit bureaus forfeits its qualified privilege and may indeed face liability under this variation of the privacy tort, but only if its disclosure is highly offensive, a standard few credit reports meet.

---

79. Martin *v.* F.I.Y. Theatre Co., 10 Ohio *op. cit.* 338 (Ohio C.P. 1938); Gregory *v.* Bryan Hunt Co., 295 Ky. 345, 174 S.W. 2d 510 (1943).
80. See, *supra* n. 67.
81. See, *supra* n. 73.
82. Reed *v.* Orleans Parish Schoolboard, 21 SO. 2d 895 (La. App. 1945).
83. Bloomfield *v.* Retail Credit Co., 302 N.E. 2d. 88, 100 (Ill. 1973).

Second, the majority rule on the extent of publicity of private facts necessary to trigger liability leaves credit bureaus free to distribute credit reports to their subscribers. Under this majority rule, defendant who publicize private facts about plaintiffs escape liability unless such communication reaches the public at large or reaches so many persons that the matter must be regarded as substantially certain to become one of the public knowledge.[84] Credit bureau distributions of consumer credit reports to a limited number of subscribers generally fall short of the publicity necessary to trigger liability.

Third, the consumer consent negates the public disclosure tort. Even if a consumer claims that a credit bureau's disclosure exceeded the scope of his consent, the defendant may still escape tort liability. In the absence of express consent, the defendant may imply consent from the plaintiff's conduct if the defendant does not reasonably and reasonably relies upon the implication. These generous rule of consent help to render the public disclosure tort as ineffectual against credit bureau privacy invasions as the intrusion tort is.[85]

VI. CONSENT

If a person consents, either expressly or by conduct or seeks publicity or is a public figure, he may be said to have waived his right to prevent some or all of the publicity which he receives.[86] Consent may be conceived simply as another way of describing the limitation on the substantive 'right to privacy' or as a defence to an action for invasion of that right. Right to privacy may, however, be waived for one purpose and still assented for another, it may be waived on behalf of the class, and retained as against another class, it may be waived as to one individual and retained as against all other persons.[87]

---

84. Scott Shorr, Personal Information Contracts: How to Protect Privacy Without Violating The First Amendment, 80 *Cornell Law Review* 1780-81 (1995).
85. *Id.* at 1781.
86. Warren and Brandeis, *op. cit.*, p. 218.
87. Pavesich *v.* New England Life Ins. Co., SO SE 68 (1905).

In order for waiver by consent to be asserted as a defence to an action for invasion of privacy, the consent must be as broad as inclusive as the act or publication complained of. Consent may be asserted as a defence only where it has not been exceed. Consent which has been exceeded cannot be a defence.[88] Truly admitting, that a claim to privacy may be undercut by a plea of consent to publicity. Anyone appearing in public place wearing strange clothes must expect to be looked at: if he wants privacy, he should stay indoors. If someone openly and indiscriminately publishes personal facts about himself, he cannot complain if someone else extends the publication. Someone who goes into public life, or adopts a profession like the stage which unavoidably attracts public notice, can be said, reasonably (and sometimes literally), to have asked for it. Still, implied consent to publicity need not be total, whether as a subject-matter, duration or the extent of the public. The consent implied must be to a waiver of privacy claims naturally and relevantly consequent upon the act in question—not to infringements after the occasion is well and truly past. Of course, restriction of implied consent would not rule out other counter-claims.[89]

Under the common law, one who expressly or impliedly consents to an invasion of one's privacy, in any of its forms, has recourse against the privacy-invader only if the invader exceeds the scope of one's consent. The intrusion tort is inapplicable when the allegedly intrusive activity consists of "viewing, observing, or recording matters which occur in a public place or a place otherwise open to the public eye."[90] Hence, there should be a defence similar to the defence of *volenti non fit injuria,* namely, that the plaintiff either expressly or by implication consented to the infringement.

---

88. Continental Optical Co. *v.* Reed 119 Ind. App. 643; Grossman *v.* Frederick Bros. Acceptance Corp., 34N.Y.S. 2d 785 (Sup. Ct. App. T. 1942); Jenkins *v.* Dell Pub. Co., 143 F. Supp. 953 (W.D. Pa. 1956); Tanner-Brice Co. *v.* Sims, 174 Ga.13, 161 S.E. 819 (1931); and Porter *v.* American Tobacco Co., 140 App. Div. 871, 125 N.Y.S. 710 (1910).
89. S.I. Benn, The Protection and Limitation of Privacy, 52 *The Australian Law Journal*, 688-689 (December 1978).
90. David A. Elder, The Law of Privacy, 387 (1991).

VIII. PRIVILEGE

The right of privacy does not prohibit the communication of any matter, even though in its nature private, when the publication is made under circumstances which would render it a privileged communication according to slander and libel law. Thus, actions for invasion of privacy are subject to the defence of privilege. A statutory privilege for the publication of information in a judicial proceeding is applicable to a claim for invasion of privacy. However, the statute does not provide blanket immunity for disclosure of constitutionally protected privileged communication, where the constitutional right of privacy is at stake, a careful balancing of the relevant statutory and constitutional interests is appropriate.

In defamation, there are also the important defences of absolute and qualified privilege. These are available to a defendant in the many situations where some obligation owed to another, or to society, make it important that he should be able to act freely, without fear of the legal consequences if at the time what he said honestly should afterwards prove to be wrong. The employer giving reference, the citizen making a report to the police, the witness in court, are all obvious examples. These privileges appear to be equally important in the field of privacy that the exception, i.e. any circumstances which provide such a defence in the field of defamation should provide one in the field of privacy also. The exception stems from the fact that there exist common law defences of privilege which, if abused, might enable long buried skeletons to be "raked up" with impunity in situations where there was no conceivable public benefit to be served from so doing. Hence, absolute or qualified privilege is a defence to an action for infringement of privacy to the private citizen, but the publishers of the mass media are required to show, in addition, that the matters were of public concern and their publication for the public benefit.[91]

91. Marklittman and Peter Cater-Ruck, *op. cit.*, pp. 37-38.

The rule has been laid down that a communication of even a private matter does not violate the right of privacy when the publication would be a privileged communication under principles governing libel and slander.[92] Privileges is of two kinds, i.e., absolute and qualified. These privileges are explained as under:

(A) Absolute Privilege

Communications made in the regular course of, or as part of, judicial or court proceedings are absolutely privileged where they are pertinent and material to the redress or relief sought, or pertinent and relevant to the issues. Such privilege serves either to protect or insulate the author from liability for invasion of privacy, so long as the communications bear a proper relationship to the issues. In matters of absolute privilege no action lies for the invasion of privacy, even though the statement is made to private matters of any individual. It may be false or it may be made maliciously. In such cases the public interest demand that an individual's right to privacy should give way to freedom of speech. Article 105(2) of the Constitution of India provides that (a) statements made by a member of either House of Parliament, and (b) the publication by or under the authority of either House of Parliament of any report, paper, votes or proceedings cannot be questioned in the court of law. Similarly, privilege exists in respect of the State legislature under Article 194 of the Constitution of India. Besides this, no action for invasion of privacy lies against judges, counsels, witnesses or parties for words written or spoken in the course of any proceedings before any court recognized by law, even though the words written or spoken were written or spoken maliciously, without any justification or excuse, and from personal ill will and anger against the person whose right to privacy is violated.[93] Judicial officers in India has been

---

92. Brents *v.* Morgan 221 KY 765.
93. Royal Aquarium and Summer and Winter Garden Society Ltd. *v.* Parkinson, (1892) 1 Q.B. 431 (This case was relating to defamation which equally applies for privacy cases).

granted protection by the Judicial Officers Protection Act, 1850 and Judges Protection Act, 1985. The advocates have also been granted absolute privilege by the Advocates Act, 1961. Hence whatever stated above in relation to judicial proceedings is out of the purview of right to privacy. Further, it has been held that the publication of a letter by attaching it to pleadings to which it had reasonable relevancy is absolutely privileged.[94] Further, a statement made by one officer of the State to another in the course of official duty is absolutely privileged for reason of public policy.[95] Such privileges also extends to reports made in the course of military and naval duties. Communications relating to State matters made by one Minister to another or by a Minister to the Crown is also privileged.[96]

(B) Qualified Privileges

A communication made in good faith and on a subject-matter in which a person making it has an interest, or in reference to which he has a duty, is privileged if it is made to a person or persons having a corresponding interest or duty, even though it invades the privacy interest of another. The truth or falsity of a qualifiedly privileged communication is not material to liability for invasion of privacy, so long as there is no bad faith or malice. However, the qualified privilege does not extend to material which defames another and is not reasonably necessary to the development of the privileged subject-matter of the publication.

In certain cases the defence of qualified privilege is also available. Unlike the defence of absolute privilege, in this case it is necessary that the statement must have been made without malice. The presence of malice destroys this defence. The malice in relation to qualified privilege means an evil motive. Generally such a privilege is available either when the statement is made in discharge of a duty or protection of

---

94. Hagan *v.* Fairfield (2nd Dist.) 238 Cal. App. 2d 197.
95. Chatterton *v.* Secy. of State for India in Council, (1875) 2 Q.B. 189.
96. *Ibid.*

an interest, or the publication is in the form of report of parliamentary, judicial or other public proceedings.

It is generally agreed that the right of privacy is subordinate to the police power. The privilege of enlightening the public is not, however, limited to the dissemination of news, it extends also to information or education, or even entertainment and amusement, by books, articles, pictures, films and broadcasts concerning interesting phases of human activity in general. Similarly, a television broadcast has the same privilege accorded to other media where the right of privacy is in issue.[97]

VIII. THE DEFENDANT'S MOTIVE

There is less justification for protecting publications which serve the interests of the defendants than those which have wider objectives such as providing news. The arguments against restraining the former are attenuated by the general rationale for free speech. A similar distinction may be drawn between publications which merely titillate and those which seek to educate. The Younger Committee Report on Privacy, 1972 resisted such distinction pointing out that "it may be that at the lower end of the scale an invasion of privacy could be justified merely to establish news for entertainment or to satisfy curiosity."[98] But where it is "prurient or morbid curiosity"[99] even the Press Council would not seek to justify its satisfaction.

IX. DEGREE OF SERIOUSNESS

In general principle of right of privacy always consider the degree of seriousness. "It is only the more flagrant breaches of decency and propriety that could in practice be

---

97. Youssoupoff *v.* Columbia Broadcasting System Inc. 48 Misc. 2d 700.
98. The Younger Committee Report (Report of the Committee on Privacy), 1972 at para 157.
99. See, *supra* n. 9 at 151.

reached and it is not perhaps desirable even to attempt to repress everything which the nicest taste and keenest sense of the respect due to private life, would condemn.[100] The disclosure must offend the reasonable man of ordinary sensibilities: "The law of privacy is not intended for the protection of any shrinking soul who is abnormally sensitive about such publicity.[101] The Untied States Law applies a 'Mores' test under which liability arises only for publicity given to matters which would be objectionable to the ordinary person.[102] And the British Bills on Privacy recognize that the invasion must be "substantial and unreasonable"[103] to give rise to a cause of action. The content, style and truthfulness of the publication may all be relevant considerations in determining the reasonableness or the degree of infringement.

X. MODE OF ACQUISITION

The fact that the defendant acquired the information by improper or illegal means ought not to affect the consideration of whether its publication is justified. The Untied States Courts have, however, occasionally ruled that the disclosure of information unlawfully obtained is not permitted,[104] but sometimes publication has been justified 'in the public interest' or because it was newsworthy.[105] The latter seems to be the preferred approach; but the former is adopted implicitly by the Younger Committee which recommended a legal remedy only in those circumstances where information unlawfully required was used or disclosed.[106]

---

100. *Supra* n. 98 at para 157.
101. *Supra* n. 33 at p. 216.
102. William L. Prosser, *op. cit.*, p. 383.
103. Mr. Walden Bill Cl. 1; Mr. Lyon Bill Cl. 2; N.C.C.L. Bill Cl. 7(2).
104. Corliss *v.* Walker 37F 434 (1893).
105. New York Times *v.* United States, 403 US 713 (1971).
106. Younger Committee, *op. cit.*, para 632.

It is, therefore, apparent from the foregoing discussion that privacy is not an absolute right. Like other rights it is also subject to some limitations, certain limitations are imposed by the provision which provides this right. The right may be lawfully restricted for the prevention of crime, disorder or protection of health or morals or protection of rights and freedom of others. In the absence of any express constitutional or statutory provisions recognizing the right to privacy, the Indian courts have seized the opportunities whenever they came and tried successfully to bring the privacy right within the purview of fundamental rights. In the course of interpretation of constitutional rights it is found within Constitution, particularly in Articles 19(1)(d) and 21. Similarly, 'dignity' clause of the Preamble to the Constitution is an accepted shelter for this right. Reasonable restrictions are allowed under these rights which applies with regard to privacy rights as well. It is clear, however, that the public figure loses his right of privacy only to a limited extent, and that the privilege of reporting news and matters of public interest is likewise limited. The decisions indicate very definitely that both privileges apply only to one branch of the tort, that of disclosure of private facts about the individual. In India, though, in some cases, privacy has been recognised as fundamental right, its content, extent and limits are not still clear. Statutory protection is piecemeal. It cannot cover the whole aspects of privacy.

The recent order of the Department of Telecommunication relating to the snooping of SMS and e-mails, issued to all private cellular service providers, requiring them to provide "monitoring" on all value added services, will give unfettered power to government and its intelligence agencies for example intelligence Bureau, the Research and Analysis Wing (RAW), the Enforcement Directorate, Military Intelligence, etc., to tap SMS, e-mails, etc., in addition to tapping of phone calls. The new order effectively circumvents the existing safeguards put in place by the Apex Court in *Amar Singh case* which ensures that phones are tapped only after a signed order from the Union Home Secretary after convincing grounds disclosed. While, abuse has been rampant, the new order virtually makes it official since the providers are not sure if the same rules and safeguards will be followed. As far as e-mail is concerned it raises questions about the citizen's right to privacy. The move according the official version is justified on security considerations, the problem of Naxalites and the huge "market manipulations."[107]

107. Swati Chaturvedi, Snooping Order to Bare Your SMS, E-mails, The Tribune, April 10, 2006, p. 1 also see, Editorial, The Tribune, April 11, 2006.

6

Privacy: The Judicial Response

I. INTRODUCTION

Today, all democratic societies have come to realize that privacy is at the heart of all human rights. Though, in England there is no constitutional guarantee of human rights against the State, the ordinary law does recognise that an individual has certain rights, such as the right to freedom of speech, to personal liberty and the like which the State would protect against invasion by other persons, in so far as the ambit of such rights is not abridged by legislation. There is, however, no such recognition of any right to privacy as such, in spite forceful advocacy by progressive thinkers such as Lord Denning.[1] Privacy rights in the United States, Great Britain and India supply an interesting range for comparison because of differences among them in terms of industrial and technological as well as Constitutional development. If the existence of privacy safeguards depends upon the stimulus provided by some degree of threat, then the legal responses should be greatest in the United States, nearly as great in Britain, and nearly non-existent in India, because the level of

1. Denning, What Next In Law? 219 (1982); Bridge *et. al.*, Fundamental Rights, 56 (1973).

technological and economic development of India, compared to the other two countries does not establish the conditions necessary for the legal safeguard of privacy rights. Privacy as a basic human right touches upon fundamental needs and values associated with man's gregarious nature. Certainly the level of technological and economic development creates pressures to protect these privacy values through legal enforcement techniques. But even in the absence of such development, the value and the basic human right to privacy may prevail irrespective of legal recognition.

It is true that common law was not able to introduce the right to privacy as an inherent and inalienable right. The American law, however, made a substantial progress in the area of right to privacy. In India we follow the English system of law in its content and procedure. Inherently our courts were not ready to recognize the right to privacy due to the influence of the English Law. But the constitutional provisions are potential enough to introduce the right to privacy by an active judiciary. The issue of right of privacy in India is in premature stage. Hence, an attempt has been made in this chapter to study how far this right can be regarded as constitutional right and the scope is confined to United States of America, United Kingdom and India.

II. JUDICIAL RECOGNITION OF PRIVACY IN UNITED STATES

In United States of America the courts have refused to be obsessed by the dignity and conservation of the English law of torts as an actionable wrong under particular circumstances where English law as yet offers no remedy, for example interception of telephonic or other conversations, publications of a person's photograph without his or her consent (irrespective of defamation or infringement of copyright). The Supreme Court of United States has recognized privacy as a constitutional right. In varying contexts the American judges have found the roots of this right in the First Amendment,[2] the Fourth and Fifth

2. Stanley *v.* Georgia, 394 US 557.

Amendments,[3] in the penumbras of the Bill of Rights[4] and in the Ninth Amendment or in the concept of liberty guaranteed by the first section of the Fourteenth Amendment.[5] Privacy interests of the individual are also protected under the law of torts in United States of America. Evolution of the right to privacy has taken place from case to case development and it appears that the doctrine of "due process of law" has largely helped the American Supreme Court to identify, recognise and protect different kinds of privacy interest.

Prior to 1965, references were frequently made to "privacy" or the "right to privacy," but these phrases were used as little more than flourishes of rhetoric. They added nothing to already existing rights. Legal researchers could look in vain for a case the outcome of which rested strictly upon privacy concepts. Not surprisingly, most references to privacy have occurred in fourth amendment litigation. In declaring the right of all "to be secure in their persons, houses, papers and affects, against unreasonable searches and seizures," the Constitution provides the primary support for a privacy right.

In *Boyd* v. *United States*,[6] the Supreme Court recognised privacy as the underlying principle of the Fourth Amendment prohibition against unlawful searches and seizures. Justice Bradley noted the inter-relationship between the Fourth and Fifth Amendments, his significant conclusion was that the purpose of the Fourth Amendment was to protect the security and privacy of "persons, houses, papers, and effects"; as a corollary, police could seize only instrumentalities of a crime but never an individual's papers as mere evidence of a crime. Justice Bradley's conclusion followed from his construction of the reasonableness clause of the amendment. He argued that the individuals have an indefeasible property right at common law and under the Fourth amendment, which renders unreasonable any governmental search and seizure of private papers or other property for mere evidence of a

---

3. Katz *v.* U.S., 389 U.S. 347 (1967)
4. Griswold *v.* Connecticut, 381 U.S. 479 (1965).
5. Meyer *v.* Nebraska, 262 U.S. 390 (1923).
6. 116 U.S. 616 (1886).

crime. Accordingly, no warrant or subpoena could reasonably issue for items not already owned by or forfeited to the State. In this connection Justice Bradley comments: "The unreasonable searches and seizures condemned in the Fourth Amendment are almost always made for the purpose of compelling a man to give evidence against himself, which in criminal cases is condemned in the Fifth Amendment."[7]

Use of the Fourth Amendment as a vehicle for the right of privacy was inhibited in the 1920s because of the heavy reliance placed on it by bootleggers during prohibition. Law is never created in a vacuum, and the interpretation of law, like the making of it, is shaped by the pressures and prejudices of the times. During the 1920s much "bad" law was written by judges anxious to support the "noble experiment." In particular, Chief Justice Taft narrowed the Fourth Amendment to assist federal agents in keeping America dry.[8] The high point of his fight for prohibition came in the court opinion in *Olmstead* v. *United States*.[9] In this landmark case, the majority view expressed by Chief Justice Taft felt that there were essentially property principles underlying the amendment and thus before determining the reasonableness of the search and seizure, it had to be proved that the 'search' involved 'physical trespass' and the 'seizure' included 'tangible material.' Justice Brandeis, however, dissented to give a liberal construction to the amendment. He warned that wiretapping represented a serious threat against privacy under the Fourth Amendment. Had he been heeded by a majority of the court, the most serious invasion against privacy might have been uprooted in its infancy. In the area of traditional searches and seizures, the Supreme Court has had little trouble in recognising a right of privacy as the underlying interest protected by the Fourth Amendment. *With Wolf* v. *Colorado*,[10] the Court extended the federal right against unreasonable search and seizure to the States through the

7. *Id.* at 633.
8. *Id.* at 630 in reference to Entick *v.* Carrington 19 How. St. Tr. 1029 (1765).
9. 277 U.S. 438 (1927).
10. 338 U.S. 25 (1949)

fourteenth amendment. Justice Frankfurter's opinion of the court then recognised "the security of one's privacy against arbitrary intrusion by the police" as being "at the core of the Fourth Amendment" and "therefore implicit in the concept of liberty."[11] Justice Douglas in *Frank* v. *Maryland*[12] said, "Indeed, during the last two decades the Fourth Amendment right to be free from unreasonable searches and seizures had become, in shorthand terminology, right to privacy." Wolf was overruled seven years later by *Mapp* v. *Ohio*,[13] a decision that clearly equated the fourth amendment with the right of privacy.

In *Mapp* v. *Ohio*, the appellant had been convicted of knowingly having in her possession and under control certain lewd and lascivious books, pictures and photographs in violation of Ohio's revised code. The United States Supreme Court held, "having once recognized that the right to privacy embodied in the Fourth Amendment is enforceable against the States, we can no loner permit that right remain an empty promise. Because it is enforceable, in the same manner and the like effect as other basic rights, secured by the due process clause, we can no longer permit it to be revocable at the whim of any police officer who in the name of the law enforcement itself, chooses to suspend its enjoyment. Our decisions, founded reasons and truth gives to the individual no more than the right which the Constitution guarantees him, to the police officer, no less than that to which honest law enforcement is entitled and to the courts that judicial integrity so necessary in the true administration of justice."

Griswold v. *Connecticut*[14] presents the first judicial activist role to enthrone the right to privacy as a constitutional right, wherein, the Supreme Court invalidated a Connecticut law prohibiting the use of contraceptives by a married couple. By a 7 : 2 majority the Supreme Court ruled that the governmental measure was against the right of marital privacy. Speaking for the majority Justice William J.

11. *Id.* at 27-28.
12. 359 U.S. 360 (1959).
13. 367 U.S. 643 (1961).
14. 381 US 479 (1965).

Douglas asked whether we would, "allow the police to search the precinct of marital bedrooms for tell-tale signs of the use of contraceptives"[15] but the learned judge did not applied his mind to the problem—whether the State could bar the use of contraceptives. For the first time, the court found the right of privacy to be of sufficient importance to overturn a State law, that is, the Connecticut law prohibiting sale or distribution of contraceptives to any person. The unique nature of the Griswold decision is more apparent when we realize that the court did not have to create a new right to overturn the oft-attacked 1879 statute and could have reached the same result on more traditional grounds. In fact, the appellant's brief devoted only ten out of one hundred pages to the right of privacy, the least documented section of the brief. Griswold's attorney centered their argument on the contention that the law violated the due process clause of the fourteenth amendment, because it was not reasonably related to a legitimate legislative purpose, and was otherwise unreasonable, arbitrary, and capricious. The brief also contended that by prohibiting instruction in birth control methods, the statute violated the first and fourteenth amendment by abridging freedom of speech. Privacy contention had been dismissed by the appellee's brief in a sentence that relied on the Connecticut appellate division's decision that there was "no invasion of anyone's privacy in this case."[16] The Connecticut Supreme Court of errors had not even considered the issue of privacy but had unanimously found the contested statute to be a legitimate exercise of the legislature's police power to "conserve" the public health and morals.[17]

In his opinion for the court in Griswold, Justice Douglas went a step beyond the incorporation theory of Justice Black. The latter had looked to the written guarantees for the first eight amendments for explicit definition of the liberty and due process provision of the fourteenth amendment. Although Justice Douglas examined the wording

15. *Ibid.*
16. State *v.* Griswold, 3 Conn. Cir. 6, 47 (1964).
17. State *v.* Griswold 157 Con. 544 (1964).

of the Bill of Rights to define the liberties of State and federal citizens in Griswold he found that these amendments mean more than they specifically say. For the first time, the court found the right of privacy to be a substantial constitutional right formulated not by any one amendment but by the specific guarantees of at least five amendments (the first, third, fourth, fifth and ninth) that "have penumbras, formed by emanations from those guarantees that help give them life and substance . . . various guarantees creates zones for privacy."[18]

The most surprising aspect of Griswold was its use of the ninth amendment as an important source of the right of privacy. Justice Goldberg, joined by Chief Justice Warren and Justice Brennan, wrote a concurring opinion, "to emphasize the relevance of that (the ninth) amendment to the court's holding."[19] Justice Black was most critical of the newly created right of privacy and of the process by which it was created, warning that its creation actually detracted from the protections provided by the Bill of rights. He wrote: "The court talks about a constitutional right of privacy as though there is some constitutional provision or provisions forbidding any law ever to be passed which might abridge the privacy of individuals. But there is not."[20] Justice Black's complaint emphasized that "one of the most effective ways of diluting or expanding a constitutionally protected right is to substitute for the crucial word or words of a constitutional guarantee another word or words, more or less flexible and more or less restricted in meaning."[21] Justice Stewart also wrote a dissenting opinion in the case expressing the view that while the Connecticut statute seemed "silly" to him, he could not find any way that it violated the Constitution.

In 1967, the Supreme Court delivered two famous decisions that decisively changed the concept of search and seizure under the fourth Amendment. Physical penetration was no longer necessary to be considered a intrusion. In

18. Griswold *v.* Connecticut, 381 US 479, 484 (1965).
19. *Id.* at 487.
20. *Id.* at 508.
21. *Id.* at 509.

Burger v. *New York*,[22] conversations recorded by electronic devices in the defendant's office were introduced as evidence in court. The court held that eavesdropping was unconstitutional under the Fourth Amendment. Also the court found that the New York statute that authorized the bugging was likewise unconstitutional. In *Katz* v. *United States*,[23] the Supreme Court in 1967 effectively overruled Olmstead's twin requirement of a physical trespass or penetration of a constitutionally protected area. In Katz federal agents acting without a warrant attached an electronic listening device, similar to a detectaphone, to the outside of a glass public telephone booth in which the defendant was making incriminating calls by relating gambling information. Counsel for the both sides argued the issues of whether the telephone booth was constitutionally protected area in which Katz had a reasonable privacy claim. The Supreme Court held:

> The government's activities in electronically listening to and recording the petitioner's words violated the privacy upon which he justifiable relied while using the telephone booth and thus constituted a "search and seizure" within the meaning of the Fourth Amendment. The fact that the electronic device employed to achieve that end did not happen to penetrate the wall of the booth can have no constitutional significance.[24]

Justice Stewart rejected that implication by noting that the amendment should not be translated into a general constitutional right of privacy. The doctrine was deceptive because recognizable claims to privacy were contingent upon the locus of individuals activities. He dispelled that idea by saying that "the Fourth Amendment protects people, not places. What a person knowingly exposes to the public, even in his own home or office, is not a subject of Fourth Amendment protection. . . . But what he seeks to preserve as private, even in an area accessible to the public, may be

---

22. 388 U.S. 41 (1967); see also Almedia *v.* United States, 413 U.S. 266 (1973).
23. 19 L. Ed. 576 (1967); 389 U.S. 347 (1967).
24. *Ibid.*

constitutionally protected."[25] Simply because Katz was in a public telephone booth did not imply that he had forgone all privacy expectations and could not assert recognisable privacy claims.

In *Stanley* v. *Georgia*,[26] Justice Marshall delivered the opinion of the court. The fact of the case were: an investigation of the appellant's alleged bookmaking activities led to the issuance of search warrant for appellant's home. Under the authority of the warrant, federal and State agents secured entrance. They found very little evidence of bookmaking activities, but while looking through a desk drawer in an upstairs bedroom one of the federal agents, accompanied by the State Officer, found three reels of an eight milimetre film. Using a projector and screen found in an upstairs living room, they viewed the films. The State Officer concluded that they were obscene and seized them. The appellant was later indicted for 'knowingly having possession of obscene matter' in violation of Georgian law. The Supreme Court held:

> Whatever may be justification for other statutes regulating obscenity, we do not think they reach in to privacy of one's own home. If the First Amendment means anything, it means that a State has no business telling a man, sitting alone in his house, what books he may read or what films he may watch. Our whole constitutional heritage rebels at the thought of giving government the power to control men's mind.

The right of privacy was further expanded by the court in *Eisenstadt* v. *Baird*.[27] Here in a Masschussets statute made it illegal for a single person to obtain contraceptives in order to prevent pregnancy. The court held that the statute is neither a health measure nor deterrent to pre-marital sexual relations but a prohibition resting upon moral judgments. The court held that it was a violation of equal protection for the State to legislate that different treatment be accorded to persons placed by a statute into different classes on the basis of

25. *Id.* at 351.
26. 394 U.S. 557 (1969).
27. 405 U.S. 438 (1972)

criteria wholly unrelated to the objective of the statute. Furthermore, it is said that if the right to privacy means anything, it is the right of individual, married or single to be free from unwarranted governmental instructions into matters so fundamentally affecting a person as the decision whether to bear or to get a child."[28] Next to the Baird decision came in 1973 the decision of the court in *Jane Roe* v. *Henry Wade*[29] which disallowed a Texas statute for bidding abortion except to save life of the mother. Justice Blackmun who delivered the majority opinion upheld the right to privacy in the following words:

The Constitution does not explicitly mention any right or privacy. In a line of decisions, however . . . the court has recognised that a right of personal privacy does exist under the Constitution.[30]

He further said that the State regulation violated the due process clause of the fourteenth amendment which was found to protect the right of privacy against State action. The right of privacy was said to be the basis of woman's qualified right to procure an abortion free from State interference during most of her pregnancy. His decision for the court did not clarify the definitional basis of that right. In some ways, the decision seemed to narrow the scope of the right by cataloguing "certain areas of zones of privacy." The list of areas in which the right of privacy was found to have some application included marriage,[31] procreation,[32] contraception,[33] family relationship,[34] and child rearing and education.[35]

The United States Supreme Court in *Planned Parenthood* v. *Danforth*[36] held that the Constitution protects a minor's

---

28. *Id.* at 453.
29. 410 U.S. 112 (1973).
30. *Ibid.*
31. Loving *v.* Virginia 388 U.S. 1, 12 (1967).
32. Skinner *v.* Oklahoma 316 U.S. 535, 541-42 (1942).
33. Eisenstadt *v.* Baird 405 U.S. 438, 453-54 (1972).
34. Prince *v.* Massachusetts 321 U.S. 158, 166 (1944); See also United States *v.* Kahn, 415 U.S. 143 (1974).
35. Pierce *v.* Society of Sisters, 268 U.S. 510, 535 (1925).
36. 428 U.S. 52 (1976).

right to privacy to abort her pregnancy. However, the United States Supreme Court's determination to extend the right to privacy protection to encompass a woman's right to abortion was received with heavy criticism by many commentators, because the court declined to recognise during the first trimester the right of the husband to participate in the abortion decision and the interest of the State in protecting the life of the foetus. Further, in an attempt to restrict the scope of constitutionally protected right of abortion the United States Supreme Court in *Webseter* v. *Reproductive Health*[37] held that it was legal for the State to prohibit abortion in the State funded public hospitals, and it could also ban publicly paid employees from performing abortions. In 1992, the United States Supreme Court in *Planned Parenthood of Southern Pennsylvania* v. *Casey*[38] held that the State is empowered to impose medical or emotional barriers to abortion, so long as these do not become an undue burden in opting for abortion.

In *Bowers* v. *Hardwink*,[39] it was held that the State can make homo-sexualism and sodomy criminal offences without violating the right of privacy. Further, law also prohibits the use of the illegally interception communications if the user knows, or has reason to know, the source. Courts have split the question of whether the first amendment nevertheless enables a party who receives an illegally intercepted communication but was not involved in the interception to disclose the information.[40]

It is, therefore, crystal clear from the foregoing study that the Supreme Court of United States of America has recognised privacy as a constitutional right. The Judges has found the roots of this right in the First, Fourth, Fifth Amendments in the penumbras of the Bill of Rights and in the Ninth Amendment or in the concept of liberty guaranteed by the first section of Fourteenth Amendment.

---

37. 109 S. Ct. 3040 (1989).
38. 112 S. Ct. 2791 (1992).
39. 478 U.S. 186 (1986).
40. Bartinicki *v.* Vopper, 200 F3d109, 118-29 (3d Cir 1999); Peavy *v.* New Times Inc. 976 F. Supp. 532 (ND Tex 1997); Boehner *v.* McDermott, 191 F3d 463 (DC Cir 1999).

III. RIGHT TO PRIVACY IN UNITED KINGDOM

Though, in England there is no constitutional guarantee of human rights against the State, the ordinary law does recognise that an individual has certain rights, such as the right to freedom of speech, to personal liberty and the like which the State would protect against invasion by other persons, in so far as the ambit of such rights is not abridges by legislation. There is, however, no such recognition of any right to privacy as such, in spite of forceful advocacy by progressive thinkers such as Lord Denning.[41]

In the result, law does not protect any unauauthorised intrusion into a man's privacy or a disclosure of information regarding a man's private affairs, even though it causes injury or suffering to the person wronged, unless he can establish that such invasion constitutes any one of the recognised torts. Thus, it would be actionable if it constitutes—trespass,[42] defamation,[43] nuisance,[44] infringement of copyright,[45] or breach of confidence arising from contract or equitable relation, for which injunction may be available.[46] This follows from the archaic nature of English common law, which is allergic to new causes of action. But, in view of the rapid development of the law in these cases, some progressive judges have come to regard it as a 'fundamental human right', following the provision in Article 8 of the European Convention of Human Rights.[47]

---

41. Denning, What Next in the Law?, 219 (1982); Bridge *et. al.*, Fundamental Rights, 56 (1973).
42. Malone *v.* Commr. of Police (1979) 2 All E.R. 620 (631, 640, 643, 645) Ch.D.
43. Dunlop Co. *v.* Dunlop (1921) 1 A.C. 367 (H.L.); Tolly *v.* J.S. Fry Sons Ltd. 1931 A.C. 333 (H.L.).
44. Kruse *v.* Johnson (1898) 2 Q. B. 91; Hubbard *v.* Pitt (1976) Q.B. 142.
45. William *v.* Settle (1960) 1 W.L.R. 1072.
46. B.S.C. *v.* Granada Television (1981)1All E.R. 417 (455, 460, 482) H.L.; Albert *v.* Strange (1849) 1 H&T.1; Seager *v.* Copydex (1967) 2 All. E.R. 415 (417) C.A.; D. *v.* N.S.P.C.C. (1978) A.C. 171 (H. L.); Science Research Council *v.* Nasse (1980) A.C. 1028 (H.L.); Argyll *v.* Argyll (1967) 1 Ch. 302.
47. Schering *v.* Falkman (1981) 2 All.E.R. 321 (C.A.).

Hence, it is crystal clear that there is no general right to privacy under English common law.[48] This has been recognised as a gap in English law, but this is unlikely to change significantly in the near future[49] as United Kingdom governments have been reluctant to introduce such a right. The Government and the U.K. judiciary does, however, believe that the Human Rights Act, 1998 will allow a common law right of privacy to develop.[50] To do so the court will need to review existing cases such as *Kaye* v. *Robertson* where a tabloid journalist ignored notices prohibiting entry to a room where a well-known actor was recovering from extensive head injuries, and interviewed and photographed him. An interlocutory injunction was sought on behalf of the action to prevent the paper from publishing the article which claimed that Kaye had agreed to give an exclusive interview to the paper. There being no right to privacy under English law, the plaintiff could not maintain an action for breach of privacy. Justice Glidewell said *obiter* in that case that there had been a gross invasion of privacy which highlighted a failure in English law. Other judges have agreed with this conclusion and suggested that a general right of privacy should be recognized.[51] In the absence of such a right of privacy, the claim was based on other rights of action such as libel, malicious falsehood and trespass to the person, in the hope that one or the other would help him protect his privacy. Eventually, he was granted an injunction to restrain publication of the malicious falsehood. The publication of the story and some less objectionable photographs were, however, allowed on the condition that it was not claimed that the plaintiff had given his consent. The remedy was clearly

48. Bernstein *v.* Skyviews and General Ltd. (1978) Q.B. 579.

49. Kaye *v.* Robertson (1991) FSR 62. Such a right was also considered by the Younger Committee in 1972; 'The Report of the Committee on Privacy and Related Matters' chaired by David Calcutt in 1990; 'The Review of Press Self-Regulation' (1993) and 'The Report of the National Heritage Committee on Privacy'.

50. Lord Irvine, Hansard House of Lords, 24 November 1997, Col. 784.

51. SI 1999/2093. For example, Lord Scarman in Morris *v.* Beardmore (1981) AC 446 and Lord Keith in A.G. *v.* Guardian Newspapers (No. 2) 1990 AC 10 at 281-282.

inadequate since it failed to protect the plaintiff from preserving his personal space and from keeping his personal circumstances away from public glare. The court expressed its inability to protect the privacy of the individual and blamed the failure of common law and statute to protect this right. However, no cases currently establish such a right although its development has been envisaged.[52]

Issues of privacy dealt with by English law include privacy of private property; the right to be let alone, the right to communicate privately and the right to respect for private life. As a matter of public policy, any law relating to privacy must strike a proper balance between preserving privacy and confidentiality and preserving freedom of speech and access to public information which are central to a modern democracy. Indeed the Human Rights Act also contains the right of freedom of expression. Some degree of protection of privacy is found in English law which is examined in the following cases.

In the case of *Wilkinson* v. *Downton,*[53] a close affinity is found in respect of some aspects between right to privacy and the law of defamation, it is due to the fact that although libel and slander are primarily concerned with reputation, namely, an interest in relation with others. It also safeguards the individuals in the sense of honour and self respect. But inspite of all that the law of defamation does not confer protection against non-statements which would not constitute wrongful act of defamation but the same would certainly amount to unauthorized exploitation of one's name or reproduction of one's choice of commercial purposes. Similarly, with regard to privacy it was observed as early as the last decade of the nineteenth century that this right should be recognized in favour of the parties in order to preserve their emotional values and to maintain their mental peace and tranquillity. There is no doubt that the law recognizes not only the causation of physical injury rather presently it considers it tortuous to cause emotional disturbance and resulting in mental agony to a person. In this

52. Hellewell *v.* C.C. Derbyshire (1995) 1 WLR 804.
53. (1887) 2 Q.B. 57.

regard it has been observed by Warren and Brandeis in their article as under:

> Recent inventions and business methods call attention to the next step which must be taken for the protection of the person, and for securing to the individual what Judge Cooley calls the 'right to be let alone'. Instantaneous photograph and newspaper enterprise have invaded the sacred precincts of private and domestic life; and numerous mechanical devices threaten to make good the prediction that "what is whispered in the closet shall be proclaimed from the house-tops." For years there has been a feeling that the law must afford some remedy for the unauthorized circulation of portraits of private persons; and the evil of invasion of privacy by the newspapers.[54]

The right to privacy was also protected in the case of *Prince Albert* v. *Strange*[55] wherein the common law rules prohibited not merely the reproduction of etching made by the Prince Albert and Queen Victoria or their private amusement. The etching, which represented members of the Royal family and matters of personal interest, were entrusted to a printer for making impressions. An employee of the printer made unauthorized copies and sold them to the defendant who in turn proposed to exhibit them publicly. Prince Albert succeeding in obtaining injunction to prevent the exhibition. The Court's reasoning was based on both the enforcement of the Prince's property rights as well as the employee's breach of confidence.

The right to privacy was recognised in *Tuck* v. *Priester*[56] wherein the court prevented the defendant who was required to make copies of the picture belonging to the plaintiff by keeping copies of the picture and selling such copies to the customers. The court held that the plaintiff was entitled to get

54. Samuel D. Warren and Louis D. Brandeis, The Right to Privacy, 4, *Harv. Law Review,* 195 (1890).
55. 1 MCN & G 23 (1849): 41 ER 1171 (1849).
56. 19 Q.B.D.

injunction as well as damages for the breach of contract. Similarly, in the case of *Pollard* v. *Photographic Co.*[57] a photographer was restrained from exhibiting a photograph of a lady and selling the copies of the photograph, on the ground that it was breach of contract as well as confidence.

The case law discussed above leads us to form an inference that the right to privacy in some respect is being recognised in the form of breach of confidence. It is mainly due to the fact that one of the parties to the contract tries to take undue advantage of this contractual relationship and tries to have undue benefit without taking into account that undue enrichment on his part resulting into the loss of the other party.

IV. JUDICIAL RECOGNITION OF PRIVACY IN INDIA

There is no guaranteed right to privacy in the Indian Constitution and it could not be found in any other statute. However, interests similar to that are protected both under statutory law, that is, under the Indian Penal Code or the Indian Evidence Act, and under the Constitution of India. These rights have been given different nomenclature in the form of privileged communication, withholding of documents, domestic affairs, matrimonial rights, etc. The Supreme Court has evolved through decisions various rights, interests in all cases similar to privacy, for example right of free enjoyment, right to sleep, right to human dignity, right to have access to justice, right to speedy trial, emanating from the concept of personal liberty in Article 21 of the Constitution. But it does not cover, at one place, all the interests of privacy which need protection. Cases of privacy in India are either related to police surveillance or matrimonial rights and sexual autonomy, etc. To reiterate that in the absence of any express constitutional or statutory provisions recognising the right to privacy, the Indian courts have seized the opportunities whenever they came and tried successfully to bring the privacy right within the purview of fundamental rights. Even though right to privacy is not enumerated as a fundamental

---

57. 40 Ch.D. 345 (1888).

right in our National Charter it has been inferred from Article 21.

There are many aspects of privacy found in the contemporary Indian legal system.[58] There is ample evidence to show that the right to privacy was broadly recognised in India at least half a century before the United States of America conceived the idea in 1890 There are several cases decided by British India Courts which recognised the right to privacy in India. In the year 1855, a case was decided by the Sadar Diwani Adalat of the North-Western Provinces in which the question of a right to privacy arose. The case was *Nuth Mull* v. *Zuka-Oollah Beg*[59] in which Begbie, Smith and Jackson, JJ. held an appeal from the decree of the principal Sadar Amin of Delhi, that the erecting by the defendant of a new house, so that the plaintiff's premises were overlooked from the roof of the new house and their privacy thereby interfered with, gave the plaintiff a cause of action against the defendants.

Thus, in Indian law there are many aspects of privacy which require a thorough examination and an endeavour is made by the author in the following pages:

(i) Privacy as a Customary Right

Indian judicial history indicates that privacy, as a right was recognised as a part of custom from ancient times and received statutory recognition in Section 18 of the Easements

---

58. (i) Section 509 of the Indian Penal Code, 1860 specifically makes it a crime to intrude upon the privacy of a woman; (ii) Sections 26, 164(3) and 165 of the Code of Criminal Procedure, 1898; (iii) Sections 121 to 129 and 132 (privileged communications) and Sections 24 to 29 (confession) of the Indian Evidence Act, 1872; (iv) Section 33 of Special Marriage Act, 1959 and Section 53 of the Indian Divorce Act, 1869; (v) Section 18 of the Indian Easement Act, 1882; and (vi) Under the Indian Telegraphs Act, 1833, no disturbance or interference of communication was allowed. However, in 1972, Parliament amended the Act and authorised certain officers to intercept such massages or stop their transmission if it was considered to be in the interest of the country or the public or for maintenance of friendly relations with foreign states, etc. {vide Section 2 of the Indian Telegraph (Amendment) Act, 1972}.
59. Sr. D.A.N. W.P.R. 1855 at p. 92.

Act, 1882. To reiterate, the first case,[60] which was decided by the Sadar Diwani Adalat in 1855 deals with the question of privacy right. Reference to this case was made by Chief Justice Edge in *Gokal Prasad* v. *Radho*,[61] the court observed:

> Owing to the destruction of records during Mutiny of 1857 I am unable to ascertain whether the existence of custom of a privacy in this part of India had ever been proved or called in question prior to 1855; and owing to the same cause and to the absence from the report of the case of *Nuth Mull* v. *Zuka-Oollah Beg and Kureem Oollah Beg* of information on the point, I am unable to ascertain whether the Judges of the Sadar Diwani Adalat of the North-Western Provinces were in that case following the law as they found it existing, or were deciding the case on facts found.

Justice Edge further observed:

> Having given the best consideration which I can to this question, I am of the opinion that such a right of privacy as that to which I have already referred exists and has existed in these provinces, apparently but usage, or to use another word, by custom and that substantial interface with such a right of privacy . . . affords a good cause of action.[62]

Justice Mahmood concurred with all the views expressed by C.J. Edge. In Gokal Prasad's case Chief Justice Edge referred to a number of cases[63] on privacy. All the

60. *Ibid.*
61. ILR 10 All. 358 (1888) at p. 384.
62. *Id.* at 387.
63. In 1862 in an Allahabad case in Gunga Pershad *v.* Salik Pershad S.D.A.N.W.P. Rep. 1862 Vol. II, 217 Ross and Roberts, JJ. did not suggest any doubt that a right to privacy could exist. In 1867 in a Banaras case in Door Das *v.* Manohaur Das—N.W.P.H.C. Rep. 1867, 269, Morgan C.J. and Spankie, J. Expressly recognised the existence of a right of privacy. In 1868 in Moradabad case in Ram Baksh *v.* Ram Sookh N.W.P.H.C. Rep. 1868, 253. In 1886 Mata Prasad *v.* Bihari Lal, S.A. No. 8 of 1856 (unreported), Straight and Mahmood, JJ. evidently considered that the right of privacy could exist in respect of a house in the city of Allahabad.

above observations in this area go to establish the fact that in a middle of the nineteenth century, privacy in India was a public issue and could be enforced through the courts of law with whatever little contents privacy was known in those days.

The concept of right to privacy was again discussed by Sulaiman, C.J. in *B. Nihal Chand* v. *Bhagwan Dei*[64] case. He interpreted that the right of privacy which is based upon social custom and *purdah* system is quite different from the right of privacy based on natural modesty and human morality. According to him the latter is not confined to any class, creed, colour or race and it is the birth right of a human being and is sacred and should be observed, though the right should not be exercised in an oppressive way. It automatically leads to the conclusion that even if we discard the right to privacy based upon *purdah* system, this right can survive as based upon natural modesty and human morality. Therefore, the recognition of right to privacy based upon natural modesty and human morality seems to be more fair wider in its operation because it is not based upon narrow considerations like class, creed, colour, race, etc. It can be uniformly applied to everybody whether they are subject to *purdah* system or not. Further, natural modesty and human morality not only relates to women but also to men folk. It means in *purdah* system right to privacy was exclusive right to women whereas this based upon modesty and morality is available to everybody.

In *Bholan Lal* v. *Altaf Hussain*,[65] it was held that the customary right of privacy could be claimed only in respect of apartments which might be occupied by females. The court categorically observed that the customary right is usually claimed in respect of houses or apartments generally occupied by females and does not extend to apartments ordinarily used by males. But at the same time the Avadh High Court in Maharaj Kumar Mohammad *Husan Khan* v. *Hafaz Abdul Hague*,[66] observed that the right to privacy would

64. AIR 1935 All. 1002.
65. AIR 1945 All 335.
66. AIR 1945 Avadh 15.

not be carried to oppressive length. But in spite of it, the High Court of Avadh granted injunction to protect the privacy of a Chabutra which was used by women. Further, in *Jivraj* v. *Keshavji*,[67] it was held that the customary right is therefore, available only in respect of premises, which are secluded from observation and cannot be claimed in respect of a garden, a courtyard or a verandah not intended to be so secluded from observation. It was, therefore, held that a person cannot claim privacy in respect of an extensive vacant site, which is used as an open air privy and bath.

However, in *Gulab Chand* v. *Manikchand*,[68] the court was of the opinion that the right based on *purdah* entitled the owner of one property to compel the owner of another to modify the design of architecture of his property so that the women residing in the dominant tenement could be protected. According to the court, the right is based on natural modesty of human morality. The court, however, held that the customary right of privacy can be claimed only in respect of apartments, which are generally occupied and used by females and does not extend to apartments ordinarily used by males, the basis of the customary right of privacy being the *purdah* system, which was confined to the protection of *purdahnasin* women and those parts of a house, which were ordinarily occupied by females. The court ruled that new constructions cannot be made to overlook apartments, which are generally occupied and used by women and have been so occupied and used for a period sufficiently long to establish a right of privacy. It may be that the custom once established does not extend only to women who are in the habit of observing *purdah*, because women of all races are entitled to a certain degree of privacy beginning on the custom of their class and even those who expose their faces in public, expect

67. AIR 1952 Kutch 22; see also Maniklal *v.* Mohanlal, AIR 1920 Bom. 141 in which it was recognised that privacy as a custom existed in Gujarat and its invasion was an actionable wrong. Further, in Bai Govind *v.* Harilal, AIR 1942 Bom. 217, the court held that the right of privacy existed not merely in some parts of Gujarat, but in the whole of Gujarat, Orissa High Court, however, recognized existence of such a right in only those houses, which are utilised by females.
68. AIR 1963 MP 63

to have their privacy respected in their more private apartment.

In *Sri Bhagwan Ramchandraji* v. *Babu Purshottamdas*,[69] the court considered this right in the erstwhile state of Bhopal where *purdah* among Muslims are observed to the extreme and to a great extent amongst the Hindu subjects as a part of their culture. The court was of the opinion that "so far as right of privacy is concerned, that is a valuable right and no person can by his action violate the right of privacy of other persons. In this connection, the custom prevalent amongst a particular community, as also their ways of life may have to be taken into consideration while deciding the right of privacy. No person has a right to act in a manner, which would violate the right of privacy of the other persons, but it is equally true that the right of privacy cannot be extended to an oppressive length." The court, therefore, ruled that "it would have to be decided in each case whether the right of privacy violated is substantial or material or whether the right of privacy claimed by a plaintiff is on an oppressive extent." The court was also of the opinion that the "plaintiffs right of privacy was not violated merely because a person standing in the door or window of the plaintiff's house could be seen through the windows of the defendant's house."

In *Keshav Sahu* v. *Dashrath Sahu*,[70] it was held that the easement right of privacy cannot be stretched to oppressive lengths. It protects only those parts of a house, which are usually utilized by females such as latrines, open bathing places for females, etc. and its extension to cover other parts of the house, which are not generally used by females is not to be countenanced.

Further, in 1863, about 75 years after the decision of Gokul Prasad's case, in another case *Basai* v. *Hasan Raza Khan*,[71] court also discarded the right to privacy based upon *purdah*. It was the case for an injunction against opening of a hole in a wall which would overlook the *Zenana* of the

69. Second Appeal No. 191 of 1959. Decided on 25.11.1960 by P.K. Tare, J. (as he then was).
70. AIR 1961 Orissa 154.
71. AIR 1963 All. 340.

plaintiff. Such relief was denied by Justice Dhavan. It was held in this case that *purdah* has been no part of Hindu religion and civilization.

In *Gulam Mohd.* v. *Aziz Sheikh*,[72] plaintiff owned a two storeyed house which was contiguous to the defendant's three storeyed house. The defendant projected three windows on the third storey of his house and also eavesdrops towards the compound of the plaintiff after the later had removed his dewarkhana and had annexed the land beneath said dewarkhana with his lawn. The defendant constructed the wall of his house towards the compound of the plaintiff and by opening the three windows on the side of the plaintiff's land invaded his right of privacy. The court held that observing *purdah* by the ladies on the plaintiff's house would not entitle him to claim any privacy right. On the other hand one could claim right to privacy as attached to one's property. In this regard court observed:

This brings us to the consideration of the question of the projection of eavesdrops on the compound of the plaintiff as also the throwing of dirt and refuse by the defendants on the former's compound. As already pointed out above, there is evidence to show that eavesdrops project on the compound of the plaintiff and these have been recently constructed. No owner of a house is entitled to project the eavesdrops on the compound of the owner of another house without the latter's permission. No such consent of the plaintiff has been obtained by the defendants. It is also in evidence of the plaintiff's witness which has not been rebutted by the defendant in any way that the defendants throw dust, dirt and refuse on the compound of the plaintiff to the annoyance of the latter. The defendant cannot be permitted to do like that and restrict the plaintiff's right to enjoy his compound without any annoyance or inconvenience to him. No owner of a house can be allowed to cause nuisance to his compound.

According to the court, the right is not based on "natural modesty or human morality." The Jammu and Kashmir High Court has, however, held that this right can be

72. Gulam Hussain *v.* Aziz Sheikh, AIR 1966 JK 49.

claimed on the basis of "natural modesty and human morality" apart from any custom of the locality.

Existence of this right in India recongised the prevalent truth that no one irrespective of the caste and creed likes to countenance his ladies while in their homes busy in the domestic routine of life being watched, observed or stealthily stared by strangers. In *Ganeshilal* v. *Rasul Fathima*,[73] the court noticed that the Indian women have always been jealous of intrusion in their privacy in their homes. It is not always that the women inside their houses are clothed with the attire which they normally use while appearing in public. Therefore, privacy inside the house is a right of every woman and much more so far a woman who has inhibitions by custom or religious notions to appear in public and keep herself in seclusion by observing *purdah*. The court, therefore, held that the defendant had infringed the right of privacy of the plaintiff, who was purdahnashin lady by having religious sanctity has formed the cornerstone of this customary right.

In *Abirchand* v. *Manik Ramnarayan*,[74] the Madhya Pradesh High Court insisted on strict proof of the custom of privacy in the State and refused to judicially recognize it unless proved. However, in *Anupam Kumar* v. *Shantibai*,[75] the court held that the demand for legal protection of the right of privacy would emanate from an emotional disturbance in the user by the member of her family of the property on the ground that they are being watched by the neighbour. It has been shown that this conduct would per se be offensive and calculated to annoy and cause emotional distress. Factors, such as, rights of the family, the *purdah* observed by them, the faith that such intrusion affects the modesty, dignity, or decency of the person living in the neighbourhood may have a bearing on the question. The mere assumption that a view of their house was exposed from the windows would not in itself suffice to establish infringement of this right.

73. AIR 1977 All. 118
74. 1978 MPLJ 204.
75. 1978 (1) MP Weekly Note p. 369.

In *Shri Krishna Murthy* v. *U. Ramlingam,*[76] it was held that a custom in order to be valid should be ancient, certain and reasonable besides being enjoyed openly and peaceably. There is no such thing as a natural right of privacy and such a right can be acquired only as a customary easement. So, where a person alleges that another has infringed his right of privacy, he has to establish that a customary right of privacy existed in the neighbourhood in which he lives and that he is individually or as a member of a particular class entitled to claim such a right on the basis of custom before he can be heard to complain that it is infringed. In other words, the courts insisted on plaintiff showing that the customary right of privacy not only existed in a locality, but also that the plaintiff had been actually enjoying the right.[77]

(ii) Privacy as a Fundamental Right

The Constitution of India does not specifically confer a right to privacy. But such a right can be carried out from different articles of the Constitution. There are several customary rules prevailing in India which protect privacy interest of an individual. Similarly, constitutional provisions have provided a protective umbrella to this right. Besides, constitutional and customary rules several other statutes recognize right to privacy directly or indirectly. The framers of the Constitution of India secured an elaborated scheme of protection of individual liberties under the heading of fundamental right, but strange enough it did not included right to privacy. Under the constitutional law of India, the right to privacy is implicit in the fundamental right to life and liberty guaranteed by Article 21 of the Constitution. This has been interpreted to include the right to be let alone. The constitutional right to privacy flowing from Article 21 must, however, be read together with the constitutional right to publish any matter in public interest, subject to reasonable restrictions. It is in this context the author shall examine various cases involving constitutional issues in the following pages.

76. AIR 1980 Andhra Pradesh 69.

77. Padumadas *v.* Smt. Parwati, AIR 1985 All. 648.

(A) Right to Privacy vis-à-vis Searches and Seizures

The right to privacy *vis-à-vis* police method of crime control is, therefore, subject to police method of surveillance and the crime control to be effective the proviso in the decision of the Supreme Court in Govinda's case should also go. Besides, the Supreme Court in *M.P. Sharma* v. *Satish Chandra*,[78] has frowned upon elevating the right to privacy to the status of fundamental right. The instant case was the first case before the Supreme Court wherein the court had the opportunity of considering the constitutional status of the right to privacy in context of state power of search and seizure. The police on information that Dalmia Group of Companies were engaged in fraudulent practices carried out a search and seized voluminous documents under of validly issued search warrant. The petitioner challenged the very search warrant under Article 32 of the Constitution contending that the search warrants were violative of Articles 20(3) and 19(1)(g) of the Constitution. The search warrant were issued under Section 96 of the Criminal Procedure Code and the court upheld the constitutional validity of this section by observing that:

> . . . the power of search and seizure is in any system of jurisprudence an overriding power of the State for the protection of social security and that power is necessarily regulated by law.

Justice Jagannadhadas speaking for the Court observed:

> When the Constitution-makers have thought fit not to subject such regulation to constitutional limitations by recognition of a fundamental right to privacy, analogous to the American Fourteenth Amendment, we have no justification to import it into a totally different fundamental right by some process of strained construction.[79]

78. AIR 1954 SC 300
79. *Id.* at 306-307.

The above observation of Justice Jagannadhadas can be considered valid in so far a different aspects of this particular case were concerned, but since there is an increasing tendency to life judgments out of their relevant context for citation in other cases having entirely different merits on the part of litigants, there is possibility that such generalization may harm the theme of privacy as a fundamental right. With regard to the concept of privacy, therefore, the author can draw the following conclusions:

(i) The right to privacy can only be read directly but impliedly in Article 21 of the Constitution, and indirectly in Article 19, and (ii) whether they be the safeguards under Section 96 of the Code of Criminal Procedure or under Article 20(3) of the Constitution, they suffer from inherent defect that they do not grant privacy so far as they also remain limited and confined to criminal cases. These safeguards do not extend to parties and witnesses in civil proceedings or proceedings other than criminal. They do not have any utility in other proceedings and it is only Article 21 which can ensure right to privacy.

In *Board of Revenue, Madras* v. *R.S. Jhavar,*[80] the Supreme Court held that the power of search and seizure can be exercised by an administrative authority only when it is conferred on it by a statute. The stipulations made by the statutes in question regulating the power of search and seizure must be observed by the authority concerned, otherwise search and seizure will be declared illegal and nothing recovered at such a search can be made use of an evidence against the individual concerned.

In *Pooran Mal* v. *Director Inspection,*[81] also the Supreme Court itself frowned upon such construction holding that neither by invoking the spirit of our Constitution nor by a strained construction of any of the fundamental rights can we spell out the exclusion of evidence obtained by an illegal search.[82] The Supreme Court thus restricted the right to privacy *vis-à-vis* search and seizure. Further, in the case of

---

80. AIR 1968 SC 59.
81. AIR 1974 SC 348.
82. *Id.* at 361.

Deena v. *Union of India*,[83] the Supreme Court held that as judges they ought not to assume that they are endowed with a divine insight into the needs of society. On the contrary they should heed the warning that history simply proves that judiciary is prone to misconceive the public good by confounding private notions with constitutional requirements.[84]

(B) Right to Privacy and Police Surveillance

The first few cases that presented the Indian Supreme Court with the opportunity to develop law on privacy were cases of police surveillance. The court examined the constitutional validity of legislations that empowered the police to keep a secret watch on the movements of an individual. The first of these cases, *Kharak Singh* v. *State of U.P.*[85] was a challenge to the constitutional validity of Rule 236 of U.P. Police Regulations which permitted surveillance. The petitioner Kharak Singh was challaned in a case of decoity in 1941, but was released under Section 169, Code of Criminal Procedure as there was no evidence against him. On the basis of accusation made against him the police had opened a 'history sheet' which was the personal record of the criminals under surveillance. On many occasions the *chaukidar* and police constables entered his house, knocked and shouted at his door, woke him up during the night and thereby disturbed his sleep. Petitioner urged that his freedom guaranteed by Article 19(1)(d) to move freely throughout the territory of India and also personal liberty guaranteed in Article 21 are infringed.

The sole question for determination before the court was whether 'surveillance' under Chapter XX of the U.P. Police Regulations constitutes an infringement of any of the citizens fundamental rights guaranteed by Part III of the Constitution. The government justified the exercise of the power on the ground that it is exercised only against those

83. AIR 1983 SC 1155.
84. *Id.* at 1188, para 93.
85. AIR 1963 SC 1295.

who are suspected to be proved anti-social habits and tendencies in the interest of the protection of the society from these elements. The issue whether right to privacy is included in Article 21 was also directly raised. N. Rajagopala Ayyangar, J. speaking for the majority of the court held that the right to privacy is not a guaranteed right under the Constitution and therefore, the attempt to restrain the movements of an individual which is merely a manner in which privacy is invaded is not an infringement of any fundamental right guaranteed by Part III of the Constitution. No matter the court showed an awareness to right to privacy when Ayyanger, J. highlighted the lack of provision in the Constitution of India like those of Fourth Amendment of the American Constitution. The Court also conceded that the common law maxim *'et domus sua chique est tussimum refugium'* (every man's house is his castle) lays down the right valued most by civilized men. But at that time the court was not prepared to give wide meaning to the expression 'personal liberty' in Article 21 as to include within it the right to privacy.

This residual and halting approach of the apex court in not giving a constitutional status to the right to privacy provoked Subha Rao, J. to write a forceful dissent. The learned Judge though conceded that the Constitution of India does not expressly declare a right to privacy as a fundamental right, but observed that the said right is an essential ingredient of personal liberty. Subha Rao, J., supporting his views by citing Frankfurter, J. in *Wolf* v. *Colorado*,[86] further observed that every democratic society sanctifies domestic life; it is expected to give him rest, physical happiness, peace of mind and security. In the last resort a person's house, where he lives with his family is his 'castle', it is rampart against encroachment of his liberty. He further observed that the right to personal liberty guaranteed by the Constitution of India encompasses not only the right to move about the country, but also to be free from encroachments on personal liberty and accordingly held that surveillance was unconstitutional.

86. (1948) 338 US 25.

A decade later, the above consideration was judicially recognized in *Gobind* v. *State of M.P.*[87] The three Judge Bench of the Supreme Court unanimously speaking through Mathew, J. revitalized and extended the minority opinion of Subha Rao, J. in Kharak Singh's case asserting the right of privacy of individual citizens. In this case the facts were similar to that of Kharak Singh's case. The police had put the petitioner under surveillance and were making domiciliary visit both by day and night at frequent intervals and secretly picketing his house and watching his movements. The M.P. Police Regulations 855 and 856 authorizing such a surveillance was challenged before the Supreme Court as violating his right to privacy forming a part of freedom of movement guaranteed under Article 19(1)(d) and personal liberty under Article 21 of the Constitution. Mathew, J. cited authority from learned writings[88] and judicial opinion[89] from U.S.A. in order to establish a separate zone of right to privacy under our Constitution and observed:

> There can be no doubt that the makers of our Constitution wanted to ensure conditions favourable to the pursuit of happiness. They certainly realized as

87. AIR 1975 SC 1378.
88. Mathew, J. quoted following passage from Warren and Brandeis famous work on the Right to Privacy: "Once a civilization has made a distinction between the 'outer' and the 'inner' man, between the life of the body, between spiritual and the material, between the sacred and the profane, between the realm of God and the realm of Ceasar, between Church and the State, between rights inherent and inalienable and rights that are in the power of Government to give and take away, between public and private, between society and solitude, it becomes impossible to avoid the idea of privacy by whatever name it may be called—the idea of 'private space' in which man may become and remain himself." 4 *Harv. L. Rev.* 193; The learned Judge also quoted from Bonn, Privacy Freedom and Respect for Person in J. Pennoak and Privacy, *Nomos* XIII, J. Chapman (ed.) 1, 15-16, i.e. "The liberal individualist tradition has stressed, in particular, three personal ideals to each of which corresponds a range of 'private affairs'. The first is ideal of the political free man in a minimally regulated society; the third, the Kantian ideal of the morally autonomous man acting on principles that he accepts are rational."
89. Olmstead *v.* United States, 277 US 438 .

> Brandeis, J. said in his dissent in *Olmstead* v. *United States,* the significance of man's spiritual nature, of his feelings and of his intellect and that only a part of the pain, pleasure, satisfaction of life can be found in material things and therefore, they must be deemed to have conferred upon the individual as against the government a sphere where he should be let alone.[90]

Hence, the Supreme Court for the first time in India located a separate zone of right to privacy in the Constitution of India emanating from the freedom of speech and expression, Article 19(1)(a); freedom of movement, Article 19(1)(d) and right to personal liberty, Article 21. After firmly bestowing a constitutional status on right to privacy, the learned Judge was quick to add that like any other fundamental right, this right is also not absolute, and could be subjected to reasonable restrictions on the basis of compelling State interest. The court allowed domiciliary surveillance of suspected criminals but gave note of caution that such provisions can be held valid only when it is supported by material fact that the suspects are addicted to such crimes as to "involve public peace or security" and they are dangerous to security risks. According to the court "any right to privacy must encompass and protect the personal intimacies of home, the family, marriage, motherhood, procreation and child bearing." It however, felt that the right to privacy in any event will necessarily have to go through a process of case-by-case development and therefore, held that, "even assuming that the right to personal liberty, the right to move freely throughout the territory of India and the freedom of speech create and independent right of privacy as an emanation from them which one can characterize as a fundamental right, we do not think that the right is absolute." The court, therefore, applied 'reasonable restriction test' to judge the vires of the impugned regulations and observed that drastic inroads directly into privacy and indirectly into fundamental rights of a citizen will be made if impugned regulations were to be read widely. The regulations,

---

90. AIR 1975 SC 1378 at 1384.

according to the court, were capable of being read down so that over-flowing expressions remain constitutionally valid. The court, therefore, held "surveillance against persons determined to lead a life of crime was justified for dangerous security risks." The court also held that domiciliary visits and picketing by police, if undertaken for "community security" and not for routine follow up, would also be valid.

There are some who feel that subjecting these police works to clearest case of danger to community security would mean that there would be no crime control as day-to-day programme.[91] They feel that it is wrong to presume that suspects are placed on surveillance on whim or caprice of police officers. They also hold that clearest case of danger to community security does not take into consideration the police role of prevention of crime. The criminal control measures do not allow events to occur or situations to develop right on the eve of actual breach of peace for the police to take action. Any police organization which allows situation to so develop and does not nip the trouble in the bud is guilty of gross dereliction of duty. Such critics therefore, feel that the test of clearest danger to community security should go.

Govind's case is certainly a pace-setter value-judgment because it shows an awareness to the sacred privacy-dignity claims of the people in India by protecting individual autonomy which is the central concern of any system of limited government by plugging all subtle and far-reaching means of invading privacy which makes it possible to be heard in the street what is whispered in the closest.[92]

To what extent may be the citizen's right to be alone and not to be invaded by the duty of the police to prevent crime is the problem which was raised in *Malak Singh* v. *State of P&H.*[93] The following two important questions were raised for consideration of the court: (i) whether a person was

91. See Pannalal Dhar, Right to Privacy, 145 *AIR 1987 Journal Section*.

92. *Id*,. at 1384; F.S. Nariman, The Right To Be Let Alone, XVII, *The Indian Advocate* 79 (1977); See also Malak Singh *v*. State of Punjab, AIR 1981 SC 760.

93. AIR 1981 SC 760.

entitled to be given an opportunity to show cause before his name was included in surveillance register, and (ii) whether in the instant case the appellants, names were included in the register without any grounds for reasonably believing them to be habitual offenders or receivers of stolen property, as required by Rule 23.4 (3)(b) of the Punjab Police Rules.

The vires of the Punjab Police Rules, which provide for maintenance of surveillance register were, however, not challenged by the appellants.

To the first question, the court answered that making any entry in the surveillance register is so utterly administrative that the rules of *audi altram partem* cannot be applied. The application of the rule in this case will defeat the very object of the rule providing for surveillance. Answering the second question, the court seems to have taken the view that it may not be necessary to supply the grounds of belief to the persons whose names are entered in the surveillance register. It may become necessary in some cases that there are no justification to entertain such belief. The court rejected the appeals making certain observations regarding the mode of surveillance. The court observed:

But all this does not mean that the police have a licence to enter the names of whoever they like (dislike) in the surveillance register, nor can surveillance be such as to squeeze the fundamental freedom guaranteed to all citizens or to obstruct the free exercise and enjoyment of those freedoms, nor can the surveillance so intrude as to offend the dignity of the individual. Surveillance of persons who do not fall within the categories mentioned in Rule 23.4 or for reasons unconnected with the prevention of crime of excessive surveillance falling beyond the limits prescribed by the rules, will entitle a citizen to the court's protection which the court will not hesitate to give. The very rules which prescribe the conditions for making entries in the surveillance register and the mode of surveillance appear to recognize the condition and care with which the police officers are required to proceed . . . Surveillance, therefore, has to be unobstrusive and within bounds . . . Organized crime cannot be successfully fought without close watch of suspect. But surveillance may be intrusive and it may so seriously encroach on the privacy of a citizen as to infringe his fundamental rights to personal liberty guaranteed by Article 21 of the Constitution and the freedom of movement guaranteed by Article 19(1)(d).[94]

Therefore, surveillance does not mean a licence to the police authorities to interfere with personal liberty. The power of the police officer to enter one's name in surveillance register must be based on reasonable grounds with justifications enumerated and recorded and in suitable cases this power is subjected to judicial scrutiny. Interference with privacy in accordance with law is permissible which also means that the right to privacy, is recognised by law.

Thus, the cases discussed above enable the author to conclude that the Supreme Court has to review and consider its decisional law to hold that privacy is a part of personal liberty read with freedom of movement and that law trenching on privacy should be reasonable and should lay down a fair procedure. The new constitutionalism that the court gave in recent years justifies such a course of action. There are scholars who subscribe to this view[95] and try to read privacy as a fundamental right in our Constitution.

(C) Right to Privacy and Sexual Autonomy of Women

Apart from statutory provisions, the judiciary also protected the right to privacy of rape victims by pronouncing a catena of landmark judgments. The first case which came before the court, in which the right of privacy even of a prostitute was recognised as an important right in *re-Ratanmala*.[96] The behaviour of a police officer who, while raiding a brothel, proceeded to the bed room of a girl, and pushed open the door even without the civility of a knock to prepare her for intrusion, was accordingly held legally inexcusable. The court further held that there can be no doubt

94. *Id.* at 763-764.

95. For more details see, Govind Mishra, Privacy: A Fundamental Right Under the Indian Constitution, *Delhi Law Rev.* 134, 1979-82; Pannalal Dhar, Right to Privacy, 145 *AIR 1987 Journal Section*; Anirudh Prasad, New Dimensions of the Right to Privacy Under the Indian Constitution, XIV *JCPS* 752 (July-September 1980).

96. AIR 1962 Mad. 31.

that such conduct implies an outrage on the modesty of the girl. Justice Anantanarayanan further reiterated that the modesty of a prostitute is entitled to equal protection, with that of any other woman. The technique of such raids must be totally altered; otherwise grave abuses of the law might enter into the very attempt to enforce the law.[97]

Similarly, in *State of Maharashtra* v. *Madhukar Narayan Mardikar*,[98] the Supreme Court of India held that even a woman of easy virtue is entitled to privacy and no one can invade her privacy and when one likes. So also it is not open to any and every person to violate her person as and when he wishes. She is entitled to protect her person if there is an attempt to violate it against her wish. She is equally entitled to the protection of law. Therefore, merely because she is a woman of easy virtue, her evidence cannot be thrown overboard. At the most the officer called upon to evaluate her evidence would be required to administer caution up to himself before accepting her evidence.

In the instant case, the respondent, Madhukar Narayan Mardikar (Police Inspector) visited the house of one Banubai in uniform and demanded to have sexual intercourse with her. On her refusing, he tried to have her by force. She resisted his attempt and raised a hue and cry. When he was prosecuted he told the court that she was a lady of easy virtue and therefore, her evidence was not to be relied. Thus, the court rejected the argument of the respondent and held him liable for violating her right to privacy under Article 21 of the Constitution.[99]

Further, the Supreme Court in *State of Punjab* v. *Gurmit Singh*,[100] held that a woman of easy virtue also could not be raped by a person for that reason. The court observed that "even if the prosecutrix, in a given case, has been promiscuous in her sexual behaviour earlier, she has a right to refuse to submit herself to sexual intercourse to anyone because she is not a vulnerable object or prey for being

97. *Id.* at 35.
98. AIR 1991 SC 207.
99. *Ibid.*, para 8.
100. AIR 1996 SC 1393

sexually assaulted by anyone and everyone."[101] Similarly, in the *State of Andhra Pradesh* v. *Gangula Satya Murthy*,[102] a girl of sixteen years was raped and throttled to death. In this case it was held that even if the court formed an opinion, from the absence of hymen that the victim has sexual intercourse prior to the time when she was subjected to rape by the appellant she had every right to refuse to submit herself to sexual intercourse by the appellant, as she certainly was not a vulnerable object or prey for being sexually assaulted by anyone.[103]

(D) Right to Privacy vis-à-vis Natural Modesty and Morality

In order to protect the privacy of women intruding upon the privacy of woman is made as an offence and is punishable under Section 509 of the Indian Penal Code. The criminal action is envisaged by Section 509 of the Indian Penal Code for violating the privacy of women. Where the offence charged consists of the accused's intrusion upon the privacy of a woman, it must show that the intrusion was made with intent to insult the modesty of any woman.[104] The accused, a stranger, though a neighbour, entered at night into the room where four women were sleeping and on an alarm being given and attempt made to capture him, the accused escaped. It was held that the intrusion upon the privacy was sufficient to bring it within the scope of this section.[105]

In *Neera Mathur* v. *Life Insurance Corporation of India*,[106] the petitioner was appointed in respondent's service and was on probation. She was pregnant at the time and took maternity leave for three months. She was discharged subsequently from service. It was alleged that she gave false declaration regarding the last menstruation period and thereby suppressed the fact of pregnancy. The Supreme Court

---

101. *Id.* at 1403, para 15.
102. AIR 1997 SC 1588.
103. *Id.* at 1593, para 25.
104. Phaiz Mohammed 5 *Bom. L.R* 502, Hopper 1192 reported in Law of Crimes and Criminology, R.P. Kathuria, Vol. 3, p. 4035 (2000).
105. 1895 ILR 22 Cal. 994.
106. AIR 1992 SC 392.

observed:

> The real mischief though unintended is about the nature of the declaration required from a lady candidate. The particulars to be furnished under columns (iii) to (viii) in the declaration are indeed embarrassing if not humiliating. The modesty and self-respect may perhaps preclude the disclosure of such personal problems like whether her menstrual period is regular or painless, the number of conceptions taken place; how many have gone full terms, etc. The Corporation would do well to delete such columns in the declaration.

Hence, any querry with respect to above nature would adversely affect the modesty and self-respect and would attract the right to privacy of a woman.

In *Nihal Chand* v. *Bhagwan Dei*,[107] the Allahabad High Court while emphasizing the importance of right to privacy, observed that the right to privacy is based on natural modesty and human morality. It is not confined to any class, creed, colour and is very sacred.

(E) Right to Privacy vis-à-vis Freedom of Press

Freedom of Press has been acclaimed as the cornerstone of modern democratic State. It is often described as fourth estate.[108] The Press enjoys a prestigious position in democratic countries where constitutions guarantee freedom or press. The freedom, like all other liberties, cannot be absolute and is subject to restrictions in public interest. Privacy of individual is a right to be protected even from the gaze of press. Invasion of privacy may arise when information about private affairs of a person is published by newspaper.[109] James Michael elucidates the difference between privacy and defamation thus:

---

107. AIR 1935 All 1002.
108. Himachal Pradesh *v.* Umed Ram, AIR 1986 SC 847
109. P. Rathinam *v.* Union of India, AIR 1984 SC 1844.

> Some complaints about invasion of privacy by the press are about the techniques used in attempting to get information, others are about the publication of personal information, and many are about both. Concern about invasions of privacy by the press are often mixed with concern about defamation, and it is perhaps worthwhile to recall the difference. Invasion of privacy, in the sense of informational privacy, by the press is, in Prosser's terms, the disclosure of embarrassing private facts. Defamation is the publication of damaging information which is false. Without going into details about the burden of proving truth or not, privacy is about the true information, defamation about false.[110]

Is there a right to publish true or unwelcome or damaging information about the people? Geoffrey Marshall states:[111] "anybody asked to answer this question in a particular case would want to know and weigh four considerations assuming the information to be true. They are, (a) was the information acquired properly or innocently, or by wrongful means; (b) was there any consent to disclosure or would any be implied; (c) was the activity described exposed itself innocent or disreputable; and (d) was there any actual damage caused to just annoyance? These questions must arise in cases of unwarranted disclosure of information. It is obvious that they necessitate the making of choice between different values. The law cannot, by itself, decide them finally by legal principles alone.[112] It is to be borne in mind that "free speech is sabotaged from within by fouling the fountains of information."[113] When the court or legislatures expand the protection given to privacy they may

110. James Michael, "Privacy" in Individual Rights and Law In Britain in Christopher Mc Crudden and Gerals Chambers (ed.), p. 3.

111. P.M. Bakshi, Defamation and Privacy in Law of Defamation: Some Aspects 20 (1986) quoted from Geoffrey Marshall, The Right to Privacy—A Sceptical View, *MC Gill L.J.*, p. 252.

112. *Ibid.*

113. V.R. Krishna Iyer, The Right to Know is Fundamental in Salvaging Democracy, 119 (1990).

limit the media's freedom to report and the public's right to know.[114]

The protection against breach of privacy and protection against defamation cover two different areas of the people's life.[115] The law of defamation protects the reputation of an individual. The law of privacy protects the feeling of an individual. The same statement may injure a person's reputation and also hurt his feelings. At the same time one can also conceive statements that injure one's feelings,[116] without causing any harm to reputation where the statement is true. In such situations no action for defamation would lie, because the information that is disclosed is merely embarrassing, not false.[117] Therefore, there is a need to evolve a new cause of action that is, the tort of privacy.

The press and right to privacy came for the first time under notice in *R. Rajagopal* v. *State of Tamil Nadu*.[118] In this case the right of privacy of a condemned prisoner was in issue. One Auto Shankar, a condemned prisoner, wrote his autobiography will confined in jail and handed it over to his wife for being delivered to an advocate to ensure its publication in a certain magazine edited, printed and published by the petitioner. This autobiography allegedly set out close nexus between the prisoner and several officers including those belonging to IAS and IPS some of whom were indeed his partners in several crimes. The publication of his autobiography was restrained in more than one manner. It was on these facts that the petitioner challenged the restrictions imposed on the publication before the Supreme Court. The Court held that right to privacy is implicit in right to life and personal liberty guaranteed to the citizens of this country by Article 21. It is a right to be let alone. A citizen as a right to safeguard the privacy of his own, his family,

114. William A. Hachten, The Supreme Court on Freedom of the Press: Decisions and Dissents, 166 (1970).

115. *Supra* n. 111.

116. Chidananda Reddy, Piety of Privacy After Death, *The Lawyers Collective*, 12 (August 1991).

117. *Supra* n. 111 at 21.

118. AIR 1995 SC 264: JT 1994 (6) SC 514.

marriage, procreation, motherhood, child bearing and education among other matters. None can publish anything concerning the above matters without his consent whether truthful or otherwise and whether laudatory or critical. If he does so, he would be violating the right to privacy of the person concerned and would be liable in an action for damages. But public men like officials stand on a different footing and the remedy is not available with respect to criticism pertaining to discharge of their public duties expecting in the case of reckless disregard for truth.

It is a fact that government and is instrumentalities have a lot of private or confidential information which in the event of getting published may infringe the privacy and adversely affect the reputation of individuals or betray the trade secrets of business. Rajagopal craves an exception to any information gathered from official records. The result will be that the individual has to apprehend the publication of such information by private individual including the Press other than the government. This is a serious situation and the law cannot wash its hands by saying that only collector[119] or information is liable and not others who make use of it subsequently with tacit permission of the collector or even steals it.

To keep the Press as a strong medium that can safeguard public interest it must observe self-censorship with a set of norms based on sound principles that due regard to both freedom of expression and right to privacy. In this regard, Press Council can play an effective role by giving proper direction to the print media. Professor Rajeev Dhavan opines that the court is giving recognition to the institutional right of press to act as a watchdog on the effective governance of administration.[120] According to Soli J. Sorabjee, the major premise of the ruling in R. Rajagopal is that uninhabited discussion of public affairs is essential in a

119. If the government as the collector of information can escape liability for subsequent publication by another, private individuals can also raise such a defence.

120. As cited in Rakesh Bhatnagar, An Extraordinary Bold Verdict, *Times of India*, 16 (Oct. 15, 1995).

democracy and the possibility of error is inevitable. If media were to be held liable for every error inaccuracy, absent malice or reckless disregard for truth, the consequent 'chilling effect' would generate self-censorship in media about matters of public concern.[121] In case the publication has no relation to official conduct and is defamatory, the public official has the same remedy available to an ordinary individual.

(F) Telephone-Tapping and Right to Privacy

Interception of telephonic communication or wire tapping also pose a serious danger to the right of privacy. In the United States of America the court refused to accept the evidence obtained by wire tapping. The Congress passed the Federal Communication Act, 1934, which forbade a person to intercept any communication and to disclose any such intercepted communication to any person, without authorization by the sender.

Individuals, politicians, professionals, officials and others talk a lot in private over telephone. It is gross invasion if everything that it talked on telephone by them is tapped and published in public forums. Except for the reasons of public safety or security of the nation or for the detection and prevention of serious crimes, a State cannot have any lawful excuse to invade human privacy. Without any reasonable cause of justification neither the State nor any private individual can legally claim to have any right to intercept telephonic communication of any person. In a democratic country, telephone-tapping without any lawful excuse at the behest of the government, Central or State, is far more deplorable than telephonic-tapping by a private individual. A man feels loss of his privacy, i.e. loss of his personal liberty when he comes to know that his telephonic talk is being tapped by somebody. Every individual should have a free private zone. His ideas, thoughts, beliefs, views, etc. should be inviolable. There are certain provisions in different legislations which permits interception of any communication sent by telegraph or any postal article on the occurrence of

121. Soli J. Sorabjee, Privacy and Defamation: SC Defines Parameters, *Indian Express*, 8 (November 12, 1994).

any public emergency or in the interest of the public safety or tranquillity.[122] The Law Commission has observed in its Forty-second Report, 1971: "As the law on the subject is still rudimentary even in advanced countries, we would not advice comprehensive legislation to deal with all aspects of invasion of privacy. It is better to make a beginning with those invasions which may amount to what is known as eavesdropping and unauthorized publication of photographs and leave the rest to be considered later on in the light of the experience gained and legislation introduced."

Telephonic-tapping is a serious invasion of the right to privacy. One can tap the telephone lines and listen to others talking. Some persons may use it for their personal pleasure, some for commercial gains and we find the Government using it on the pretext of surveillance. In all these instances, right to privacy was the victim. There is however, no express guarantee against the telephone-tapping under the Constitution of India.

In *Yusuf Ali Ismail Nagree* v. *State of Maharashtra*,[123] the court was faced with the question whether tapping of the appellant's conversation without his knowledge offended his right under Article 21. In this case, the police inspector tapped the conversation between Nagree and Sheikh, a municipal clerk whom Nagree wanted to bribe. Nagree had no knowledge of this. Nagree challenged the admissibility of such evidence. The court evolved two directions for guidance in admitting such evidence. First, the court will find out whether it is genuine and free from tampering or mutilations. Secondly, the court may also secure scrupulous conduct and behaviour on behalf of the police. The reason is that the police officer is more likely to behave properly if improperly obtained evidence is to be viewed with care and caution by the judge. In every case the position of the accused, the nature of investigation and the gravity of the offence must be judged in the light of material facts and the surrounding circumstances.

---

122. See Section 5(2) of the Indian Telegraph Act, 1885; Section 2(1) and (2) of Indian Post Office Act, 1898.

123. AIR 1973 SC 157.

The court further rejected the appellant's arguments that it violated procedures established by law and the appellant was incriminated. Conversation was voluntary and without any compulsion. The attaching of tape recording machine was known to the appellant, that fact does not render the evidence inadmissible. The tape was only a mechanical contrivance to play the role of eavesdropper. The court also rejected the appellant's argument that his right to privacy was violated. It said Article 21 contemplates procedure established by law with regard to deprivation of life or personal liberty. The telephonic conversation of an innocent citizen would be protected by courts against wrongful or highhanded interference by tapping the conversation. The protection is not for a guilty citizen against the efforts of police to vindicate the law and prevent corruption in public servants. It must not be understood that the courts would tolerate safeguards for the protection of the citizen to be imperiled by permitting the police to proceed by unlawful or irregular methods. In the present case, no unlawful or irregular method was adopted in obtaining the tape-recording conversation.

In *Rama Reddy* v. *V.V. Giri*,[124] the Court held that the tape-recording conversation is admissible provided first the conversation is relevant to the matter in issue, secondly, there is identification of voice, thirdly, the accuracy of the tape recorded conversation is proved by eliminating the possibility of erasing the tape recorded. Further, in *Megraj Patodia* v. *R.K. Birla*,[125] the Supreme Court clearly stated that a document which was procured by improper or even illegal means could not bar its admissibility provided its relevance and genuineness were proved.

The challenge to telephone-tapping under Article 21 was considered in *R.M. Malkani* v. *State of Maharashtra*.[126] In this case, the telephonic conversation between two parties was tape-recorded by the police with the consent of one of the parties. The Supreme Court observed that the

124. AIR 1968 SC 147.
125. (1971) 1 S.C.R. 399.
126. AIR 1971 SC 1295.

conversation could be used in evidence as it was voluntary and there was no duress or compulsion to extract the same. The fact that the tape-recording instrument was attached without appellant's knowledge does not make the conversation inadmissible against him. The Supreme Court further observed that it would not tolerate safeguards for the protection of citizen to be imperilled by permitting the police to proceed by unlawful or irregular methods. At the same time the court held that even stolen evidence was admissible if it was not tainted by an inadmissible confess of guilt.

In *Peoples Union for Civil Liberties* v. *Union of India*,[127] the Supreme Court examined in detail the challenge to the right to privacy by way of telephone-tapping. The court looked into the constitutional validity of Section 5(2) of the Indian Telegraph Act, 1885, by virtue of which the government has tapped some telephonic conversations. After holding that privacy is an essential ingredient of personal liberty, Kuldeep Singh, J. came to the conclusion that telephone tapping is a serious invasion of an individual's privacy. He observed that with the growth of highly sophisticated communication technology, the right to hold telephone conversation in the privacy of one's home or office without interference, is increasingly susceptible to abuse. It was held that telephone-tapping, a form of "technological eavesdropping" infringed the right to privacy. Finding that the Government had failed to lay down a proper procedure under Section 7(2)(b) of the Act to ensure procedural safeguards against the misuse of the power under Section 5(2), the court prescribed stringent measures to protect the individual's privacy to the extent possible.

Taking cue from the earlier decisions, in this public interest litigation, the Supreme Court had no hesitation in holding that right to privacy is part of the right to 'life and personal liberty' enshrined in Article 21 of the Constitution and the said right cannot be curtailed, except according to procedure established by law.[128] In this case, the constitutional validity of "tapping of politician's phones" by the Central

127. AIR 1997 SC 568.
128. *Id.* at 574.

Bureau of Investigation was challenged as it amounts to violation of right to privacy. It was contended that right to privacy is a fundamental right guaranteed under Article 19(1) and Article 21 of the Constitution of India. The Supreme Court after reviewing the earlier cases in this field held that "we have, therefore, no hesitation in holding that right to privacy is a part of the right to life and personal liberty enshrined under Article 21 of the Constitution. Once the facts in a given case constitute a right to privacy Article 21 is attracted. The said right cannot be curtailed "except according to procedure established by law."[129] It may thus be summed up that in India constitutional provisions of telephonic interception lack the clarity and depth of its American counterpart. This can be attributed to three main reasons, viz. firstly, the courts have never defined the parameters of right to privacy with regard to electronic interception in the way American courts have done in the Katz case. Telephonic conversation has been taken out from the overall context of electronic snooping and dealt with. But even there the exact right to privacy *vis-à-vis* wiretap has been dealt in a superficial manner. Secondly, the telephonic interception has been treated as infringement of Article 19(1)(a). This prevents wiretap for any other purpose than those enumerated in Article 19(2) causing hindrance to law enforcement. Lastly, in India wiretap does not require a judicial warrant, nor is there any exclusionary rule of evidence. This leaves the aggrieved person without a remedy in case a violation of this right occurs. The law of wiretap in India is therefore, satisfactory neither from the point of view of the law enforcement nor the accused. One can only hope that the legislature and the courts take notice of this.

(G) Privacy and Restitution of Conjugal Rights

The conjugal right that is, the right of the husband or the wife to the society of other is not the creature of statute. But it is inherent in the very institution of marriage itself. The Law Commission of India in its 71st Report stated that the essence of marriage is a sharing of common life, a sharing of

129. *Ibid.*

all the happiness that life has to offer and all the miseries that has to be faced in life, an experience of the joy that comes from enjoying the common things of the matter and of the spirit and from showering love and affection of one's offsprings. The remedy of restitution of conjugal rights and its origin in the ecclesiastical law of England. But now it has been abolished in England by the Matrimonial Proceeding Act, 1970. In India, it was applied as a part of justice, equity and good conscience. However, Hindu Marriage Act, 1955, enacted it as statutory remedy.

Fundamental rights jurisprudence witnessed another development in the first half of 1980s wherein constitutionality of Section 9 of the Hindu Marriage Act, 1955 providing for restitution of conjugal rights was challenged on the ground of violation of Article 21 in *T. Sareetha* v. *T. Venkata Subbaiah*.[130] The court declared Section 9 as *ultra vires* and violative of Articles 14 and 21 of the Constitution. Chaudhary, J. while examining restitution of conjugal rights in relation to right to personal liberty opined:

> A decree of restitution of conjugal rights constitutes the grossest form of violation of an individual's right to privacy. It denies women her choice whether, when and how, her body is to become the vehicle for the procreation of another human being.

Justice Chaudhary has no hesitation in characterizing the remedy of restitution of conjugal rights as a savage and barbarous remedy, violating the right to privacy and human dignity guaranteed by Article 21 of our Constitution. The court was prepared to accord zones of privacy to each spouse even in the marital relationship. It was observed:

> . . . a court decree enforcing restitution of conjugal right constitutes the starkest form of government invasion of personal identity and individual's zone of intimate decisions. The victim is stripped of its control over the various parts of its body subjected to the

130. AIR 1983 AP 356.

> humiliating sexual molestation accompanied by a forcible loss of the precious right to decide when if at all her body should be allowed to be used to give birth to another human being. Clearly the victim loses its autonomy of control over intimacies of personal identity. Above all, the decree for restitution of conjugal rights takes the unwilling victims body of soulless and a joyless vehicle for bringing into existence another human being. In other words, pregnancy would be foisted on her by the State and against her will. There can therefore be little doubt that such a law violates the right to privacy and human dignity guaranteed by and contained in Article 21 of our Constitution.[131]

The issue again cropped up in *Harvinder Kaur* v. *Harminder Singh*.[132] Justice Avadh Bihari Rohtagi of Delhi High Court has expressed a contrary view and upheld the validity of Section 9 of the Hindu Marriage Act. The court opined that though sex constitutes an important element in marriage but it does not constitute the sole object. Court opposed the introduction of constitutional principles in the privacy of a home. The court observed that in the privacy of a home Articles 14 and 21 have no place whatsoever, matrimonial relations are rather based on love, affection, care and like considerations.

The Supreme Court finally set the controversy at rest in *Saroj Rani* v. *Sudarshan Kumar*[133] by approving the judgment of Delhi High Court in Harvinder Kaur's case. Supreme Court ruled that Section 9 serves social purpose as an aid to the preservation of marriage and therefore, satisfies Articles 14 and 21.

(H) Right to Privacy of AIDS Infected People

In the present era AIDS has posed a new problem before courts regarding conjugal rights, right to privacy and

131. *Id.* at 370.
132. AIR 1984 Delhi 66.
133. AIR 1984 S 1526

right to information. The much appreciative step towards the protection of right to privacy of HIV infected persons is the direction of the court to suppress the identity of the AIDS patients in proceedings before the court because after disclosure of name they suffer from several embarrassments including bad publicity and consequential discriminations in every walk of life. The appeal for suppression of identity before court was made in the case of *MX of Bombay Indian Inhabitant* v. *M/S ZY*.[134] In this case, the Division Bench passed an order permitting the petitioner to prosecute by suppressing the identity and therefore, to be named as "Mr. MX" and also directed the respondent corporation to be named as "ZY". The learned counsels for the respondent addressed the court on the aspect of requirement of non-disclosure of identity of the petitioner in such matters and submitted that in view of the stigma which is attached to HIV infection, the persons infected with HIV may be reluctant to approach the court of law with fear that the disclosure of his HIV status may expose him to social astracisation and also discrimination in every walk of life. Hence, the apex court has categorically observed and permitted the suppression of density of the medically acquired HIV or AIDS cases. This decision protected privacy from the society. Another dimension or right to privacy, i.e. right to privacy of AIDS infected people has received judicial attention during the recent times. The question here arises is whether AIDS infected people have a right to privacy, i.e. whether they have right that their HIV should be kept secret. The question has acquired immense importance in the present time. It will not be an exaggeration to say that the whole community is sitting on AIDS bomb ready to explode anytime.[135] In view of this, it is pertinent to examine the right to privacy of AIDS infected people.

In *Mr. 'X'* v. *Hospital 'Z'*,[136] the Supreme Court was seized on an issue concerning an AIDS patient and his right

---

134. AIR 1997 Bom 406.

135. Sureder Kumar Singh, Human Rights of AIDS Infected People *vis-à-vis* Healthy People, AIR Journal Section 199 (2003).

136. AIR 1999 SC 495.

to privacy and confidentiality regarding his medical condition, and right of the lady to whom he was engaged to lead a healthy life. In this case, a person was found to be HIV positive and the information was disseminated by the doctor to his prospective wife. The person preferred a suit against the doctor for breach of right to privacy and damages as well.

Doctor-patient relationship though basically commercial is professionally a matter of confidence and therefore, doctors are normally and ethically bound to maintain confidentiality. In such a situation public disclosure of even true private facts may amount to an invasion of the "right to privacy" which may sometimes lead to clash of one person's "right to be let alone" which another person's "right to be informed." Disclosure of even true private facts has a tendency to disturb a person's tranquillity. It may generate many complexes in him and may even lead to psychological problems. He may, thereafter, have a disturbed life all through. In the force of these potentialities the right of privacy is an essential component of right envisaged by the Article 21. The right, however, is not absolute and may be lawfully restricted for the prevention of crime, disorder, or protection of health or morals or protection of rights and freedom of others. As such, when the patient was found to be HIV positive, its disclosure by the doctor would be violative of either the rule of confidentiality or the patient's right to privacy. However, there is another face of the coin also. Its disclosure would have saved the lady with whom the patient was likely to be married otherwise she too would have been infected with the dreadful disease if marriage had taken place and consummated. In such a situation public disclosure of even true private facts may amount to an invasion of the right to privacy which may sometimes lead to the clash of one person's right to be informed. The right is not absolute and may be lawfully restricted for the prevention of crime, disorder or rights and freedom of others.

It is to be noted that the court in this case has not just laid down that the right to life includes right to privacy. The other important part of the principle is that the "Right to life" includes right to healthy life. It has further laid down that where there is a clash of two fundamental rights, as in the instant case, namely the appellant's right to lead a healthy life which is her fundamental right under Article 21, the right which would advance the public morality or public interest, would alone be enforced through the process of court, for the reason that moral considerations cannot be kept at bay.[137] The Supreme Court was of the opinion that the life of the fiancee would be endangered by her marriage and consequent conjugal relations with the AIDS victim, and consequently she was entitled to information regarding the medical condition of the man she was to marry.

In a recent case of *Sharda* v. *Dharmpal,*[138] the Supreme Court was confronted with the issue whether subjecting a person to a medical test be in violation of Article 21 of the Constitution. The court outlined the concept of the law of privacy in India and was of the opinion that the right to privacy in terms of Article 21 of the Constitution is not an absolute right. The Supreme Court has given a potentially contrary view from the existing policies while answering the question whether a party to the divorce can be compelled to undergo a medical examination, in order to ascertain whether she is of unsound mind. It is said to be potentially contrary, because, in the light of the facts of the case, right of a HIV positive person was not directly in issue, but can be used to ascertain their rights. because various statements and judgments regarding the right of the persons living with HIV/AIDS are relied on to come to a conclusion regarding the issues of the present case. In this case, one of the issues was whether subjecting a person to a medical test be in violation of Article 21 of the Constitution. While answering this question, the court relied on various decisions while relying on *M. Vijaya* v. *Chairman and Managing Director, S.C.C. Ltd.*[139] case the court highlighted those parts of the judgment which say that the power of the State to ensure public health to all, will prevail over the right to privacy of the suspected

137. *Id.* at 503.

138. (2003) 4 SCC 493, per V.N. Khare, C.J. and S.B. Sinha and Dr. A.R. Lakshmanan, JJ.

139. AIR 2001 Andhra Pradesh 502.

of HIV not to submit himself forcibly for medical examination. The other part of the judgments the court relied on was that under the Immoral Traffic (Prevention) Act, the sex workers can be compelled to undergo HIV/AIDS test and that under Sections 269 and 270 of the Indian Penal Code, a person can be punished for negligent act of spreading infectious diseases, and that in these circumstances Article 20(3) of the Constitution will not be violated. The Court thus came to the conclusion that a Matrimonial Court has the power to order a person to undergo medical test, and that passing of such an order by the court would not be in violation of the right to personal liberty under Article 21 of the Constitution of India.

It is heartening to note that recently in *"Mr. X"* v. *"Hospital Z"*,[140] the apex court has partly overruled the earlier decision. The petitioner raised the question whether a person suffering from HIV positive contracting marriage with a willing partner after disclosing the factum of disease to that partner would be committing an offence within the meaning of Sections 269 and 270 of the Indian Penal Code. In other words, the clarification was sought by the petitioner that there was no bar for marriage, if the healthy spouse consented to marry after knowledge of the HIV positive status to the other spouse. The court held that the earlier decision of the court was based on the facts of the case that it was open to the hospital to reveal such information to persons related to the girl whom he intended to marry and she had a right to know about the HIV positive status of the appellant. However, further observations of the court to declare in general as to whether such persons were entitled to be married or not, or if they married they would commit an offence, or whether right to marry was suspended during the period of illness, were unnecessary and uncalled for. The development is being seen as an affirmation by the highest court in the country of rights based response to HIV/AIDS.

(l) Right to Abortion vis-à-vis Female Foeticide

Abortion has become a very controversial and

---

140. AIR 2003 SC 664.

debatable issue in the modern world of today since the recent movement towards liberalization of abortion in the western countries. Before the recent movement towards liberalization of abortion in the United States of America and England, abortion in most countries declared illegal unless necessary to preserve the life of the mother. In 1867, England and some American States liberalized their statutes to allow abortion when pregnancy is caused by rape, or to prevent the birth of a deformed child.[141] In 1973, the United States Supreme Court in *Roe* v. *Wade*[142] and *Doe* v. *Balton*[143] ruled that a woman's decision to terminate her pregnancy, at least until the foetus is viable, in a personal matter protected from State interference by her constitutional right to privacy. In effect, these two decisions legalized abortion in the United States of America,

In 1971, India liberalized its abortion law with the enactment of the Medical Termination of Pregnancy Act. With the enactment of this Act, the features of Indian abortion law have changed. In fact, the MTP Act, has been modelled on English Abortion Act of 1967. It provides for termination of pregnancy by a registered practitioner acting in good faith under the following circumstances:

(a) where the continuance of the pregnancy would involve a risk to the life of the pregnant woman or of grave injury to her physical and mental health;
(b) where there is a substantial risk that if the child was born, it would suffer from such physical or mental abnormalities as to be seriously handicapped;
(c) where the pregnancy results from rape; and
(d) where the pregnancy has occurred as a result of the failure of a contraceptive device or method (in this case, the anguish caused by such unwanted pregnancy may be presumed to constitute a grave threat to mental health of the pregnant woman).

---

141. James George, The Evolving Law of Abortion, 23 *Case W. Res. L. Rev.* 708; 732-49 (1972); Mohr James, Abortion in America: The Origin and Evolution of National Policy, (1978).
142. 410 US 113 (1973).
143. 410 US 179 (1973).

The Constitution of India further liberalised the Act by an Amendment in 1975. A woman is now competent to terminate pregnancy without the consent of even her husband. Only the consent of pregnant woman is mandatory.[144]

The Constitution of India guarantees right to life and personal liberty to all which implies that even the unborn child has the right to life under Article 21. Females however, argue that the choice to rear and bear children or not belongs to the woman concerned if Article 21 as to have any meaning for them. The State has enacted Pre-Natal Diagnostic Techniques (Regulations and Prevention of Misuse) Act, 1994. The Act has been strictly enforced in order to stop female foeticide. The Act has made registration of Ultra Sound and other sex diagnostic techniques compulsory and the prenatal sex determination has been made a punishable offence. In our patrilineal society, desire to have son has created this complex problem forcing the females to kill the female foetus. Hence, it is submitted that once the woman enters the marriage relation, her right to privacy must be seen in the context of family life. Therefore, the father's participation in the abortion decision is necessary to protect stability in family life, and after viability that State should prohibit to protect the life of the unborn child, except when abortion is needed to preserve the life of the mother or to protect her health when it is threatened by a substantial risk if the pregnancy is allowed to continue.

(J) Surrogate Motherhood

Development in medical science have also affected the otherwise complex and broad concept of personal liberty. The new developments in medical science as seriously affected the right of privacy of women. Surrogate motherhood or surrogacy is one of such aspect whose denial or approval may become a complex phenomenon. The relevant question which arises in whether surogacy be allowed or not or

144. The consent of the woman alone is required if she is above 18 years of age, but if she is a minor or a lunatic, consent of the guardian is necessary.

whether woman can claim it as a right under the broad umbrella of personal liberty. There is a diverse of opinion among the different jurists and medical professionals over this issue. Some people support surrogacy under the garb of personal liberty whereas some other people opposed such claims and that too under the garb of personal liberty coupled with ethical and moral norms prevalent in society. Therefore, suitable legislation should be framed to take care of the plight of infertile women. Further, women may be allowed surrogacy since she has an inherent and constitutional right to have control over his body and thus the reproductive process.

V. PRIVACY AS A TORT

The aforesaid analysis should indicate that the law concerning invasion of privacy of an individual though ancient in origin as developed both as a part of constitutional law and also the Law of Torts. However, in India Kharak Singh and Govind established this law as a part of our constitutional right of life and liberty. Apart from these decisions, there are no reported cases on privacy as part of law of torts. During British rule Indian courts considered it to be part of their obligation to act according to justice, equity and good conscience if there was no specific statutory law applicable to the dispute before them. In regard to suits for damages for torts, Indian Courts followed the English common law in so far as it was consonant with equity, justice and good conscience. They departed from it only when any of its rules appeared unreasonable and unsuitable to Indian conditions. Inspite of it, there is very little tort litigation in India and therefore, very scanty opportunity for applying principles evolved elsewhere and evolving principles appropriate to Indian conditions. This is, however, not to say that whenever there had been an opportunity, our courts have not done anything in the matter. Our constitutional values which have become part of our judicial culture, have been responsible for many a changes in this law. Though the English common law of torts is treated to be the law of torts in India, notable instance of such modification is the decision of Supreme Court in *M.C. Mehta* v. *Union of India*,[145] wherein the court considered famous English decision in *Rylands* v. *Flectcher*[146] to adopt it to Indian conditions and develop the law of strict liability. According to the court, the rule of strict liability as contained in this judgment was evolved in 19th century at a time when scientific and technological developments had not taken place and therefore, cannot be accepted as affording any guidance in evolving the standard of liability consistent with the constitutional norms and needs of the present economy and the social structure. The court felt that "as new situation arises the law has to be evolved in order to meet the challenge of such new situation. Law cannot afford to remain static nor can courts allow the judicial thinking to be constricted by reference to law as it prevails in England or for that matter in any other foreign country." The court, therefore, modified the principles of strict liability contained in *Rylands* v. *Fletcher* by holding that the liability was not subject to any exception. This case, therefore, indicates the Indian approach to the law of torts. Indian law of torts is, therefore, the same as the law of England except where it needs modification or changes to suit Indian conditions and do justice between parties.

Though there are no decided cases about the invasion the right of privacy, the invasion of this right has been dealt with as a part of law of trespass or nuisance where it is well developed. Intrusion cases which is the first classification of right of privacy overlap the law of trespass. Kharak Singh and Govind both deal with this aspect of the matter and provide the limit within which a person can enjoy this right. However, both these cases deal with public authority and not with private individuals. Though this right can be and has been enforced against public authorities covered within the definition of 'State' under Article 12 of the Constitution of India, the remedy of writ petition would not be available against a private individual. Civil suit would, therefore, be the only remedy. The person suffering the invasion of his right may bring the suit for damages or injunction as he may

145. AIR 1987 SC 1086.
146. (1868) L.R.3 H.L. 330.

deem fit and proper. Injunction is available to prevent an attempted trespass or continuing the same. Grant of injunction is however, discretionary and is regulated by Specific Relief Act, 1963. Invasion of incorporeal right to immovable property is related as a private nuisance and gives rise to an action for damages. A private nuisance can however become legal by prescription though a public nuisance cannot so become. Rights violated either by trespass or by private nuisance do not always disturb enjoyment of privacy though its disturbance cannot always be ruled out.

Similarly appropriation cases are usually dealt with as a part of law of libel and defamation. In fact, defamation is generic name for the wrong and libel and slander are its particular forms. Libel is treated as a criminal offence but slander is not except when it is blasphemous, seditious, obscene or amounts to contempt of court. Though the appropriation cases have similarly with the law of libel they are really different. Though American Courts and many occasions to deal with appropriation cases of privacy, Indian Courts have not faced them so far and therefore, the law has not yet developed. But as our civilization becomes more complex and varied, these cases are bound to arise and therefore, it may be useful to study some of the facets of this right with reference to cases decided by American Courts.

In *Melvin* v. *Reid*,[147] a producer of motion depicted true incidents of earlier life of a reformed prostitute. She complained of invasion of her privacy rights and sued the producer for damages which were awarded. The Court held that the right to pursue and obtain happiness is guaranteed to all by the fundamental law of our State. This right, by its very nature includes the right to live free from unwarranted attacks of others upon one's liberty, property and reputation. Any person living a life of rectitude has that right to happiness which includes a freedom from unnecessary attacks upon his character, social standing or reputation. Therefore, the court held that the right to privacy implies the right not merely to prevent the incorrect portrayal of private life but the right to prevent it being depicted at all and the court held

147. 112 Cal. App. 285.

that the depiction of her previous life of shame as the violation of right to privacy.

In *Pavesich* v. *New England Life Insurance Co.*,[148] the court held that the constitutional guarantee of freedom of the press does not include the privilege of taking advantage of the incarceration of a person accused of crime to photograph his face and figure at his will. In this case the facts were the Insurance Company published in a newspaper likeness of a man, recognizable as the picture of the plaintiff, placed by the side of an ill-dressed and sickly looking person, with caption indicating that the other man was one who did not have insurance policy and that the plaintiff was protected by insurance in the defendant Insurance Company. The court held that such a publication constituted an invasion of plaintiff's right of privacy and is actionable. Hence, any intrusion of right to privacy was held to be an actionable claim in torts throughout the country.

In *Foster Milburn Co.* v. *Chinna*,[149] a manufacturer of kidney-pills, published a booklet advertising the products, a picture of a prominent citizen together with a sketch of his life and a forged letter falsely stating that such a person has used the pills and recommends them. This manufacturer was held liable for damages. The court observed that a person is entitled to the right of privacy as to his picture and that the publication of picture of a person without his consent, as a part of the advertisement for the purpose of exploiting the publisher's business, is a violation of right of privacy and the plaintiff is entitled to recover without proof of special damages.

In *Deon* v. *Kirby Lumber*,[150] the court held that one who maliciously and with the intent to injury violates the right of privacy, is liable for damages. In this case, the defendant with a social standing and character forbade and prevented his employees and their families for visiting the defendant and his family and from the society of their friends and neighbours thereby bringing about practical ostracism of the

148. 122 Ga. 190-50 S.E. 68 (Ga. 1905).
149. 120 SW 364.
150. 162 La. 671.

plaintiff and his family, was liable in damages to the plaintiff. The court observed that it is the legal right of every man to enjoy social relations with his friends and neighbours. He is entitled to visit them and their families and to have them visit him and family. The free and unhampered exercise of the right is necessary to his happiness and comfort and well being. If he is unlawfully deprived of this right by others, he is entitled to redress.

Similarly, in some States of America, there statutes which make it a criminal offence to open or read a sealed letter or telegram without the authority or to publish the contents of one so opened and read. Also the eves dropping, the tapping of telephone wires and listening to private conversation constitute an invasion of right of privacy. The courts have also held, the sale of photograph of the plaintiff, the unauthorized exhibition of X-ray-pictures showing a part of plaintiff's body or of pictures showing the performance of an operation upon the plaintiff or the effect of the disease upon the plaintiff's appearance, or the publication of the name and picture of a woman in bed in hospital, in connection with a story concerning her unusual ailment as violative of the right of privacy. In *Olmstead* v. *United States*, it was held that any unjustifiable intrusion in the right to privacy (right to be alone) by Government irrespective of means would amount to violation of Constitution.

The right of privacy also accrues to a householder as a protection against door to door solicitation of vendor of magazines; or against the loudspeakers being operated on streets so as to cause nuisance. The right of married couples to use contraceptives and the right of a woman to terminate her pregnancy is within the right of privacy. In *Eisenstadt* v. *Baird*,[151] the court made remarkable observations. It stated that right of privacy means "anything", it is the right of individual, married or single to be free from unwarranted Government intrusion into matters of fundamentally effecting a person as the decision whether to bear or beget a child. In *Stanley* v. *Georgia*,[152] the court proclaimed the right of private

151. (1972) 405 US 438.
152. (1969) 394 US 557.

possession, for private use, of obscene material. In *Hinish* v. *Meier and F. Co.,*[153] the unauthorised use of a person's name in a petition, a remonstrance or other governmental or political matter has been held to amount to an actionable invasion of the right of privacy.

Time v. *Hill,*[154] is a much widely discussed American decision of our age. The Hill family had been held hostage in their home by three escaped convicts and the incident was widely reported in the press at that time. A fictionalised account of their experience later became the story line for a book "The Desperate Hours" followed by a broad-way play of the same name and author. An article in Life Magazine about the play illustrated with photographs of some of the scenes taken at the former Hill home indicated that the story had been "inspired by the family's experience". However, the book, play and magazine photographs depicted the Hills as having been brutalise by the convicts and having resisted their attacks, when in reality they had been treated courteously and there had been no violence, the Hills sued "Time Incorporated", the owners of Life Magazine for invading their privacy, reviving a painful episode and causing them severe emotional distress. It was in response to this suit that the Supreme Court ruled that publisher could be liable only if proven to have published the material knowing it to be false or with reckless disregard for its truth and falsity. The court, therefore, laid down that in order to succeed a false light invasion of privacy suit involving communication about newsworthy subjects the plaintiff must establish "actual malice on the part of the communicator, just as in cases of alleged libel of public officials and public figures."

Cantrell v. *Forest City Publishing Company,*[155] is yet another important case on the subject supporting the reasoning in *Time* v. *Hill*. In that case, the Cleveland Plain Dealer printed the story with photographs about the life situation of a Cantrell family five months after. Mr. Cantrell

153. 166 Or 482.
154. (1974) 491 US 245.
155. Reported in 1974.

had been killed in a collapse of a bridge over the Ohio river. The story which portrayed the family as living in abject poverty and Mrs. Cantrell as unwilling to talk with a reporter about their conditions contained a number of admitted inaccuracies and false statement not the least of which was the fact that Mrs. Cantrell was not even at home when the Reporter made his visit. The Publisher was sued for false light invasion of privacy, making the Cantrells "the object of pity and ridicule" and "causing them to suffer outrage, mental distress, strain and humiliation". The trial court, using the standard of actual materials laid down in *Time* v. *Hill*, decreed the suit in favour of the plaintiffs and the U.S. Supreme Court affirmed that judgment. The debate whether these cases adopt correct legal standards is still going on in the United States. The debate is, however, irrelevant in our context as there is hardly any reported case of any court in India available for our consideration. Though likelihood of such cases coming to our law courts in near future cannot be ruled out because of yellow journalism, which is becoming fashionable, the matter can be left to the wisdom of our law courts to be decided as and when the situation arises according to the needs of the time. Now the study of first third, fourth and ninth amendments reveals that right to privacy derives its sanction from the Constitution. The United States Supreme Court as held the publication of wrong facts leading to death of husband of a lady as violative of right to privacy in *Central* v. *Forest City Publishing Company* reported in 1974.

Though reading of decided cases may justify discovering different guidelines, the guiding principle appears to be the concept of "theft" which can provide the key in resolving the conflict between freedom of expression and privacy. Application of this principle may permit not only damage suit, but also a suit for permanent injunction if the material is taken from a private conversation, or from a private place without consent and perhaps even without the awareness of the person involved as in such a situation, any one who publicises it knowing it to be stolen property can be lawfully sued for these reliefs. American society has been so sensitive to their right of privacy that large number of cases have gone to law courts for decision resulting in development of the law. As early as in 1903, the New York Legislature reacting against a decision rendered in 1902 by the State's highest Court denying common law relief to an individual whose picture had been appropriated to advertise a product, passed the law providing protection against such communication. The Supreme Court of Gorgia in 1905 ruled in favour of the plaintiff in a common law claim against appropriation and thereafter many courts in that country followed the rule. Today either in common law or by virtue of State statue, it is generally accepted that one has a legal remedy if any ventures to use ones name or picture without consent for personal gain. Dean Prossers classification only indicates its development in different directions and amply proves that privacy right is really a bi-product of developing civilization. Though this right is yet to crystalise in India, a beginning has already been made. Those who profess to preserve the rich cultural heritage of tribals living in remote areas, can find this right useful to preserve and protect the same. The unavoidable intrusion by outsiders and photographing intimate human relationship can be checked, restricted and regulated on the touch-stone of this law. Photography at bathing places or of religious ceremonies can also be regulated by application of this law. It is wrong to assert that every thing in life and human relationship deserves publicity. Indeed, by not publishing or permitting publication of several aspects of human relationship, little more dignity and decency can be inducted in the society and social relationship. Considered in this view, the right of privacy may by an integral part of civilized behaviour, deserving effective legal sanction and protection.

VI. SUM-UP

It may, therefore, be summed up that the concept of privacy has been recognised throughout the world. It is an essential requisite of human personality embracing within it the high sense of morality, dignity, decency and value orientation. For preservation of the society the moral and social values cannot be ignored. The importance of the concept of right to privacy though not specifically worded in the Constitution or in the statute, carved out through process of judicial interpretation can be appreciated by the fact that any sort of unjustifiable intrusion either by the Government or individual is forbidden and breach of which is redressable through a recourse of law. Thus, the decisions discussed above enables the author to conclude that the courts have taken the cherished concept of right of privacy to a new and unprecedented height with a zeal to translate the philosophy of right of life and personal liberty into reality. Frankly admitting, the privacy right in India is still in a state of evolution. It has to go through a case to case development. The technological discoveries in modern times pose a serious threat to citizen's privacy. In the age of computer, it is very difficult to identify the infringement of the right for the purpose of taking legal action. Privacy, in such situations, dies an unnatural death. Further, in an age of revolutionized communications, privacy is clearly under seize but law-makers have shown scarce concern on the issue. While in many other countries, there are now a variety of statutes[156] in place that seek to protect those rights, Indian laws on the subject lag behind. In fact, the attitude of the legislators and the executive has been rather regressive. So far the law of privacy has been relegated to a penumbral status and has never enjoyed the status of a well-defined right. Hence, we need to take some concrete legislative action before we lose control of our overdoings of bringing crisis under control.

156. Such as the Privacy Act, 1988 (Commonwealth); the Data Protection Act, 1988 in the United Kingdom and the Information Technology Act, 2000.

7

Appraisal and Suggestions

I. APPRAISAL

Privacy is a part of the vocabulary of every society. It is a concept based on human behaviour. It is the notion of original sovereignty over oneself. It stands for individual autonomy which ensures human dignity. It maintains social processes which helps to safeguard one's sacred individuality. It protects a person from being manipulated or dominated wholly or partly by others. Similarly, it provides relief from physical and emotional stress. It shields the individual from having always to comply with social norms. Privacy enhances self-evaluation capability as well. Therefore, every civilization has recognized it as a human value. It gives sixth sense to every society and it preserve human autonomy under the umbrella of human dignity. Ancient Indian society was conscious to protect it. Similarly, it was not unknown to ancient Hebrews, Chinese and Greek. Analysis of the concept of privacy in India proves that the rules respecting the privacy of individuals in ancient Hindu society were relevant. A person was not be disturbed while he was sleeping, meditating or studying. Enjoyment of sex and food were recommended in secluded place, away from the sight of other persons. Further, a male was enjoined not to see, touch or meet other woman in a lonely place. The texts of the epics, that is, the Ramayana and Mahabharata also establish that privacy is the essence of human beings. The ancient law-giver of the Hindus declared "Sarvas sew sew Grihe Raja" which means every man is a king in his own house. The Dharmasastras and commentaries thereon expounded the laws of privacy in the Indian sub-continent. The kings were bound to uphold Dharma and to respect the privacy of the citizens.

Kautilya, in his Arthashastra advocated privacy for the king while consulting with his ministers. He prescribed procedure to ensure privacy in consultations. The *Griha Sutras* contain comprehensive rules for construction of house. Those rules are supportive of privacy of a family and individual. There were stringent rules punishing those who used to disclose or divulge the confidential information. Over-hearing confidential conversation was strictly prohibited.

The Muslims always maintained the distinction between public and private and a high level of consciousness about privacy is reflected in their language, culture, architecture and other aspects of everyday life. The more focus under Islamic law was that the privacy of home is guaranteed as a core value and fundamental human right.

During the colonial period, the Indian legal system provided for inviolability of one's person, his family, home and correspondence. The Telegraph Act, 1885 and the Indian Post Office Act, 1898, both make interception of messages punishable except during the public emergency. The sanctity of home is preserved in the various provisions spread over in several statutes which make unreasonable searches and seizures punishable. Entering into one's home, even under the authority of law, is regulated to avoid embarrassment or annoyance to the inmates. The Indian Penal Code, 1860 and the Indian Evidence Act, 1872 provide sufficient measures to preserve inviolability of family life. Those in profession, such as, lawyers, medical doctors, dentists, chartered accountants and cost and works accountants are obligated by law not to divulge the personal informations of their clients and patients which they happen to know in discharge of their professional duties. Further, the corporate bodies such as, banks, financial institutions and the like, have also been put under obligation to maintain secrecy in respect of the informations of persons having business relations with them. There are provisions which preserve one's honour and reputation. The Indian Penal Code, 1860 makes it a crime to intrude upon the privacy of woman.

The post-independence period in India witnessed the emergence of many constitutional rights, the right to privacy is one of such right which has of late been accorded constitutional recognition in this period. In the Constituent Assembly a clause was proposed which was in substance similar to right to privacy and against search and seizure as guaranteed in the Fourth Amendment of the U.S. Constitution. But Dr. B.R. Ambedkar's support was a little reserved one and not forceful enough to secure incorporation of right to privacy in the Constitution. After the framing of the Constitution, the anti-privacy strategies came to be challenged although interception of postal and telegraph communication and telephone taps, also part of the police kit, have escaped judicial review.

Privacy is a culturally limited concept. It varies with the times, the historical context, the state of culture and the prevailing judicial philosophy. The customs related to privacy differ greatly from culture to culture, from situations to situations and from social system to social system. So there is no uniform and universal definition. However, a number of attempts have been made to define it. The long search for a definition of privacy has produced a continuing debate that is often sterile and ultimately futile. The debate is sterile for four main reasons. First, the premises upon which the proposed definitions are based are materially different. Those who assume privacy to be a right have not really joined issue with those who conceive it to be a 'condition', 'state', 'area of life' and so on. Secondly, the objectives of the arguments tend to differ. Dean Prosser sees four interests in privacy which were protected by American law. Edward J. Bloustein finds a single interest which privacy protects, that is human dignity. Thirdly, the arguments as to the desirability of privacy frequently proceed from different stand points. Some see privacy as an end in itself, while others regard it as instrumental in the securing of other desirable social ends such a creativity, love, emotional release. Fourthly, the definitions usually beg more questions than answers.

The debate is ultimately futile for, in those legal system which recognise a common law right to privacy. Privacy is entrenched in the vocabulary of the courts. And where it is accorded statutory protection then privacy is simply what the legislature says it is. Though, the oriental concept of privacy, particularly in India, is different from western concept in its historical perspective, they are more akin at the philosophical level. They profess same value. Therefore, any contribution made by western scholars to develop this right is equally justifiable in relation to Indian privacy jurisprudence.

Privacy in general means 'the right to be let alone'. The expression was used by Justice Thomas M. Cooley in 1888. According to him the right to respect for private life is the right to be let alone. A couple of years later in 1890 Samuel D. Warren and Louis D. Brandeis cultivated the notion with the initial analysis of the concept of privacy. They wrote an article which was published in *Harvard Law Review* which gave rise to the current of independent right to privacy. The view expressed in this article supplies legal thoughts to establish separate right to privacy. The article attempted to create a general right of privacy independent from traditional common law right of property, contract or implied trusts. Warren and Brandeis wanted to extend the scope of jurisprudence to protect not the reputation already covered by libel law but the feelings of individuals who had been subjected to some form of intrusion. Their deep concern was to protect one's feelings and consequent mental anguish. They ultimately advocated 'right to be let alone'. Later a number of scholars tried to discuss the topic from different angles which is supportive to enrich and refine the concept. William L. Prosser, reviewed more than two hundred American cases and found four different torts which protect the right of privacy. These torts were: (i) intrusion upon the plaintiff's seclusion or solitude or into his private affairs, (ii) public disclosure of embarrassing private facts about the plaintiff, (iii) publicity which places the plaintiff in a false light in the public eyes, and (iv) appropriation for defendant's advantage of the plaintiff's name or likeness.

Dean Prosser's analysis clearly highlighted four interests represented by four torts which questioned the view of Warren and Brandeis. Prosser's classification of privacy interests raised much controversy over the theoretical and legal foundations of privacy. If Prosser's analysis was correct, the Warren and Brandeis were wrong. Instead of a single interest, there were four interests represented by four torts, none of which bore a distinctive interest in privacy. Edward J. Bloustein does not agree with the view of Dean Prosser. He says there are no four interests. Privacy preserves human dignity and individuality, a single interest. Somewhere between Prosser's specific torts and Bloustein's human dignity concept, Alan F. Westin comes. He defines privacy as "the claim of individuals, groups or institutions to determine themselves when, how and to what extent information about them is communicated to others." He classifies four states of individual privacy: solitude, intimacy, anonymity, and reserve. But defining privacy Hyman Gross appears to oscillate between viewing it as a "condition of life" and as a "form of control." His analysis of 'control' is open to criticism, for he uses two different senses of 'control' viz., (a) the control on individual has over the flow of information about himself from himself, and (b) the control over the communication of information about oneself by others. Even though others are obliged not to disclose the information, it can hardly amount to 'control' the information. This duality of senses exists for all those who define privacy in terms of control over information (e.g. Charles Fried, Aurther Miller and Richard B. Parker) except Edward Shils who defines it as the existence of a boundary through which information does not flow from the person who possess it to others. Likewise, Gary L. Bostwick describes privacy right as repose, sanctary and intimate decisions. He holds that intimate decisions are more dynamic privacy concepts as compared to repose and sanctuary.

Communication, scholar Judee K. Burgoon identifies broad dimensions of privacy namely, physical privacy, social privacy, psychological privacy and informational privacy. Her's former two dimensions are similar to Westin's concept. First resembles with solitude and second is similar to limited or protected communication. Psychological privacy is dependent upon the interpretation of each individual. Informational dimension is most problematic aspect of privacy today. It is in what most people have in mind when they speak of privacy intrusion.

From the conceptual point of view, Dean Prosser and Gary L. Bostwick describe the application of law to personal autonomy, property and other liberties that have come to be associated with privacy. William L. Prosser's torts become Bostwick's generic rights in translation. Edward J. Bloustein, however, is not satisfied with it. He insists that there is a single interest behind the law's protection, what he calls human dignity. Alan F. Westin wants a narrow but absolute 'claim' to control individual group, and institutional information. His approach seems to be normative and descriptive. The Indian writers who have written articles on privacy, have preferred to rely upon the definition given by the western scholars rather than contributing their own. In May 1967, an attempt has been made to cover most of the definitions of the privacy in Nordic Conference of Jurists on the Right to Respect for Privacy. Privacy is not made of one particular interest only. This consists of many interests. The western scholars have also subscribed to the view that privacy is very closely knitted with the life-style of the people. People have different life-styles in different civilizations. And so long there are different civilizations existing on the globe, there cannot be uniform human behaviour. This is the reason which defies a universally accepted definition of privacy.

Privacy has grown into a large and unwieldy concept. Synonymous with autonomy, it, as colonized traditional liberties, becomes entangled with confidentiality, secrecy, defamation, property and storage of information. It would be unreasonable to expect a notion so complex as 'privacy' not to spill into regions with which it is closely related, but this process has resulted in the dilution of 'privacy' itself, diminishing the prospect of its own protection as well as the protection of the related interests.[1]

---

1. Raymond Wacks, The Poverty of Privacy, 96, *The Law Quarterly Review*, 88 (Jan 1980).

In this attenuated, confused and unworked condition, privacy seems beyond redemption. Any attempt to restore it to what is quintessentially is—an interest of personality—seems doomed to fail for it comes too late. Privacy has become as nebulous a concept as 'happiness' or 'security'. Except as a general abstraction of an underlying value, it should not be used as a means to describe a legal right or cause of action. The more honest, effective and rational course is to approach the subject from the standpoint of the protection of personal information. The problem of privacy is essentially three-fold: the first concerns those activities which intrude, physically or electronically, into home or office and are best regulated by legislation of the kind advanced by the Younger Committee[2] without recourse to privacy. The other two problems really concern personal information: publicity given to personal information and the use and potential misuse of personal information by data banks.

The cultural dimensions of right to privacy with reference to traditional Indian scene is quite different from other western world. A vast majority still live traditionally in large joint families. These families are like mini-states. The autonomy of decision-making is not availed by an individual member. The head of the family decides important matters of the family and members of the family are obedient to the head and they recognise his wisdom. The growth of urbanization, the spurt in population and various kinds of shortages caused a contradiction in the living as a result of which the old lifestyle could not be sustained. Emancipation of women, urbanisation and deficient resources have acted as catalysts to the inherent craving for privacy to bloat it up in a magnified form that we have witnessed in the recent times. Things have changed greatly with the social, political, scientific and industrial advancements and today man is asserting his right to privacy in all its dimensions.

It may be pertinent to mention here that the right to privacy as an independent and distinctive concept originated in the field of tort law, wherein an unlawful invasion of privacy was recognized as a cause of action for a remedy in

2. Younger Committee, paras 562-563.

damages. Privacy as an actionable right has a relatively new existence in India. The law regards the right to privacy in two separate and distinct fields, which are but two sides of the same coin, private law and public law, i.e., the general law of privacy that affords a tort action for damages resulting from an unlawful invasion of privacy and the constitutional recognition given to the right of privacy which protects personal privacy against unlawful government invasion.

On attaining her independence, India adopted the Constitution which ushered in a new society based on values enshrined therein. The Preamble to the Constitution resolves to secure to all citizens justice, liberty, equality of opportunity and of status assuring their dignity. The fundamental rights, observes the Supreme Court of India, represent the basic values cherished by the people of this country since the vedic times and they are calculated to protect the dignity of the individual and create conditions in which every human being can develop his personality to the fullest extent.[3] The right to life, guaranteed under Article 21 of the Constitution, has been interpreted as the right to live with human dignity.[4] By virtue of his dignity, each individual has a right to a private enclave where he may lead a free life without any let or hindrance.[5] This is precisely in tune with the declaration of the Nordic Conference held in Stockholm in 1967.

Though, there is no express provision in the Constitution of India, right to privacy has got a secure position under it. Article 21 miraculously has been playing a major role in the safeguard of privacy as an essential ingredient of personal liberty. It is further to note that Article 21 by itself has not been a potent enough weapon in defence of privacy until it is sharpened and made effective by judicial activism. The case law reveals that this right emanates from Articles 19(1)(d) and 21 of the Constitution of India. Similarly, some scholars find right to privacy in 'dignity' clause of the Preamble of the Constitution of India. However,

---

3. Maneka Gandhi *v.* Union of India, AIR 1978 SC 597 at 620.
4. Francis Coralie Mullin *v.* Union Territory of Delhi, AIR 1981 SC 746 at 753.
5. Nandani Satpatti *v.* P.L. Dani, AIR 1978 SC 1025 at 1045.

the content and extent of this right is not still clear. First, defining right of privacy is very difficult. It is always left to be decided by the court, or in other words, privacy means what the court says it is. Second, there is always a possibility of avoiding right to privacy because of its confusing boundary. The protection of privacy under human dignity enshrined under Article 21 is not sufficient to include all aspects of privacy. Similarly, the harm caused by violation of privacy cannot be repaired by awarding damages.

Most of the cases of privacy in India are either related to police surveillance or matrimonial rights, sexual autonomy, freedom of press, phone-tapping and AIDS infected people. So the area of privacy which is often questioned before the court is limited. Privacy is, further an emanating right under the certain constitutional provisions. For this reason it cannot go beyond the particular Article or Provision under which it emanates. Sometimes, the restriction imposed on particular provision may not be reasonable for the restriction of privacy. One of the Articles which is often referred for this right is Article 21 which is already overburdened with recent developments.

Though, there are several customary and constitutional provisions for right of privacy, without statutory protection this right cannot be protected in a meaningful way. The Constitution provides only framework and constitutionally protected fundamental rights cannot be enforced against private person alone. Customary rules are very limited and inadequate. Statutory provisions, therefore, are more important to safeguard the privacy interest.

There is no single unifying legislation relating to right to privacy in India. There are several statutes which directly or indirectly protect right to privacy. How and at what extent right of privacy is well guarded in India is a question answered by several legislations? The Indian system provides protection of person through various legal provisions contained in several penal laws. Due attention is paid to maintain privacy while making an arrest. Protection is extended while conducting search and seizure so as to ensure privacy. Section 509 of the Indian Penal Code, 1860 makes it a crime to intrude upon the privacy of woman intending to insult her modesty. Indian laws do not allow the right to die in the name of right of privacy. The dignity clause of right to privacy does not support destroying life. Most of the cases support the view that the court may order medical examination whenever it is essential in a case to determine disputed questions of fact, but a person may not be compelled to undergo such examination. The court may be justified in drawing an adverse inference, in case of such refusal.

Protection against breach of privacy and protection against defamation cover two different areas of a person's life. The law of defamation protects the reputation of an individual. The law of privacy protects the feelings of an individual. The same statement may injure a person's reputation. A man's reputation is his property and possession, more valuable than other property. If a person injuries the reputation of another he is liable to be punished under the law. To that extent, the Indian law of defamation protects privacy of an individual. Although closely related, invasion of privacy is distinct from defamation (libel and slander). An action for invasion of privacy differs from a libel action in that in the former, truth is not a defense,[6] and it is not necessary for sustenance of the cause of action, to allege or prove special damages.[7] A libel may arise from publication of a defamatory statement to only one person whereas the invasion of privacy, at least by false light publicity, requires publicity of a falsehood to a substantial number of people.[8] In privacy cases, the primary damage is the mental distress from having been exposed to public view, although injury to reputation may be an element bearing upon such damage.

A number of legal provisions and case law[9] exist in India which protect privacy of home. Case law reveals that even a prostitute is entitled to be informed before entering

---

6. Smith *v.* Das, 251 Ala 250, 37 SO 2d 118.
7. *Ibid.*
8. Fellows *v.* National Enquirer, Inc. 2nd Dist., 165 Cal App. 3d 512, 211 Cal Reptr. 809.
9. Re- Ratanmala, AIR 1962 Md. 31. 31; State of Maharashtra *v.* Madhukar Narayan Mardikar, AIR 1991 SC 207.

into her bedroom. Unauthorized entry into a person's home for the purpose of learning the secrets of his private life can amount to violation of Article 8 of the European Convention on Human Rights which the United Kingdom has implemented through the Human Rights Act of 1998 even if the natural law the essential conditions for the offence of violation of domestic privacy have not been met. Further, Indian Easement Act, 1882 provide protection to a person's privacy of home.

If privacy has any social focus, it is in the family, a set of intimate relationships that can flourish when sufficiently protected from public scrutiny. The family has been the ultimate foundation of every civilization. It is the economic and productive unit of society. It is the political and cultural unit of society, it is moral unit as well. In many ways family is more essential than other institutions. Sociologists say that if the family dissolves, civilization itself disappears. Family life is protected under several statutes in India. No person is compelled to disclose any communication made between husband and wife. Similarly, no person is forced to be a witness against her/his spouse, father, mother, daughter and son. The underlying rationale of this provision is that the admission of such testimony have a powerful tendency to disturb the peace of families and weaken the mutual confidence upon which the happiness of married life depends. Further, Article 17 of the International Covenant on Civil and Political Rights, 1966 *inter alia* provides right of privacy of family. This Covenant is equally applicable in India because India is a party to the Covenant.

Sexual privacy is closely connected with privacy of home and family. Sex has been a natural urge of all the creatures of the world. Nature has imbibed this instinct so that the process of procreation is continued, and this would have been the reason for addition of element of pleasure with sexual intercourse. Nearly all societies have sought privacy for sexual relation. Indian law protects privacy of sex even in brothel. Case law reveals that even a woman of easy virtue deserves right of privacy. Some of Indian tribes practise polygamy either polyandary or polygyny. Even in case of plurality of partner sexual privacy is desirable. However, sexual privacy does not protect unnatural sexual relation. Unnatural sexual activities conducted in private are also punishable in India.

Whether the right of privacy extends in relation to the conjugal rights? Whether a wife can say no to have a sexual relation with her husband? It is clear that the question of woman as an individual having separate entity from her husband having the right to privacy against her own husband, while matrimonial bond continues, has attracted judicial attention. There are different opinions in this matter. Andhra Pradesh High Court in *T. Sareetha* v. *T.V. Subbaiah,*[10] adopted the extreme positive view recognising the right to privacy. But Delhi High Court did not go into the question of the right of privacy.[11] The Supreme Court of India has passed the issue of privacy in *Saroj Rani* v. *Sudershan Kumar.*[12]

Law of trespass and nuisance also protect privacy interest. The tort of nuisance is underdeveloped in India. It does not protect sufficient privacy interest. It is also limited as trespass. It protects from physical interference only. It does not protect photography, bugging, tapping, snooping from the distance without entering to other's land. Prying neighbour with binoculars, electronic eavesdropping and spying by electronic devices do not amount to trespass. Thus, trespass protects privacy of a person in certain respect. It restricts, physical intervention so its scope is limited to protect privacy. Indian legal system protects such types of privacy which is derived out of trespass law.

Freedom of speech and expression is guaranteed by the Constitution of India. It includes freedom of press. Freedom of Press has been acclaimed as the cornerstone of modern democratic state. It is often described as fourth estate. It is debatable as to whether freedom of press is superior to that of privacy interest? It varies according to circumstances. Press is not allowed to publish any matter which is of private nature. Press is entitled to publish only those matters which are of legitimate public interest. To keep the Press as a strong

10. AIR 1883 SC 350.
11. Harvinder Kaur *v.* Harmender Singh Chaudhary, AIR 1984 Del. 66.
12. AIR 1984 SC 1562.

medium that can safeguard public interest it must observe self-censorship with a set of norms based on sound principles that offer due regard to both freedom of expression and right to privacy. The encroachment by Press and other mass media into privacy rights of individuals through the help of modern technology is the new threat. The concept of privacy is multidimensional and ever widening with every advancement in technology. Hence, it seems that evolution of the concept step by step through judicial decisions would be a prudent course. The judiciary can take note of the ever widening concept and use it as a parameter for deciding disputes that involve the question of privacy rights.

Indian jurisprudence recognizes the sanctity of mail and it protects correspondence and communication by law. However, legal provisions contained in Post Office Act, 1898, Telegraph Act, 1885 (Indian Telegraph Amendment Act, 1972), and Inception of Telecommunication Act, 1985 are sufficient to protect privacy interest. There are a number of safeguards against interception or censuring mails in other developed countries which are lagging in Indian laws. Indian Telegraph Act, 1885 did not allow disturbance or interference of communication when it was enacted. However, with little public debate or scholarly scrutiny of policy, the right to privacy suffered a set back in 1972 when the Parliament amended the Act and authorised certain officers to intercept such messages or stop their transmission if it was considered to be in the interest of the country or the public or for the maintenance of friendly relations with foreign states. For the sake of public interest, national security and well-being of the country interception is justified. Even on justifiable grounds the government should not exercise its authority arbitrarily but should exercise power judiciously. The sender or sendee should be informed properly before interception.

There are certain confidential relations which are privileged under the law whereby the persons falling within such relationship are not bound to disclose the communications which has taken place between them. There are two common rationales which justify the existence of privileges. The first is utilitarian rationale which focuses on justifying confidential communications within the context of various professional relationships. This approach holds that these privileges are justified in order to encourage full communication within these relationships. The second justification for privileges is that they protect certain privacy interest. While the utilitarian justification looks only to prevent widespread systematic harms to a class. The privacy rationale is concerned with harm to the individual communicant. Thus communication within certain relationship should not be pried into, not because the privileges promote communication but because the relationship is an essentially private one. The confidential relationship between doctor and patient is recognized in India. Doctor should not disclose the matter of medical concern which is confidential. However, the duty of a doctor is not an unqualified one. This duty may have to succumb to the countervailing public interest in protection of third parties against infectious disease or violence or in the administration of justice. The Indian Evidence Act, 1872 provide privileges of certain relations. Similarly, judicial privileges state secrets and professional privileges are recognized under the Act. These privileges undoubtedly protect privacy interest but are not adequate to protect privacy of all relations. Privacy interest is not limited to relations only but it can be related to any one whomsoever he interacts in a private affair.

A general principle of rule of law is open justice. Justice should not only to be done but should also seem to be done. However, in certain situation, trial in camera is more justifiable than in open court. The rationale behind camera proceeding is that in some cases the administration of justice of those qualities of individuals which inhibit them to speak out certain facts in front of general public. Further, it is coupled with a policy consideration that certain matters of intimate and personal nature or prejudicial to the safety of the State ought not to be discussed in general public. One of the goals of privacy is to protect family relations. It can be preserved if certain matters of family could be kept private. For this reason Indian law provides camera proceeding for matrimonial cases and lunacy. These cases are entirely related to private and domestic life with which public has no legitimate concern.

Privacy has become an issue in modern democratic societies which are characterized by large-scale, sophisticated bureaucratic structures and advanced technology in communication and information systems. A major factor of the privacy problem is the absence of legislation and organized rules ensuring privacy, confidentiality and due process to the subjects of computerized information. Data banks have been established at all levels of Government, business and military services without any real knowledge or concern for their potential impact over individual rights. Professor Arthur R. Miller identifies recent development that relate to the late twentieth century concern for privacy, namely, (i) massive record-keeping; (ii) decision-making by dossier; (iii) unrestricted transfer of information from one context to another; and (iv) surveillance conduct at one level or another. He further states that the modern concept of privacy does not relate to intrusion, misappropriation, embarrassing private facts or false light. These things constitute the work of lawyers in their quest to get things within rigid limits. But record-keeping and data collection represent new and different ways of disrupting solitude and seclusion as more and more institutions collect more and more information about more aspects of our lives. Data Protection law ensures protection of living individuals with respect to the disclosure of personal data relating to them which is stored on computer. The current law, the Data Protection Act, 1988 implemented in March 2000 controls the compiling, and use of data relating to living individuals processed in the United Kingdom or elsewhere under the control of a United Kingdom established person or company called the data controller. The Act limits the extent of data which may be stored, the processing of data and how it can be disclosed.

In India, there are several statutes which prohibit divulgence of information acquired. These statutes authorise collection of data for certain purposes. As regards state-led initiatives, Andhra Pradesh has proposed a Data Processing (Special Contracts) Act in the line with Global standards. The initiative is the first of its kind in the country, and a move that will comfort overseas clients on the privacy concerns over the processing of private data by third party service players in the State. Most overseas clients protect the privacy of personal data being processed in India by their preferred providers through the traditional contract route. In India, some data obtained in relation to certain transactions are made confidential.

Similarly, any information obtained in the course of employment is confidential. Any employee who has obtained information of his employer's secrets is bound to keep the information in confidence. But there is a reciprocal implied duty imposed on an employer to maintain to confidentiality. Further, law of Banking in India recognizes a contractual duty of confidences. Several statutes recognize this relationship and transaction and secrecy of banking documents should be observed. This provision extends to the protection of bank account and other banking transactions. Nobody other than the concerned account holder is entitled to get information relating to his account. But this rule does not prelude auditor and inspector of the bank for inspection. These auditors and inspectors are to maintain confidentiality of the same as the employer of the bank. However, there are four grounds under which the disclosure is justified: (i) under the compulsion of law; (ii) required in public interest; (iii) required in the protection of banker's interest; and (iv) with the express or implied consent of the customer.

Privacy of information is protected by the law relating to census as well. The Census Act, 1948, restrict information from being used for other than the collected purpose. However, there is no clear legal protection of privacy while gathering the information. Only employee's official duty of confidentiality is available. The same rule applies to other institutions which collect personal information. Further, privacy of research work is an important aspect to develop the research activities. But in India comprehensive legislation to protect research work is not available. There is a dire need to develop a code of conduct to those all who practice in any research work. However, professional codes of conduct are available to medical researchers, chartered accountants and advocates in India.

The credit bureaus are the largest information gathering

systems. Violation of the right of privacy is at the heart of the question of how much information is known about a person and how freely it is circulated to people who have no legitimate interest in knowing everything in a given file. There are a number of credit agencies. They collect personal information which is susceptible to misuse. Lindop Committee recognised that the growing number of agencies which sell information and the free circulation of information among firms in the consumer credit industry bring greater risk that information will become available to persons other than credit grantors. The Consumer Credit Act, 1974 requires the grantor of credit to supply the consumer on request with the name and address of any credit reference agency which has supplied information about him, the consumer must be issued a copy of all information about him held by the agency. However, the misuse of personal information obtained by credit agencies is not a serious problem in India. No cases are available in this respect. There are several global standards relating to privacy and data protection. The protection afforded to personal data in India may not be considered adequate, as compared to global standards set by various governments and institutions.

Privacy is not an absolute right. Like other rights it is also subject to some limitations, certain limitations are imposed by the provisions which provides this right. The Constitution of India does not speak about this right in express words. In the course of interpretation of constitutional rights it is found within Constitution, particularly in Article 19(1)(d) and 21. Similarly, 'dignity' clause of Preamble of the Constitution is an accepted shelter for this right. Reasonable restrictions are allowed under these rights which applies with regard to privacy right as well.

There are other limitations propounded by judicial interpretation, right conferring laws and reasonable standard. Public interest is the legitimate limitation on right of privacy. Right of privacy does not prohibit the publication of any matter of public or general interest. The same rule applies where the information would be of public interest which conflict with a claim to privacy must be a legitimate and proper public interest but not only a prurient or morbid curiosity. "Of interest to the public" is not synonymous of the "public interest". The public interest is widely construed to permit fair comment on a variety of matters.

Similarly, another limitation on right of privacy is concerned with the status of a person. Whether he is public figure or not? Right to privacy protects only to those persons whose affairs the community has no legitimate concern. Those who enter into public life forfeit a degree of the privacy. Such forfeiture is limited to those matters which may be legitimately necessary or appropriate for the information of the public. Public figure includes not only great personality but also others who are catapulated into public prominence for a short period. Victims of an offence, pardoned, civil litigants and other person whose acts are matters of public record come into this category. The mere fact that the someone is a public figure does not determine the extent to which his private life may legitimately be exposed.

Likewise if a person conducts something in public place then he cannot claim the right of privacy. Further, any matter recorded in public record keeps the person out of access of this right. However, law may prohibit any matter of public record from being published. Likewise, the disclosure must offend the reasonable man of ordinary sensibilities. The law of privacy is not intended for the protection of any shrinking soul who is abnormally sensitive about such publicity. Further, the right of privacy is limited to the matter of communicated within certain relations privileged by law. If there is no public disclosure of private facts it cannot amount an invasion of privacy. The simple disclosure of private information to one other person is not sufficient to state a claim for the public disclosure of private facts. Another condition which limits the right of privacy is consent. If a person consents either expressly or by conduct or seeks publicity or is a public figure, he may be said to have waived his right to prevent some or all of the publicity which he receives. Similarly, the degree of seriousness is also a factor which determines the limitation of privacy.

In the absence of any express constitutional or statutory provisions recognising the right to privacy, the Indian court have seized the opportunity whenever they came and tried successfully to bring the privacy right within the preview of fundamental rights. In other words, the seminal semantics postulated and carved out is right of privacy which inheres in the fundamental rights themselves and it is the nidus of the constitutional fabric. The Apex Courts of United Kingdom and United States made a pertinent observation in respect of the fundamental principle that any importune intrusion into one's individual life tantamount to one of infraction of one's fundamental right of privacy and the same is finely honed and tuned in its supercilious disdain and the same was rightly observed by the said apex court in *Federal Trade Commission* v. *American Tobacco Co.*,[13.] wherein one of the foremost arguments put forward was that the right of privacy is an every increasing responsibility had gone to menacing proportions of American civilization. It is a case of intrusion into one's private life and wherein it was noted down that any publication has been made falsely, slyly, wily and maliciously and even if it is made public without there being any documentary evidence it tantamount to intrusion of one's private life thereby infected constitutional mandate. The Federal Constitution of the United States of America made no mention of any right of privacy in specific, but the apex courts rendered the right of privacy is a fundamental right and it can be culled out from the very nuances and rudiments enshrined in the very Constitution itself. In India, privacy has been recognized in many cases as a fundamental right emanated under the Constitution of India, its content, extent and limit are not still clear. Statutory protection is piecemeal. The courts in India have taken the cherished concept of privacy to a new and unprecedented height with a zeal to translate the philosophy of right to life and personal liberty into reality. The right relating to privacy had to pass through a strenuous struggle during last many decades and it seems that it would still have to struggle hard. The court's treatment of this right is a matter of paramount importance because of growing invasion of this right in areas that remained away from the purview of courts. The law declared by the Supreme Court of India that right to privacy—a right

13. 264 U.S. 298.

to be let alone—is implicit in the right to life and personal liberty guaranteed under Article 21 of the Constitution—is a sign post of future development of this right.

Frankly admitting that the right of privacy in India is still in a state of evolution. It has to go through a case to case development. The technological discoveries in modern times pose a serious threat to citizen's privacy. In this age of computer, it is very difficult to identify the infringement of the right for the purpose of taking legal action. The development of the concept of privacy has gone a pace rapidly with the recent scientific and technological developments and have raised the spectre of new and frightening invasion of privacy. The recent communication explosion and revolutionary advance in communication technology which has put thrust into the hands of unscrupulous persons, gadgets by the use of which they have with impunity, pry into, intrude upon or invade the privacy of another home without his consent or even knowledge. Owing to these developments, a person's house is no longer inviolate or immune from wire-tapping, eavesdropping and bugging with the aid of sophisticated devices. Privacy, in such situations, dies an unnatural death. Further, in an age of revolutionized communications, privacy is clearly under seize but law-makers have shown scarce concern on the issue. While in many other countries, there are now a variety of statutes in place that seek to protect those rights, Indian laws on the subject lag behind. In fact, the attitude of the law-makers and the executive has been rather regressive.

II. SUGGESTIONS

In the light of discussion made in the preceding chapters, the following suggestions may humbly be put forward for future course of action:

(i) The norms of privacy should be determined and measured to a usual standard because a right without description is a right without protection. The uncertainty about the constitutional basis of privacy and its protection should be removed immediately. It is possible only when we adopt a new perspective of right to privacy. This can be achieved by making necessary constitutional amendment whereby right to privacy should either be added in Article 21 or a new clause should be added in Article 19, which would be subject to appropriate judicial control, so that balance is struck between individual's privacy and social exposure. Such an amendment is necessary so as to give recognition to the right to privacy which is most comprehensive of rights, and only then, personal liberty as guaranteed by Article 21 can be achieved in real sense. Alternatively, if constitutional amendment is more difficult, a comprehensive and separate unified right of Privacy Act is expected to be enacted which would not violate any provision of the Constitution. Even if privacy is made as a fundamental right, a separate legislation becomes necessary to regulate it. Right to privacy, therefore, should not rely on other laws. It should be developed as an independent right.

(ii) In an age of revolutionized communications, privacy is clearly under seize but law-makers have shown scarce concern on this issue. While in many other countries, there are now variety of statutes in place that seek to protect these rights, Indian laws on the subject lag far behind. In fact, the attitude of the legislators and the executive has been rather regressive. It is time our law-makers enacted laws to protect privacy rather than laws that license intrusion into private affairs. Technological development in the field of electronics and computers had made it much more difficult for the individual to preserve his privacy. Therefore, it is necessary to preserve the tenuous balance between the right of the individual to be let alone and the fundamental right to free speech, expression and information. Hence, heavy burden lies upon the judiciary to balance the tilt. It is expected from the judiciary that by playing the role of a "balance wheel," it should adjudge which interest requires to be comparatively more protected interest inherent in the "privacy right" or that which is inherent in the "information right."

(iii) Disclosure of personal information by government be prohibited: If there is any violation of personal information then remedy of injunction and damages should be provided to the aggrieved person. The right of getting information regarding governmental activities will continue to be available to the aggrieved parties.

(iv) Privacy primarily concerns with individual and it is for the individual to decide for himself how much he will share his personal thoughts, feelings and life. Further, what is private may vary from time to time, and society to society. Therefore, the development or the law relating to privacy necessarily as to be dependent on the local, cultural and other sociological factors. Awarding damages for invasion of privacy by unlawful governmental interferences and consideration of cultural, sociological and philosophical traditions in determining what is privacy are the necessary ingredients to strengthen the further development of law relating to privacy in India, where different cultural, sociological and philosophical traditions are cherished.

(v) In India, the Constitutional provisions of telephone interception lack the clarity and depth as compared to its counterpart United States of America. The law or wiretap in India is, therefore, satisfactory neither from the point of view of the law enforcement nor the accused. One can only hope that the legislature and the courts take notice of this.

(vi) Autonomy to mass media, such as, press, radio and television should be restricted and only then the right of privacy could be protected and promoted. The encroachment by press and other mass media into privacy rights of individuals through the help of modern technology is the new threat. There is no code of conduct for journalists prescribed by the Press Council of India on the lines similar to those of medical practitioners, advocates and chartered accountants. Hence, there is a dire need to formulate a code of conduct for journalists so as to ensure maintenance of high professional standards in Indian journalism. The norms of journalistic conduct as made in 2005 are to be strictly followed so that press shall not intrude or invade the privacy of an individual unless outweighed by genuine overriding public interest, not being a prurient or morbid curiosity.

(vii) Privacy claims have also come under attack qua Section 9 of Hindu Marriage Act, 1955 dealing with restriction of conjugal rights. In the present day society this provision seems to have little social purpose. The impact of this remedy works injustice to the woman who is forced to join matrimonial home under the threat of attachment. It is against the modern concept of privacy and it defies the dignity of a woman who may have to submit herself to the wishes of a man. It is submitted that Section 9 of the Hindu Marriage Act, 1955 should be abolished to effectuate the personal liberty of the women in real terms.

(viii) Indian jurisprudence recognises the sanctity of mail and it protects correspondence and communication by law. There are a number of safeguards against interception or censuring mails in other developed countries which are lagging in India laws. The right to privacy suffered a set back in 1972 when the Parliament amended the Telegraph Act and authorized certain officers to intercept such messages or stop transmission if it was considered to be in the interest of the country or the public or for maintenance of friendly relations with foreign states. For the sake of public interest, national security and well-being of the country interception is justified. Even on justifiable grounds the government should not exercise its authority arbitrarily but should exercise power judicially. The sender or sendee should be informed properly before interception.

(ix) In India, there are several statutes which authorise collection of data for certain purposes. Some of the information concerning privacy are not of such a serious nature. But some personal informations are more sensational which need protection. In modern times, the State collects a lot of information from citizens about their affairs. The information may relate to health, business secrets or financial status of an individual. The disclosure of this information may harm their reputation. However, there is no clear legal protection of privacy while gathering the information. Only employee's official duty of confidentiality is available. The same rule applies to other institutions which collect personal information. Further, privacy of research work is an important aspect to develop research activities. However, there is no comprehensive legislation to protect research work available in India. Copyright and Patent law cannot cover the whole spectrum of research work. While work is still in process, no law protects from being used by some others. Any unpublished work is not protected by copyright law. Hence, there is a dire need to develop a code of conduct to those all who practice in any research work.

(x) Female foeticide has assumed dangerous proportions in the modern day society. The male-female sex ratio has deteriorated severely. It is argued that the females have a right to have control over their reproductive process and they should be granted liberty to decide in such matter. As long as there is a clamour for the male child and the female child is considered as a burden, people will continue to seek ways and means of eliminating the female foetus. The Government should, therefore, carryout women empowerment programmes vigorously. Efforts should be made to make people aware of different aspects of female foeticide. There is a need to bring about a change in the mindset of people and create an effective awareness among the people across the nation. It is, however, submitted that in order to check female foeticide, rights of female have to give way to the societal interest in preservation of male-female ratio. It is submitted that the government has rightly banned pre-natal tests since female foeticide is violative of Article 21. Exemplary damages should be imposed upon the doctors carrying on female foeticide.

(xi) In the modern advanced sophisticated society surrogacy is a panacea to those who cannot rear and bear children for medical reasons. It has been practised in ancient times in the form of *dasi putra*. The advocates of surrogacy plead that a law should be laid down legalizing surrogacy and dealing with various situations which may arise. However, the other line of thinkers oppose it on the grounds of decency and morality. It is submitted that the surrogacy may be permitted keeping in view all aspects of the problem. The law should provide for compensation to the carrying mother if the donor mother refused to accept the baby. It should be laid down that the donor mother must accept the babies, if there happen to be twin or triplet babies. The law should also ban abortion by carrying mother against the consent of the donor mother except for medical reasons.

(xii) Privacy claims of AIDS infected people have also attracted attention of the judiciary in the recent times. The judiciary has clearly and rightly held that since the society is facing a danger of AIDS infection being spread, the privacy claims of AIDS infected people have to give way to the societal interests. The Government should take steps at the earliest to enact a law that takes into account the protection of the persons living with HIV/AIDS, aims at anti-discrimination of such persons as well as takes care of those living around them. It is encouraging that the Indian government has begun to take steps in this direction. The draft of the country's first comprehensive legislation on HIV/AIDS is in the process of being completed and will soon be presented to the Government. It is hoped that this law will provide an encouragement for health care reform and also eradicate discrimination against HIV affected persons. Taking into consideration the nature and the size of the problem, a comprehensive legislation is long over due. Undue delay in responding to this grave matter can result in adverse consequences of unmanageable proportions.

(xiii) The extent of privacy varied from time to time with the social evolution with women coming out for education, job, etc. the scope and meaning of privacy has changed. However, preserving the dignity of woman should remain for ever and it is in this context that a codified law on privacy is demanded to suit the present demand. Hence, there is a need for amending the Constitution to provide a specific definition of privacy. Such a law will protect the women from specific crimes which can be committed against woman only. The ever increasing teasing, molestation, sexual harassment at work places, etc. can be tackled and interests of women protected when a stricter law on privacy is in its place.

(xiv) Article 8 of the European Convention of Human Rights, 1950 should be incorporated in Human Rights Act, 1993. In this manner, it could be possible to protect privacy of the concerned parties in a desirable manner.

So far as the law of privacy has been relegated to a penumbral status and has never enjoyed the well-defined right. In this backdrop, the above mentioned suggestions may be taken into consideration so that we may not lose control of our overdoings of bringing crisis under control.

Table of Cases

A.G. *v.* Guardian Newspapers (No. 2) 1990 AC 10 at 281.
A.K. Gopalan *v.* State of Madras, AIR 1951 SC 27.
Abdul *v.* Bhagwan, 4. A.L.J. 445.
Abhirchand *v.* Manik Ramnarayan, 1978 MPLJ 204.
Abrams *v.* U.S., 250 U.S. 616 (1919).
Achhar Singh *v.* Pritoo, ILR 1974 Him 876.
Albert *v.* Strange, (1849) 1 Mac & G 25: 41 ER 1171.
Almedia *v.* United States, 413 U.S. 266 (1973).
Anupam Kumar *v.* Shantibai, 1978 (1) MP Weekly Note, 369.
Argyll *v.* Argyll, (1967) 1 Ch. 302.
B. Nihal Chand *v.* Bhagwan Dei, AIR 1935 All 1002.
B.S.C. *v.* Granada Television, (1981) 1 All E.R. 417 (H.L.).
Barber *v.* Time Inc., 348 MO 1199, 159 S.W. 2d 291 (1942).
Bartinicki *v.* Vopper, 200 F3d 109, 118-29 (3d Cir 1999).
Basai *v.* Hasan Razakhan, AIR 1963 All. 340.
Basheshar Nath *v.* C.I.T., AIR 1959 SC 149.
Bell *v.* Birmingham Broadcasting Co., 266 Ala 266, 96 SO 2d 263.
Bennett *v.* Norban, 396 Pa. 94, 151 A.2d 476 (1959).
Berg *v.* Minneapolis Star and Tribune Co., 79 F Supp. 957 (D. Minn 1948).
Bernstein *v.* National Broadcasting Co., 129 F. Supp. 817 (D.D.C. 1955).
Bernstein *v.* Skyviews and General Ltd. (1978) Q.B. 579.
Berry *v.* Moench, 8 Utah 2d 191, 331 P.2d 814 (1958).
Bhagwan Das *v.* Zamarred, AIR 1929 All. 676.
Bhai Govind *v.* Hari Lal, AIR 1942 Bom. 217.
Bhanwarlal *v.* Dhan Raj, AIR 1973 Raj. 212.
Bhulanlal *v.* Altaf Hussain, AIR 1945 All. 335.
Bipin Chandra *v.* Madhuriben, AIR 1963 Guj. 250.

Entick *v.* Carrington, 19 How. St. Tr. 1029 (1765).
Fellows *v.* National Enquirer, Inc. 2nd Distt., 165 Cal. App. 3d 512, 211, Cal Reptr. 809.
Flores *v.* Mosler Safe Co., 7 N.Y. 2d 276, 280, 164 N.E. 2d 853-855, 196 N.Y.S. 2d 975, 978 (1959).
Florida Publishing Co. *v.* Fletcher, 340 SO 2d 914 (Fla Sup. Ct. 1976).
Forsher *v.* Bugliosi, 6 Media L.R. 1097.
Forster Milburn Co. *v.* Chinn, 120 SW 364.
Francis Coralie Mullin *v.* Union Territory of Delhi, AIR 1981 SC 746.
Frank *v.* Maryland, 359 U.S. 360 (1959).
Frith *v.* Associated Press (DC SC) 176 F Supp. 671.
G. Venkatanarayana *v.* K. Lakshmi Devi, AIR 1985 AP 1.
Ganeshilal *v.* Smt. Rasool Fatima, AIR 1977 All. 118.
George *v.* Sundari Edward (1954) 67 Mad Law 676.
Gertz *v.* Robert Welch, Inc. 418 US 323 (1974).
Gill *v.* Hearst Pub. Co., 40 Cal. 2d 224, 253 P. 2d 441 (1953).
Givraj *v.* Keshavji, AIR 1952 Kutch 22.
Gohree *v.* Jaintee, 91 P.R. 1899.
Gokul Prasad *v.* Radho, ILR 10 All (1888) 358.
Golak Nath *v.* State of Punjab, AIR 1967 SC 1643.
Goor Das *v.* Manohar Dass, N.W.P.H.C. Rep. 1867, 269.
Gouldman-Taber Pontiac, Inc. *v.* Zerbst, 96 Ga. App. 48, 99 S.E. 2d 475 (1957).
Govind *v.* State of M.P. (1975) 2 SCC 148.
Gregory *v.* Bryan—Hunt Co., 295 Ky. 345, 174 S.W. 2d 510 (1943).
Grimes *v.* Carter (5th Dist.) 241 Cal. App. 2d 694.
Griswold *v.* Connecticut, 381 US 479 (1965).
Grossman *v.* Frederick Bros. Acceptance Corp., 34 N.Y.S. 2d 785 (Sup. Ct. App. T. 1942).
Gulab Chand *v.* Manik Chand, AIR 1960 MP 63.
Gulam Hussain *v.* Aziz Sheikh, AIR 1966 JK 49.
Gunga Pershad *v.* Salik Pershad, S.D.A.N.W.P. Rep. 1862, Vol. II, 217.
Hagan *v.* Fairfield (2nd Dist.) 238 Cal. App. 2d 197.
Harvinder Kaur *v.* Harmander Singh Chaudhary, AIR 1984 Del 66.
Harzlitt *v.* Fawcett Publications, 116 F. Supp. 539 (D. Conn. 1953).

Hellewell *v.* C.C. Berbyshire (1995) 1 WLR 804.
Himachal Pradesh v. Umed Ram, AIR 1985 SC 847.
Hinish *v.* Meier and F. Co. 166 Ot 482.
Hubbard *v.* Pitt (1976) Q.B. 142.
Hull *v.* Curtis Pub. Co., 182 Pa. Super 86, 125 A. 2d 644 (1956).
Hustler Magazine and Larry C. Flynt *v.* Jerry Falwell, 485 US 46 (1988).
Jane Roe *v.* Henry Wade, 410 US 112 (1973).
Jenkins *v.* Dell Pub. Co., 143 F. Supp, 953 (W.D.Pa 1956).
Jivraj *v.* Keshavji, AIR 1952 Kutch 52.
Kamathi *v.* Gurandan, S. 3 M.H.C.R. 141.
Kashi Nath *v.* Ram Jiwan, AIR 1933 Lah 847.
Katz *v.* U.S. 389 US 347 (1967).
Kaye *v.* Robertson, 54 M.L.R. 451 (1991).
Kerby *v.* Hal Roach Studios, 53 Cal. App. 2d 207, 127 P. 2d 577 (1942).
Kesavananda Bharti *v.* State of Kerala, AIR 1973 SC 1461.
Keshav, Ganpat Hirachand, 8 BHRC, A.C.J. 67.
Keshav Sahu *v.* Dashrath Sahu, AIR 1961 Orissa 154.
Kesho Saha *v.* Mt. Muktakimon, AIR 1931 Pat. 212.
Kharak Singh *v.* State of U. P., AIR 1963 SC 1295.
Kruse *v.* Johnson (1898) 2 Q.B. 91.
Lachman Prasad *v.* Jamna Prasad, Weekly Notes, 1887, 295 (Cawnpore Case).
Letang *v.* Cooper (1965) 1 QB 232.
London Artists *v.* Littler (1969) 2 Q.B. 375.
Lord Byron *v.* Johnston, 2 Mer. 29, 35 Eng. Rep. 851 (1816).
Loving *v.* Virginia, 388 U.S.I, 12 (1967).
Lyons & Sons *v.* Wilkins, (1899) 1 Ch. 255 CA.
M.C. Mehta *v.* Union of India, AIR 1987 SC 1086.
M.P. Sharma *v.* Satish Chandra, AIR 1954 SCR 1077.
M. Vijaya *v.* The Chairman and Managing Director, Singareni Collieries Company Ltd., AIR 2001 AP 502.
Maneka Gandhi *v.* Union of India, AIR 1978 SC 597.
Maharaj Kumar Mohammad Hasan Khan *v.* Hafaz Abdul Haque, AIR 1945 Avadh 15.
Malak Singh *v.* State of P&H, (1981) 1 SCC 420.
Manik Lal *v.* Mohan Lal, AIR 1920 Bom 141.
Mapp. *v.* Ohio, 367 U.S. 643 (1961).

Martin *v.* Dorton, 210 Miss 668, 50 SO 2d 391 (1951).
Martin *v.* F.I.Y. Theatre, Co., 10 Ohio Op. 338 (Ohio C.P. 1938).
Martin *v.* Johnson Pub. Co., 157 N.Y.S. 2d 409 (Sup. Ct. 1956).
Mata Prasad *v.* Bihari Lal, Unreported S.A. No. 8 of 1886.
Mau *v.* Rio Grande Oil Inc. (DC Cal.) 28 F Supp. 845.
Mc Connel *v.* Beverly Enters Conn. Inc. 553 A 2d 596, 601 (Conn. 1989).
Mc Kinzie *v.* Huckaby, 112 F. Supp. 642 (W.D. Okl. 1953).
Meetze *v.* Associated Press, 230 S.C. 330, 95 S.E. 2d 606 (956).
Megraj Patodia *v.* R.K. Birla, AIR 1971 SC 1295.
Melone *v.* Commr. of Police, (1979) 2 All. E.R. 620 Ch. D.
Melvin *v.* Reid, 112 Cal. App. 285, 297 Pac 91 (1931).
Metzer v. Dell. Pub. Co., 207 Misc. 182, 136 N.Y.S. 2d 888 (Supp. Ct. 1955).
Meyer *v.* Nebraska, 262 U.S. 390, 399 (1923).
Miranda *v.* Arizona, 384 US 436 (1966).
Mohd. Hussain Saheb *v.* Chartered Bank, AIR 1964 (1) Mad. 1012.
Morris *v.* Beardmore, (1981) AC 446.
Motherwell *v.* Motherwick, (1976) 73 DLR 93 SO 62 (Atla App. Div.).
Mr. 'X' *v.* Hospital 'Y', (1998) 8 SCC 296.
Mr. 'X' *v.* Hospital 'Z', AIR 1999 SC 495.
Munzer *v.* Blaisdell, 183 Misc. 773, 49 N.Y.S. 2d 915 (Sup. Ct. 1944).
Mx of Bombay Indian Inhabitant *v.* M/S ZY, AIR 1997 Bom. 406.
Nadar *v.* General Motors Corp. 31 A.D. 2d 392, 397, 398, N.Y.S. 2d 137, 143 (1969).
Nandini Satpathi *v.* P.L. Dani, AIR 1978 SC 1025.
Nanuck Chand *v.* Lolla, 21 P.R. 1169.
Nath Mull *v.* Zuka-Oolha Beg, S.D.A., N.W.P. Rep. 92 (1855).
Neera Mathur *v.* Life Insurance Corporation of India, AIR 1992 SC 392.
New York Times Co. *v.* Sullivan, 367 U.S. 254 (1964).
New York Times *v.* United States, 403 US 713 (1971).
Nihal Chand *v.* Bhagwan Dei, AIR 1935 All 1002.
Olga Tellis *v.* Bombay Municipal Corporation, (1985) 3 SCC 545.

Ruth *v.* Educational Films, 194 App. Div. 893, 184 N.Y.S. 948 (1920).
Rylands *v.* Fletcher (1868) L.R. 3 H.L. 330.
Saifudin Saheb *v.* State of Bombay, AIR 1962 SC 863.
Saiyad Habib *v.* Kamal Chand, AIR 1969 Raj 31.
Samuel *v.* Cutris Pub. Co., 122 F Supp. 327 (N.D. Cal. 1954.
Saroj Rani *v.* Sudardan Kumar, AIR 1984 SC 1526.
Schering *v.* Falkman, (1981) 2 All.E.R. 321 (C.A.).
Science Research Council *v.* Nasse (1980) A. C. 1028 (H.L.).
Seager *v.* Copydex (1967) 2 All E.R. 415 (C.A.).
Sellers *v.* Henry, 329 S.W. 2d (KY. 1959).
Seymayne's case (1603) 5 Co. Rep. 91, 916.
Sharda *v.* Dahrampal, (2003) 4 SCC 493.
Sharman *v.* C. Schmidst and Sons, Inc. (EDPa) 216 F Supp. 401.
Shibdyal *v.* Golab, 96 P.R. 1876.
Shri Bhagwan Ramchandraji *v.* Babu Purshottamdas, Second Appeal No. 101 of 1959 decided on 25.11.1960.
Sidis *v.* F. R. Pub. Corp. 138 ALR 15.
Sital Ojhu *v.* Rekha, A.W.N. 1892, 159.
Skinner *v.* Oklahoma, 316 U.S. 535 (1942).
Slim *v.* Daily Telegraph Ltd. (1968) 2 Q.B. 157.
Smith *v.* Das, 251 Ala 250, 37 SO 2d 118.
Smith *v.* Lubbers, 398 F. Supp. 777 (W.D. Mich. 1975).
Smith *v.* Stone, (1647) Stry 65.
Smith *v.* Suratt, 7 Alaska 416 (1926).
Srinarain *v.* Jadhu Nath 5 SWN 147.
Stanley *v.* Georgia, 394 U.S. 557 (1969).
State of Andhra Pradesh *v.* Gungula Satya Murthy, AIR 1997 SC 1588.
State of Maharashtra *v.* Madhukar Narayan Mardikar, AIR 1991 SC 207.
State of Rajasthan *v.* Rehman, AIR 1960 SC 210.
State *v.* Griswold, 157 Conn. 544 (1964).
State *v.* Griswold, 3 Conn. Cir. 6, 47 (1964).
State *v.* Gurmit Singh, AIR 1996 SC 1393.
State *v.* Person, 298 NE 2d 922 (Ohio).
Stryker *v.* Republic Picture Corp., 108 Cal. App. 2d 191, 238 P. 2d 670 (1951).
Superintendent of Belcher Town State *v.* Saikewiez, 370 N.E. 2d 417, 424 (Mass. 1977).

T. Sareetha *v.* T.V. Subbaiah, AIr 1983 Andhra Pradesh 356.
Tanner-Brice Co. *v.* Sims, 174 Ga. 13, 161 S.E. 819 (1931).
Taylor *v.* K.T.V.B. Inc., 96 Idaho 202, 525 F 2d. 984.
The New Swadeshi Mills *v.* S.K. rattan, AIR 1968 Guj. 117.
Thomas *v.* Thomas (1948) 2 KB 294.
Thomson *v.* Adelberg & Berman, 181 KY 487, 205 S.W. 558 (1918).
Time Inc. *v.* Firestone, 424 US 374 (1967).
Time Inc. *v.* Hill 385 US 374.
Tolley *v.* J.S. Fry Sons Ltd., 1931 A.C. 333 (H.L.).
Trammell *v.* Citizens News Co., 285 Ky. 529, 148 S.W. 2d 708 (1941).
Tuck *v.* Priester, 19 Q.B.D.
U.S. *v.* Carriger 541, Fed 545.
United States *v.* Gugel, 119 F. Supp., 897 (E.D. Ky. 1954).
United States *v.* Kahn, 415 U.S. 143 (1974).
Webster *v.* Reproductive Health, 109 S.Ct. 3040 (1989).
Wheatley *v.* Wheatley (1950)1KB 39.
Wilkinson *v.* Downton (1887) 2 Q.B. 57.
William *v.* Settle (1960) 1 W.L.R. 1072.
Wilson *v.* Brown, 189 Misc. 79, 73 N.Y.S. 2d 587 (Sup. Ct. 1947).
Wilson *v.* Layne, 526 U.S. 603 (1999).
Wolf *v.* Calorada, 381 US 508 (1965).
Wood *v.* National Computer Systems, Inc. (CA 8 Ark) 814 F 2d 544.
Youssoupoff *v.* Columbia Broadcasting System, Inc., 48 Misc. 2d 700.
Yusuf Ali Ismail Nagree *v.* State of Maharashtra, AIR 1968 SC 147.

Bibliography

(A) Books and Articles

A. David Ambrose, "Development of Right to Privacy as a Constitutional Rights in India", *Academy Law Review*, 1997, Vol. 21, pp. 195-208.

A. Manoj Krishna, "Privacy Revisited," *Academy Law Review*, 2000, Vol. 24(1), pp. 41-75.

A.G. Noorani, "Parliament and Privacy," *Economic and Political Weekly*, 1984, Vol. 19, pp. 239-40.

A.H. Robertson, Privacy and Human Rights, (1972).

A.H. Robertson, Privacy and Human Rights, *Standford Law Rev.*, (1972).

A.R. Desai and Chidananda Reddy S. Patil, "Contours of Privacy and Defamation *vis-à-vis* Free Speech," *Cochin University Law Review*, (1996), Vol. XX, Nos. 1 and 2, pp. 187-99.

Adam Carlyle Breckenridge, The Right to Privacy, (1971).

Alan F. Westin, "Privacy and Freedom", New York, Athenum, 1967.

Alka Mookerjee and Soumya Ray Chowdhary, "Information Privacy or Data Protection Laws: Scope and Ambit," *Corporate Law Advisor*, Feb. 2004, Vol. 10 (Suppl), pp. 21-29, 36.

Amit Ludri, "Recognition of Right to Privacy Through Convention Jurisprudence with Special Reference to U. K. and India," *Indian Bar Review*, Jan.-Mar. 2001, Vol. 28, pp. 113-22.

Anand Grover and Priti Patel, "Legal Aspects in the Relationship Between Doctors, Patients and HIV/AIDs," *The Lawyers Collective*, (1995), Vol. 10, No. 9.

Anila George, "Tapping Privacy: The Telephone Tapping Case," *Lawyers Collective*, Jun. 1997, Vol. 12, pp. 28-29.

Anirudh Prasad, "New Dimensions of the Right to Privacy under the Indian Constitution," *JCPS*, Vol. XIV (1980).

Arka Mookerjee and Soumya Ray, "Information Privacy or Data Protection Laws: Scope and Ambit", *Corporate Law Advisor*, Feb. 2004, pp. 21-29.

Arnold Simmel, "Privacy", 12 International Encyclopedia of the Social Sciences, 480.

B. Shanta Kumari, "Infringement of Privacy on an Actionable Tort," Year Book of Legal Studies, (1972).

B.D. Agarwala, "Right to Privacy: A Case-by-Case Development," 3 SCC (1996).

B.D. Agarwala, "Right to Privacy: A Case-by-Case Development," *Supreme Court Cases*, 1996, Vol. 3, pp. 9-12.

B.S. Jagjeevan Kumar, "Right to Privacy Under Indian Constitution", *Andhra Law Times*, 2003, Vol. 2, pp. 23-26.

Bishnu Prasad Divedi, "The Right to Privacy: A New Horizon", AIR 1991, Journal Section.

Bishnu Prasad Dwivedi, "Right to Privacy: A New Horizon," *All India Reporter*, Aug. 1991, Vol. 78, pp. 113-19.

Bloustein, "Privacy as an Aspect of Human Dignity: An Answer to Dean Prosser", (1964) 39, N.Y.U.L.R. 38.

Brain Neill, "The Protection of Privacy", *The Modern Law Review*, July 1962, Vol. 25, No. 4, pp. 395-405.

Brain V. Johnstone, "The Right to Privacy: The Ethical Perspective", *The American Journal of Jurisprudence*, 1984, Vol. 29, pp. 73-94.

Brain Zoellar, "Health and Human Services' Privacy Proposal: A Failed Attempt at Health Information Privacy Protection", 40 *Brandeis Law Journal*, 1065 (2002).

Brij Pal, "Right to Privacy and its Development in India," *M.D.U. Law Journal*, 2001, Vol. 6, pp. 171-80.

Burno Bettleheim, "The Rt. to Privacy is a Myth", *Saturday Evening Post*, July 27, 1968.

Chandra Pal, "Right to Privacy: Emerging as a Constitutional Right," *Civil and Military Law Journal*, Jan.-Mar. 1982, Vol. 18, pp. 42-53

Chandra Pal, "Right to Privacy—Emerging as a Constitutional Right", *CMLJ*, Vol. 18, Nos. 1-4.

Charles Fried, "Privacy", 77, *Yale L.J.* 475 (1968).

Chetan Nagendra, "Privacy and the Concept of Data Protection in India", *Chartered Secretary*, July 2003, Vol. 33, pp. 205-06.

Chetan Nagendra, "Privacy and the Concept of Data Protection in India," *Chartered Secretary*, July 2003, Vol. 33, pp.205-06.

Chidanand Reddy, "Piety of Privacy After Death", *The Lawyers*, August (1991).

Chidanand Reddy, "Privacy Rights of the Citizens *vs.* Executive Govt.", *The Lawyers*, Feb. 1990.

Chidananda, "Privacy Rights of Citizens *vs.* Executive Government," *Lawyers Collective*, Feb. 1990, Vol. 5, pp. 2-23.

Craven, "Personhood: The Right To Be Let Alone", (1976), *Duke L.J.*, 699, 702, n. 15.

D.S. Chauhan, "Data Surveillance, Privacy and Public Administrators," *Indian Administrative and Management Review*, Jan.-Mar. 1976, Vol. 8, pp. 1-14.

Davi's, "What Do We Mean by Rt. to Privacy?", 4, *S.D.L. Rev.*, 1929.

David Finit, "Media Power and Privacy," *Press Council of India Review*, Jan. 1995, Vol. 15, pp. 21-23.

David Flaherty, Protecting Privacy in Surveillance Societies (1989).

David R. Lipson, "Serrano *v.* Priest I and II: The Continuing Role of the California Supreme Court in Deciding Question Arising under California Constitution", 10, *University of San Francisco Law Review*, 697 (Spring, 1976).

David, M.O. Brien, "Privacy, Law and Public Policy," (1979).

Devashish Bharuka, "Piercing the Privacy Veil: A Renewed Threat", *Supreme Court Cases*, Vol. 1, 2003, pp. 23-26.

Dhrismitha Goswami, "Right to Privacy: In the Perspective of the Information Technology Act, 2000", *Gauhati Law Times*, April 2005, Vol. 2(1), pp. 1-14.

Dilbir Kaur Bajwa, "Right to Privacy—Its Origin and Ramifications", *CMLJ*, (1990), Vol. 26.

Dixon, "The Griswold Penumbra: Constitutional Charter for an Expanded Law of Privacy", 64, *Mich. L. Rev.*, 197, 204 (1965).

Durga Das Basu, Comparative Constitutional Law (1984).

Dworkin, "Common Law Protection of Privacy", 2, *Univ. Tas. L. Rev.*, 418 (1967).

Edward J. Bloustein, "Privacy as an Aspect of Human Dignity: An Answer to Dean Prosser", 39, *N.Y.U.L.*, 962 (1964).

Edward Shils, "Privacy: Its Constitution and Vicissitudes", *Law and Contemporary Problems* (1966), Vol. 31.

Ester, Greenfield, "From Equal to Equivalent Pay: Salary Discrimination in Academia", 6, *Journal of Law and Education*, 41-64.

F.S. Nariman, "Right to be Let Alone", *The Indian Advocate* (1977), Vol. XVIII.

Fainberg, "Autonomy, Sovereignty and Privacy: Morals Ideals in the Constitution," 58, *Notre Dame L. Rev.*, 445-46, (1983).

Faizan Mustafa, "Emerging Jurisprudence of Right to Privacy in the Age of Internet, Collection and Transfer of Personal Data: A Comparative Study", *Kashmir University Law Review*, 2004, pp. 13-67.

Faizan Mustafa, Constitutional Issues in Freedom of Information, International and National Perspective (2003).

Franklin E. Zimring, "Legal Perspectives on Family Violence", 75, *Cali. L. Rev.*, 521 (1987).

G. Misra, "Right to Privacy in India", (1994).

G.B. Sharma, "Federal Privacy Commissioner of Canada: Defender of Peoples Privacy," *Indian Journal of Public Administration*, Oct.-Dec. 1979, Vol. 25, pp. 1055-81.

G.D.S. Taylor, "Privacy and the Public" (1971), 34, *Mod. L.R.*, 288.

G.S. Bhargava, "Scoop Based on Phone-Tapping," *Mainstream*, 1996, pp. 19-20.

Gary Bostwick, "A Taxonomy of Privacy: Repose, Sanctuary, and Intimate Decision," 64, *California Law Review*, 1447 (Dec., 1976).

Geoffrey Marshall, "The Right to Privacy—A Sceptical View," *Mc. Gill L.J.*

George C. Chrristie, "Injury to Reputation and the Constitution: Confusion Amit Conflicting Approaches," 2175, *Michigan Law Review* (1976).

Gerety, "Redefining Privacy", 12, *Harv. C.R.C.L.L. Rev.*, 233, 274 (1997).

Govind Mishra, "Privacy and the Indian Legal System", *Delhi Law Review*, 1990, Vol. 12, pp. 46-83.

Govind Mishra, "Privacy as Public Issue," *Vidhura*, June 1981.

Govind Mishra, "Privacy: A Fundamental Right under the Indian Constitution," *Delhi Law Review*, 1979-82, Vols. 8 and 9, pp. 134-60.

H.R. Khanna, "Intercepting Letters: Invasion of Right to Privacy," *The Statesman*, September 15, 1981.

Harbert Marcuse, "One Dimensional Man", (1964).

Harbert Marcuse, One Dimensional Man, (1984).

Hargovind Shashtri, *Manusmriti*, (1970).

Harry D., Krause and Paul Marcus, "Privacy", *American Journal of Comparative Law*, Vol. 26, Supplement 1978.

Hema V. Menon, "Right to Privacy is Included in Right to Life, But is Not Absolute: Mr. X.V. Hospital 'Z' AIR 1995 SC 495 and the Right of HIV/AIDS Patients," *All India Reporter*, Sep. 2002, Vol. 89, pp. 261-67.

Hemlata Jain, "Right to Privacy: Where Does one Stop," *Lex et. Juris*, Oct. 1990, Vol. 5, pp. 40-41.

Hemlata Jain, "Right to Privacy: Where Does One Stop", *Lex Et. Juris*, Oct., 1990.

Higross, "The Concept of Privacy", (1967), 2, *Univ. of Ras. L.R.* 418.

Hyman Gorss, Privacy—Its Legal Protection, (1976).

I.P. Messey, "Constitutionalization of the Right to Privacy in India," in BPS Sehgal (ed.) *Human Rights in India*, (1995).

Jagdish Swarup, Tagore Law Lectures: Human Rights and Fundamental Freedoms, (1975).

James Rachel, "Why Privacy is Important", (1975), 4, *Philosophy and Public Affairs.*

Janusz Symonides, Human Rights Concepts and Standards, (2000).

Jed Rubenfeld, "The Right of Privacy", 102, *Harv. L. Rev.* (1989).

Jed Rubenfeld, "The Right of Privacy", *Harvard Law Review*, February 1989, Vol. 102, No. 4, pp. 737-807.

John L. Coons "Recent Trends in Science Fiction: Serrano Among the People of Number" (The Role of Social Science in School Finance Litigation), 6, *Journal of Law and Education*, 23-40, No. 1.

Judith Jarvis Thomson, "The Right to Privacy", (1975), 4, *Philosophy and Public Affairs*.

Justice R.S. Sarkaria, "Freedom of Press: Defamation and Privacy", *Press Council of India Review* (1994), Vol. 15.

K. Pattibhi Rama Rao, "Right to Privacy: A New Fundamental Right," *Andhra Law Times*, 1999, Vol. 2, pp. 16-18.

K.C. Joshi, "Right to Privacy—An Extension of Personal Liberty", *Ku. L.J.*, 1978.

K.K. Methew, "The Right to Be Let Alone", 4 SCC (1979), Journal Section.

K.K. Methew, Freedom of Speech and Right to Privacy.

Karen, DeCrow, Sexist Justice, New York: Random House, (1974).

Ken Hyder, "Phone Tapping in Britain", *CMLJ*, Jan.-Mar. 1989, Vol. 25, No. 1

Ken I. Kersch, Freedom of Speech: Rights and Liberties Under the Law.

Kenneth, Davidson, Ginsburg, Ruth and Herma, Sex Based Discrimination (St. Paul, Minn, West Publishing Co., 1974.

L. Brittain, "The Right to Privacy in England and the United States", (1963), 37, *Tulane L.R.*, 235.

L. Jyashree, "Right to Privacy of a Woman under Criminal Law", *Criminal Law Journal*, May 2003, Vol. 109, pp. 145-49.

L. Lusky, "Invasion of Privacy: A Clarification of Concepts: (1972), 72, *Columbia Law Rev.*, 693.

Law Commission 42nd Report (1971) Sections 490, 491 and 492 IPS Offences Against Privacy Protection under Sec. 50 IPC.

Louis Henkin, "Privacy and Autonomy", 74, *Column. L.R.*, 1410 (1974).

Louis J. Parker and Twiley W. Barker, Jr, "Civil Liberties and the Constitution", (1978).

M.C. Pramodan, "Right to Privacy", *Cochin University Law Review*, Vol. 14, (1990).

M.K. Bhandari, "Right to Privacy Versus Freedom of Press: Comparative Conspectus of Legal Position in USA, US and India," *Indian Journal of Legal Studies*, 1991, Vol. 11, pp. 178-91.

M.L. Upadhayay and Prashant Jayaswal, "Constitutional Control of Right to Privacy," *Central India Law Quarterly*, Jan.-Mar. 1989, Vol. 11, pp. 39-58.

M.V. Prasada Rao, "Right to Privacy—Palsied or Gauntlet", *Andhra Law Times*, 1999 (2), Vol. 97, pp. 16-18.

Madhavi Divan, "Right to Privacy in the Age of Information and Communications," *Supreme Court Cases*, 2002, Vol. 4, pp. 12-23.

Md. Ahmad, "Right to Privacy: Apex Court Case Analysis", *CMLJ*, Vol. 35, No. 2.

Medani Abdel Rehman Tageldin, "Right to Privacy and Abortion: A Comparative Study of Islamic and Western Jurisprudence," *ALIG. L.J.*, 140 (1997).

Meroyn Jones, Privacy, (1974).

Michael F. Kelleher, "The Confidentiality of Criminal Conversations on TD Relay Systems", 79, *Cali. L. Rev.* Oct 1991.

Michael Henry, International Privacy, Publicity and Personality Laws, (2001).

Milton R. Konvitz, "Privacy and the Law: A Philosophical Prelude", *Law and Contemporary Problems*, 1966, Vol. 31, pp. 272-78.

Mohd. Ahmad, "Muslim Law and Reforms: Protection of Privacy in Islam," *Civil and Military Law Journal*, Jan-Mar, 2000, Vol. 36, pp. 64-65.

Mohr James, Abortion in America: The Origin and Evolution of National Policy, (1978).

Mokey, "The Right of Privacy Emanations and Intimations", (1965), 64, *Mich Law Rev.*, 259.

Murray N. Rothbard, The Ethics of Liberty.

N. Balu, "Right to Privacy," *Calcutta Weekly Notes*, 1991-1992, Vol. 96, pp. 125-28.

N. Balu, "State of Maharashtra and Another v. Madhukar Narayan Mardikar and the Right to Privacy," *All India Reporter*, Jul. 1992, Vol. 79, pp. 104-06.

N. Balu, "The Right to Privacy" XCVI, *Calcutta Weekly Notes*, 125 (August, 1992).

N.K. Raha, "Right to Privacy under Indian Law," AIR 2001, Journal Section, pp. 51-52.

N.K.N. Iyengar, "Personal Privacy in the United States", 25 *Indian Journal of Public Administration*, 1234-41 (Oct.-Dec. 1979).

Naveen Thakur, "Right to Privacy: An Implicit Fundamental Right Under Article 21," *All India Reporter*, Sep. 1998, Vol. 85, pp. 145-46.

Nemika Jha, "Legitimacy of the Right to Privacy as a Fundamental Right: A Comparative Study of India and America", AIR 2001, Journal Section, pp. 325-31.

Nikhil Chakravarty, "Privacy of Piracy," *Mainstream*, 1997, Vol. 35, pp. 5-6.

Oscar M. Rue Bhausen and Orville G. Brim Jr., "Privacy and Behavioural Research", 7, *Colum. L. Rev.*, 1184 (1965).

P. Allan Dionisopoulos and Craig Ducat, The Right to Privacy: Essays and Cases (St. Paul, Minn, West Publishing Co., 1976).

P.H. Winfield, "Privacy", (1931) 47 LQR 23.

P.M. Bakshi, "Privacy: A House of Many Mansions," *Supreme Court Journal*, 1996, Vol. 1, pp. 14-17.

P.S. Seema, "Human Rights of Persons Living with HIV/AIDS—An Analysis of the International and National Norms", *C.U.L.R.*, 10 (2005).

P.V. Kane, History of Dharamshastra, (1968).

Panna Lal Dhar, "Right to Privacy", AIR 1987, Journal Section, pp. 145-49.

Partha Sarathi Patnaik, "HIV/AIDS Victim's Right to Privacy," *Cuttack Law Times*, 1999, Vol. 88, p. 40.

Parthsarthy, A.S. Pati, "Inner Man", *Lawyers Collective*, July 2003, Vol. 18(7), pp. 13-15.

Philip, Hanon, "From Politics to Reality: Historical Perspective of the Legal Service Corporation," 25, *Emory Law Journal*, 639-54 (Summer, 1976).

Prabhat Kumar Basumallik, "Right to Privacy: A New

Dimension," *All India Reporter*, Aug 1992, Vol. 79, pp. 120-21.

R. Santhanam, Telephone-Tapping vs. Right to Privacy, *Indian Judicial Reports*, 1988, Vol. 29, pp. 159-67.

R. Shamasastri, Kautilya's Arthashastra, (1961).

R.B. Jain, "Right to Privacy and Freedom of Information: The Search for a Balace," *Indian Journal of Public Administration*, Oct.-Dec. 1979, Vol. 25, pp. 1117-27.

R.H. Clark, "Constitutional Sources of the Penumbral Right to Privacy," *Villanova Law Review*, 1974, Vol. 19, No. 6.

Rachika Agrawal, "Privacy and Technology: Are Indian Laws Catching Up", *Lawyers Collective*, 2004, pp. 17-19.

Radabinod Pal, History of Hindu Law, (1958).

Raghavendra Kumar, "Right to Privacy: Juridical Vision," *All India Reporter*, July 2002, Vol. 89, pp. 195-98.

Rahul Saha and Surya Bala, "Sex, Property and Privacy: Testing and Constitutionality of Section 497, I.P.C.", *Criminal Law Journal*, May 2005, pp. 156-60.

Rajinder Sachar, "Phone Tapping: A Missed Opportunity," *Mainstream*, Feb 1997, Vol. 35, pp. 26-27.

Ram Narayan Duta Shastri, Valmiki Ramayan, Geeta Press (Gorakhpur).

Ranjit Lal, "Privacy or Something to Hide," *Vidhura*, February, 1981.

Raymond Wacks, "The Poverty of Privacy", Vol. 96, *LQR*, 73 (1980).

Reiman, "Privacy, Intimacy and Personhood", 6, *Phil & Pub. Aff.*, 28 (1976).

Rendall P. Bezanson, "The Right to Privacy Revisited: Privacy, News and Social Change, 1890-1990", Vol. 80, *Cali. L. Rev.*, 1133 (October 1992).

Richard Hixson, "Privacy in a Public Society: Human Rights in Conflict" (1987).

Richard P. Claude, Comparative Human Rights, (1976).

Richards, "Constitutional Legitimacy and Constitutional Privacy," 61, *N.Y.U.L. Rev.*, 800, 862 (1986).

Robert C. Post, "The Social Foundation of Privacy: Community and Self in Common Law Tort", 77, *Calif L. Rev.*, 957 (1989).

Robert F. Copple, "Privacy and the Frontier Thesis: An

American Intersection of Self and Society", *The American Journal of Jurisprudence*, (1989), Vol. 34, pp. 87-125.

Rodney D. Ryder, "Security Concerns, Trade Secrets and Privacy: Developing Trends and Legal Issues," *Corporate Law Advisor*, May 2001, pp. 57-63.

Roxanne B. Conlin, "Equal Protection *Versus* Equal Rights Amendment—Where Are We Now?" 24, *Drake Law Review*, 259 (1975).

Ruth Gavison, "Privacy and the Limits of Law", 89, *Yale L.J.* 421, 438-39 (1980).

S. Parameswaran, "Mundu (not mundae) Controversy," *Kerala Law Times*, 2001, Vol. 1, pp. 9-10.

S. Sahay, "Law of Privacy and Freedom of Expression," *Civil and Military Law Journal*, Oct.-Dec. 1994, Vol. 30(4): pp. 286-88.

S. Shivakumar, "Right to Privacy," *Academy Law Review*, 1994, pp. 191-230.

S.B. Dawarkanath, "Right to Privacy: A Need for Constitutional Status," *Andhra Law Times*, 2002, Vol. 5, pp. 42-45.

S.D. Warren and L. D. Brandeis, "The Right to Privacy", 4, *Harvard Law Review* (1890).

S.N. Parikh, "Right to Privacy and Homosexual Acts," *Central India Law Quarterly*, Oct.-Dec. 1992, Vol. 5, pp. 485-95.

S.N. Parikh, "Right to Privacy," *Civil and Military Law Journal*, Jan.-Mar. 1982, Vol. 18, pp. 42-53.

S.N. Parikh, "Right to Privacy," *Cochin University Law Review*, Mar. 1990, Vol. 14, pp. 59-72.

S.N. Parikh, "Right to Privacy-Nature and Character of the Concept of Privacy," *Gujarat Law Reporter*, 1984, pp. 41-42.

S.N. Parikh, "Telephone-Tapping and Right to Privacy," *Civil and Military Law Journal*, Jul.-Sept. 1988, Vol. 24, pp. 150-64.

S.N. Parikh, "Telephone-Tapping and Right to Privacy," *Gujarat Law Herald*, 1998, Vol. 8, pp. 12-24.

Satyan S. Irani, "Right to Privacy Inherent Freedom", AIR 2004 (Journal Section), pp. 26-27.

Saurabh Awasthi, "Privacy Laws in India: Big Brother is

Watching You," *Company Law Journal*, 2002, Vol. 3, pp. 15-23.

Sehzad Mansuri, "Testing the Test with Dignity", *Lawyers Collective*, March 2003, Vol. 19, pp. 23-24.

Sheetal Asrani-Dann, "Right to Privacy in the Era of Smart Governance: Concerns Raised by the Introduction of Biometric-enabled National ID Cards in India," *Journal of the Indian Law Institute*, Jan.-March, 2005, Vol. 47(1), pp. 53-94.

Shrinivas Gupta, "Right to Privacy is an Aspect of Human Dignity," *Lawyer*, Sep.-Oct. 1985, Vol. 17, pp. 67-73.

Shrinivas Gupta, "Right to Privacy: A Kind of Personal Autonomy," *Lex et. Juris*, Aug 1988, Vol. 3, pp. 38-41.

Simon L. Gallant, "Privacy and the Press: The English Perspective," *Indian Advocate*, July-Dec. 1992, Vol. 24, pp. 54-59.

Soli J. Sorabjee, "Privacy and Defamation: SC Defines Parameters," *Press Council of India Review*, Jan 1995, Vol. 16, pp. 17-19.

Survrajyoti Gupta, "Constitutionality of Wiretap in India and USA", *Criminal Law Journal*, December 2003, Vol. 109, pp. 379-83.

Suvendu Kumar Pati, "Right to Privacy—Whether Fundamental?" *Indian Bar Review*, Apr.-Jun. 2000, pp. 151-54.

Swarupama Chaturvedi, "Right to Privacy: Certain Cardinal Aspects", *All India Reporter*, Vol. 91, May 2004, pp. 129-35.

T. Anantha Chair, "Right to Privacy," *Seminar*, 1979, pp. 29-32.

T. Jagan Mohan and P. Ravi Joshua, "To What Extent Can an Individual Know the Secluded Life of Other?", *Supreme Court Journal*, 2000, Vol. 3, pp. 35-42.

Thriyambak J. Kannan and Subhashini Narasimhan, "Right to Privacy of Public Personalities", *Journal of Symbiosis Law Journal*, 2004, Vol. 4, pp. 74-83.

Tim Leach and Buchanan David, "HIV Litigants Right to Privacy," *Lawyers Collective*, Oct. 1993, Vol. 8, pp. 15-18.

V.R. Krishna Iyer, "Privacy is Human Right," *Press Council of India Review*, July 1990, Vol. 11, pp. 15-18.

Thriyambak J. Kannan and Subhashini Narasimhan, "Right to Privacy of Public Personalities", *Journal of Symbiosis Law Journal*, 2004, Vol. 4, pp. 74-83.

Tim Leach and Buchanan David, "HIV Litigants Right to Privacy," *Lawyers Collective*, Oct. 1993, Vol. 8, pp. 15-18.

V.R. Krishna Iyer, "Privacy is Human Right," *Press Council of India Review*, July 1990, Vol. 11, pp. 15-18.

Vany Adithan, "Right to Privacy under Article 21-B", 2, *Madras Law Journal*, 28-32 (2003).

II. Reports/Acts/Conferences/Debates

The Indian Telegraph Act, 1972.

The Information Technology Act, 2000.

Justice Report (Privacy and the Law), 1970.

Nordic Conference on Privacy of the International Commission of Jurists, Stockholm, May 1967.

Press Council Declaration of Principal of Privacy (23rd Press Council Report), 1976.

Report of Lindop Committee (1978).

The Australian Law Reform Commission Report, Uniform Publication: Defamation and Privacy (1979).

The Hindu Marriage Act, 1955.

The Indian Evidence Act, 1872.

The Law Commission of India, 38th Report (1968).

The Law Commission of India, 71st Report (1978).

Younger Committee Report on Privacy (1972).

The Fair Credit Reporting Act, 1970.

The Fair Credit Billing Act, 1974.

The Electronic Communications Privacy Act, 1986.

The Video Privacy Protection Act, 1988.

The Privacy Act, 1974.

The United States Federal Communications Act, 1934.

The Wireless Telegraphy Act, 1967.

Constituent Assembly Debates, Vol. VIII.

The Data Protection Act, 1988 (UK).

The Privacy Act, 1988 (Commonwealth).

Corpus Juris Secundum, 2004.

Index